THE TESTIMONY OF HENRY ADAMS, FREEDMAN

THE TESTIMONY OF

HENRY ADAMS, FREEDMAN

Hope, Terror, and Exodus in the Post–Civil War South

INTRODUCTION BY
Steven Hahn

LIBRARY OF AMERICA

THE TESTIMONY OF HENRY ADAMS, FREEDMAN
Introduction, notes, and volume compilation copyright © 2026 by
Literary Classics of the United States, Inc., New York, NY
All rights reserved.

Published in the United States by Library of America,
14 East 60th Street, New York, NY 10022.
Visit our website at www.loa.org.

Distributed to the trade in the United States by Penguin Random House Inc.
and in Canada by Penguin Random House Canada Ltd.

The authorized representative in the EU for product safety and compliance
is eucomply OÜ, Pärnu mnt 139b-14, 11317 Tallinn, Estonia.
hello@eucompliancepartner.com

Library of Congress Control Number: 2025942690
ISBN 978–1–59853–836–6

1 3 5 7 9 10 8 6 4 2

Printed in the United States of America

CONTENTS

INTRODUCTION
by Steven Hahn

Among the voices of America's past, few are as arresting and distinctive as that of the freedman Henry Adams. Born into slavery, he experienced emancipation as a young man, enlisted in the United States Army, and in the 1870s became a grassroots organizer of such stature in the Reconstruction and post-Reconstruction Deep South that the United States Senate summoned him to Washington, D.C., to testify about the struggles of Black Americans and a movement they were building to flee the South for safer and more secure places elsewhere. Over two grueling days before the Senate panel, sometimes in the face of hostile and skeptical questioning, Adams told of the wrenching conditions freed people faced in the post-slavery world, the economic exploitation and racist violence they suffered, and their determination through a variety of means to give the promise of freedom a reality. In so doing, Adams provides us with a revelatory window onto the lives of newly emancipated people and a powerful example of the important mark he, and others like him, left on our history.[1]

Henry Adams called himself a "laborer," an occupation encompassing the worlds of enslavement and its aftermath for most Black people in the nineteenth-century United States. Initially known as Henry Houston, he was born in rural Jasper County, Georgia, in 1843, southeast of Atlanta, and spent his first seven years there before his enslaver took him and his family west to DeSoto Parish,

Louisiana, in the northwest corner of that state. Like most enslaved children, Adams worked in the fields from a young age, although there were several developments in his early life that helped shape the course of his future. For one thing, his father preached the gospel to other enslaved people despite intimidation from local whites. Perhaps even more important, Adams's owner, Caleb Adams, died in 1858 and both he and his father became the property of his enslaver's young daughter, who hired them out to neighboring planters until emancipation came in 1865. (Adams's mother became the property of one of Caleb's sons.) Adams managed to acquire some personal property while still enslaved, and thereby brought into freedom both material resources and a very independent disposition. "I feared God but not man," he told a local planter.[2]

An independent disposition did not, however, ease Adams's transition from slavery to freedom. If anything, it invited terrorist repression from white people who demanded submission rather than independence. Refusing to sign a labor contract that would consign him to the fields, Adams traveled the roads of DeSoto and Caddo parishes, at times heading to the town of Shreveport, hoping to fashion a livelihood of his own design. For this, Adams was harassed, robbed, and beaten while witnessing many other "outrages" brought upon freed people whether they signed labor contracts or not. The United States Army was his next stop; Adams enlisted in September 1866.

Adams's time in the army proved to be another of his life's turning points. Over the course of his three-year term of enlistment, he served in three regiments and rose to the rank of quartermaster-sergeant, about as high a position as a Black man could hold in the U.S. armed forces. More significantly, Adams learned how to read and write and, feeling the inveterate hostility of white Louisianans while wearing the emblems of federal authority, he and a number of other Black soldiers ("a parcel of we men") formed a secret committee once they were discharged to take the measure of Black life in the South.

By Adams's telling, the secret committee attracted as many as 500 members, perhaps 150 of whom began to travel the southern states "to see what sort of living our people lived." In the meantime, Adams split rails and managed a plantation, bought a town lot in Shreveport with the benefit of his army bounty, and, moving around the Mississippi and Red River Valleys, helped freed people negotiate labor contracts. Although he later claimed that he never had anything to do with politics except going to vote, Adams also became a source of support and enlightenment for local freedmen after the Reconstruction Acts of 1867 and the Louisiana Constitution of 1868 extended the franchise to them. He spoke with the freed people about their new rights; introduced them to the Republican Party, which had organized the defeat of the Confederacy and the Reconstruction of the South; established Republican clubs; and served as an election supervisor.

Nonetheless, reports filtering in from secret committee members in the field confirmed Adams's own sense of Black prospects in Louisiana: they were "very bad." Black men had registered to vote in remarkable numbers and went to the polls in defiance of their white employers. Indeed, in the Red River Valley and in many other areas of rural Louisiana where Black people outnumbered whites, they also elected representatives to the state legislature and parish offices. Yet, as Adams also recognized, Black political empowerment triggered white paramilitary violence—including the notorious White League in Louisiana—to lethal and devastating effect. And it became increasingly clear that their white Republican allies, in the state and the nation, were often unwilling or unable to meet force with force, leaving Black people to the tender mercies of their former enslavers.[3]

Adams would continue to support and canvass for the Republican Party for several more years, but in 1874 he and his committee comrades called a meeting in Shreveport and established a Colonization Council. Believing it was "utterly impossible" to live with the white people of Louisiana, they sent a petition to President Ulysses S. Grant asking to be "removed to a territory where they could live" by themselves, either within the United States or to Liberia "if no better place could be given them." Three years later, the Council tried again. A meeting of five thousand people drew up a set of resolutions and sent it to President Rutherford B. Hayes requesting the appropriation of "some Territory in which we may colonize our race" or the "means whereby we can colonize in Liberia or some other country" if the rights granted them by the Constitution could not be guaranteed. Several hundred names were appended to the document, representing, according to the Council, "69,000 colored people of the South." Henry Adams and his council, that is to say, promoted and hoped to lead what could have been the first "great migration" of freed Black Americans.

Why Liberia? In 1816, white political leaders from the North and South who hoped that slavery would eventually end but feared the presence of emancipated people of African descent formed the American Colonization Society. Their plan was to set up a colony on the coast of West Africa and encourage free people of color from the United States to move there, beginning a process that would tie "colonization" to emancipation and thereby convince whites to embrace antislavery. Before the Civil War a few thousand Black people immigrated to Liberia, which became an independent republic in 1847. But once emancipation occurred, the American Colonization Society continued to work toward Black resettlement. And whereas colonization there had previously been viewed by most Black Americans as a form of expulsion, it was now increasingly seen by many as a means of escape. Thousands had learned of Liberia and the work of the American Colonization Society, and hundreds wrote to the ACS for information about how they might gain support for emigration. Henry Adams was one of them.[4]

As the efforts of the Colonization Council took shape, interest in emigration from the South grew and was in evidence well beyond

Louisiana: in North Carolina, Tennessee, Arkansas, Mississippi, and Texas most prominently, though, in truth, it was to be found throughout the South, and especially in the plantation districts. The greatest organizational activity—meetings, conventions, clubs—focused on Liberia but desperate Blacks, especially in North Carolina and the Lower Mississippi Valley, looked as well to Indiana and especially to Kansas. So widespread was this movement and so worrisome was it to southern landowners that it caught the attention of state legislatures and eventually the U.S. Senate, where in 1879 a select committee was tasked with investigating "the Causes of the Removal of the Negroes from the Southern States to the Northern States." Among the witnesses subpoenaed to appear before the committee was Henry Adams, and his deep and stunning testimony, as well as the written statements he presented to support his claims, appear in the following pages of this book.

The United States Senate committee was composed of five members and, responding to reports of growing interest in emigration and especially of specific movements that appeared to be under way from North Carolina to Indiana and from Tennessee and the lower Mississippi Valley to Kansas, they hoped to determine why this was happening. To what extent was economic and political turmoil in the South to blame? Why were destinations like Indiana and Kansas chosen and how were they to be reached? How widespread was the desire among southern Blacks to relocate and what did they hope to find? What would this mean for the southern states and for the people, Black or white, who lived there?

The Senate committee included three Democrats, Daniel Voorhees of Indiana, George Pendleton of Ohio, and Zebulon Vance of North Carolina, and two Republicans, William Windom of Minnesota and Henry W. Blair of New Hampshire. The committee began to hear testimony on January 19, 1880, and continued to do so until April 27. Appearing before them were federal officials, local men of prominence, ministers, lawyers, railroad agents, journalists, and Black political leaders. All told, the committee heard from 153 witnesses from six southern and three northern states. On June 1 the committee published three large volumes of testimony along with its majority and minority reports.

Not surprisingly, the reports reflected the deep partisan divides in Congress and the country at large. The six-page majority report, signed by the three Democrats, blamed Black emigration on the political designs of Republicans, particularly those who were interested in tipping the electoral balance in Indiana from the Democrats to the Republicans. They insisted that, while the aftermath of "a bitter and desolating civil war" continued to set hurdles in the paths of Blacks and whites alike, the rights and prospects of freed people were not being imperiled. Black people were "gradually and steadily improving in every respect," were receiving fair pay for their labor, had few grievances about their treatment by white planters, and were able to participate fully in the politics of their counties and states. There was, they argued, no need for "any further attempts at legislation or agitation of this subject"; Black people were content to stay put and had no reason to fear for their future. "The sooner they are taught to know that their true interest is promoted by cultivating the friendship of their white neighbors instead of their enmity," the majority averred, "the sooner they will gain that friendship and [achieve] civilization and advancement."

The seventeen-page minority report, submitted by the two Republican senators, offered wholly different conclusions. They rejected the Democratic claim regarding Indiana and North Carolina as gross partisanship. Instead, they emphasized the many thousands of Black people who had set their eyes on Kansas, lined the Mississippi River looking for possible transportation, and hoped to find new and better lives in the state that had long been associated with militant abolitionism, thanks to John Brown's raids and the larger antislavery struggle of the 1850s. The minority report told of the "intolerable hardships, injustice, and suffering inflicted upon" Black people "by a class of Democrats in the South." Their labor was being mercilessly exploited. They were being reduced to near peonage. They were being denied education and justice. And they were being persecuted politically.

Although one of the Republican committee members, William Windom of Minnesota, had previously introduced a resolution in the Senate calling for an inquiry into "the expediency and practicability" of encouraging Black migration from the South into the western territories, the minority report did not call for congressional action to that end. Rather, it concluded that there "is but one remedy for the exodus—fair treatment of the negro." But as the minority report began to lay out its case, the testimony that it believed could show the "real origin of the exodus movement and the organizations at the South which have promoted it" came from a man they described as "an uneducated colored laborer, but a man of very unusual natural abilities, and, so far as the committee could learn, entirely reliable and truthful." It came from Henry Adams, in many ways their star witness.

Adams sat down before the committee on March 12, 1880, and responded to their questions over the course of two long days, although Ohio's Pendleton was absent both days. Adams also introduced extensive documentation to support his claims about conditions in the South that provoked the exodus, including two lengthy narratives of "outrages" committed against Black men and women, a list of 683 specific cases of victimization, and eleven affidavits from other Black people. Indeed, he had collected, for more than a decade, a veritable archive of information from different parts of the Deep South that he managed to hold on to despite his lengthy travels along the back roads and the harassment and abuse he suffered in the process. His searing words exposed the day-to-day travails that Black people in the South endured, the denial of their civil and political rights, and their subjection to continuous violence at the hands of white terrorists. All of this in the face of the obvious doubts and hostility of the committee's Democratic inter-rogators, not least Senator Vance, previously governor of North Carolina under the Confederacy. Yet, as the testimony shows, Adams did not back down or bend the knee.[5]

Adams's testimony and archive are far more than catalogues of Black exploitation and repression at the hands of former enslavers and white Democrats. They present a multilayered picture of Black political activism and struggle, a picture that confounds long-standing assumptions about Black disorientation and submission to the ploys of white politicians, whether Democrats or Republicans. Through Adams's testimony, we can see grassroots organizing around labor relations, around voting and officeholding, around the development of party loyalty, and more generally against the repressive demands of southern whites. And we can see emerging, little by little, political knowledge of the post-emancipation South, of the experiences of Black people in different parts of it, of the debates over what freedom meant for the formerly enslaved, and of the many initiatives that leaders like Adams took to address potential allies in pursuit of their goals. We can hear of Adams and some of his fellow veterans setting out, over many miles and at considerable personal cost, to assess the condition of freedmen and -women; of the establishment of the Colonization Council and the petitions collected and submitted to Ulysses S. Grant, Rutherford B. Hayes, and both houses of Congress; of meetings that were held, discussions that took place, and plans that were devised. Quite simply, there is no other sustained documentary evidence of grassroots activism—economic, political, and social—from the perspective of a laborer to match what Henry Adams provides us here.

Adams's remarkable testimony reminds us, too, of the vast and highly significant historical record created during the Civil War and Reconstruction. Beforehand, much of what we could learn about Black life in the slave South came either from white observers (including enslavers) and fugitives from enslavement like Frederick Douglass or Harriet Jacobs who penned gripping autobiographies that energized the abolitionist movement. The Confederate rebellion and the outbreak of the Civil War, however, changed everything. The U.S. Army kept voluminous records of its military undertakings, but even though the administration of Abraham Lincoln initially hoped to keep matters of slavery and the enslaved themselves as far out of the conflict as possible—its main goal was to put down the rebellion by armed force—that proved to be impossible. As the Union army advanced into Confederate-held territory, enslaved people began to flee to their lines where they believed freedom might be obtained. The military records help document the scale and ambitions of the actions enslaved people took, their reports of life under slavery, and their understanding of the national struggle over slavery's future, including ideas about who their political allies might be. They would also provide an expansive view of the process of Black enlistment—of the formerly enslaved and of free people of color—that would help turn the tide of the war and put issues of civil and political rights on the table. And as the Lincoln administration increasingly recognized that the Confederate rebellion could not be defeated without taking slavery down along with it, government officials and social reformers began to fan out across the southern states to interview Black men and women about their experiences under slavery and their visions of freedom. The American Freedman's Inquiry Commission, created in 1863, collected especially important testimony and led to the establishment of the Freedman's Bureau in the final months of the war.[6]

Reconstruction, which effectively commenced when the Union army first marched across ground claimed by the Confederacy and continued with greater force after the Emancipation Proclamation in 1863, gave freed people more opportunities to register their experiences and perspectives. The battle between Republicans in Congress and President Andrew Johnson over federal policies initiated more investigations, like those of the Joint Committee on Reconstruction, which included Black witnesses and led to the drafting of the

Fourteenth Amendment.[7] The Reconstruction Acts of 1867, which
put nearly all of the rebellious South under martial law and enfran-
chised the freedmen, did even more to generate a historical record,
as U.S. Army officers were put in charge of registering eligible Black
voters and protecting their rights. The rise of white terrorist
organizations like the Ku Klux Klan that set their sights on Black
political leaders and voters—and thereby threatened Republican
power nationally—led to a large-scale congressional investigation
with hundreds of Black witnesses from states across the Deep South.[8]
And the mobilization of Black voters by the Republican Party and the
political power that Black people gained as a result—elected to local,
state, and national offices, selected to serve on juries—turned elections into paramilitary warfare, as Black voters were harassed and
murdered and Black officeholders were expelled or killed. As a result,
Republicans in Congress initiated investigations into a number of
elections in the South—including contests in Louisiana—and enable
us to read the accounts of Blacks and whites who bore witness to the
political turmoil and were often victimized themselves.[9] Years later,
when W.E.B. Du Bois wrote his pathbreaking *Black Reconstruction
in America, 1860–1880* (1935), he chided historians for ignoring the
many sources available in the National Archives and in print that
called into question the racist interpretations of the period that had—
like the film *The Birth of a Nation*—become the conventional wisdom
of the country. Henry Adams's testimony and the larger investigation
of the "Negro Exodus" are examples of this enormous archive and
especially vivid firsthand renderings of Black struggle.

The "great migration" that Henry Adams and his followers had
imagined and hoped for did not, in the end, occur. Although many
thousands of Black people did line the banks of the Mississippi River
for many miles, only about six thousand of them succeeded in making it to Kansas. And although hundreds of Black people, speaking
on behalf of the communities in which they lived, contacted the

American Colonization Society for information about emigrating to Liberia, only a comparative handful made it to points of departure and embarked on the journey. The costs of migrating were too considerable, the ship departure dates too difficult to manage for farming people, and the support that the American Colonization Society could provide steadily diminished after the economic panic of 1873 and the subsequent depression.[10] Nonetheless, Adams continued to promote emigration while struggling to make a living. Exiled from Shreveport because of his political activism, he found occasional work in the New Orleans custom house and mint as well as on the levees designed to protect the city against river flooding. The last written record of him is a letter to the ACS on August 27, 1884, in which he predicted that the election of a Democratic president would renew interest in Liberia among "the Laboring Classes of Color." We know nothing about when or how he died.

But for the nearly two decades that he served in the U.S. Army and organized on the ground in the Deep South, Adams—thanks to the testimony and appended evidence printed here—opens a window unlike any other onto the worlds of the newly emancipated as they battled for a freedom they had envisioned and struggled against great odds to achieve. In a sense, like his Brahmin namesake, Henry Adams gives us the fruits of his intense education about our country, an education derived not at Harvard or among the privileged and powerful in Washington and London, but on plantations and farms, in churches and homesteads, at clandestine meetings and polling places. It was an education both about some of the darkest times and failed promises of our history and about some of the remarkable efforts by some of the most "invisible" but extraordinary people to realize what we like to think our country is all about. Henry Adams's education is therefore ours as well, one of hope as well as heartbreak, and a necessary reminder that those who can best grasp the full possibilities of freedom are often those who have been most brutally denied it.

NOTES

1. Henry Adams and the movement he helped to build are best treated in Nell Irvin Painter, *Exodusters: Black Migration to Kansas After Reconstruction* (New York: Alfred A. Knopf, 1977) and Steven Hahn, *A Nation Under Our Feet: Black Political Struggles in the Rural South from Slavery to the Great Migration* (Cambridge, MA: Harvard University Press, 2003), 317–63. But also see Robert G. Athearn, *In Search of Canaan: Black Migration to Kansas, 1879–80* (Lawrence, KS: The Regents Press of Kansas, 1978); William Cohen, *At Freedom's Edge: Black Mobility and the Southern White Quest for Racial Control, 1861–1915* (Baton Rouge, LA: Louisiana State University Press, 1991); Kenneth C. Barnes, *Journey of Hope: The Back-to-Africa Movement in Arkansas in the Late 1800s* (Chapel Hill, NC: The University of North Carolina Press, 2004).

2. It was common for slaves to do extra work, sell produce from their provision grounds, and turn some of the pay from being hired out to acquire small amounts of property. See, for example, Dylan C. Penningroth, *Claims of Kinfolk: African American Property and Community in the Nineteenth-Century South* (Chapel Hill, NC: The University of North Carolina Press, 2003); *The Slaves' Economy: Independent Production by Slaves in the Americas*, ed. Ira Berlin and Philip D. Morgan (London: Frank Cass, 1991); Justene Hill Edwards, *Unfree Markets: The Slaves' Economy and the Rise of Capitalism in South Carolina* (New York: Columbia University Press, 2021).

3. On Reconstruction violence in Louisiana and the Red River Valley, see Ted Tunnell, *Crucible of Reconstruction: War, Radicalism and Race in Louisiana, 1862–1877* (Baton Rouge: Louisiana State University Press, 1984); Nicholas Lemann, *Redemption: The Last Battle of the Civil War* (New York: Farrar, Straus and Giroux, 2006); and LeeAnna Keith, *The Colfax Massacre: The Untold Story of Black Power, White Terror, and the Death of Reconstruction* (New York: Oxford University Press, 2008).

4. On the American Colonization Society and its efforts to promote the emigration of free people of color to Liberia, see Eric Burin, *Slavery and the Peculiar Solution: A History of the American Colonization Society* (Gainesville: University Press of Florida, 2005); David Brion Davis, *The Problem of Slavery in the Age of Emancipation* (New York: Alfred A. Knopf, 2014); and Floyd J. Miller, *The Search for a Black Nationality: Black Emigration and Colonization, 1787–1863* (Urbana: University of Illinois Press, 1975).

5. While serving as an undercover scout for the U.S. Army in 1875 Adams wrote an earlier version of the "Statement of Affairs and Outrages in the South, 1866" that he would submit to the Senate committee in 1880. It was included in an extensive report on political violence in Louisiana that was sent to Congress by President Grant in 1877. Adams prefaced his earlier account with a characteristically defiant note:

SHREVEPORT, LA., CADDO PARISH.

GENTLEMEN: Let me say to you and to the good people of the North, I did this with no fear. I did it with honesty, and did it because I thought that such things should be reported to the people at large; but I [word missing, probably "say"] to you, and to you, gentlemen, and to the officers of the military service, if these documents is published to the world at large and my name signed to them, I cannot live no longer in the Southern States, because I would be killed by the white people of the Southern States and never be allowed to travel through the South no more. But if it is necessary for to publish my name at the world at large, publish it, sink or swim, live or die.

Yours, truly, HENRY ADAMS

6. The American Freedman's Inquiry Commission submitted its final report to Secretary of War Edwin M. Stanton in 1864; its manuscript records are located in the Houghton Library at Harvard University. Many of the extraordinary documents from this period that are in the National Archives can be found in the multivolume *Freedom: A Documentary History of Emancipation, 1861–1867* (New York and Chapel Hill: Cambridge University Press and University of North Carolina Press, 1982–2013).

7. House of Representatives, *Report of the Joint Committee on Reconstruction,* Report No. 30, 39th Congress, 1st Session (Washington, D.C.: Government Printing Office, 1866).

8. The investigation of the Ku Klux Klan can be found in U.S. Senate, *Report of the Joint Select Committee to Inquire into the Condition of Affairs in the Late Insurrectionary States,* Report No. 41, 42nd Congress, 2nd Session (13 vols., Washington, D.C.: Government Printing Office, 1872).

9. See, for example, *Report of the United States Senate Committee to Inquire into Alleged Frauds and Violence in the Elections of 1878, with the Testimony and Documentary Evidence, Volume I: Louisiana,* Report No. 855, 45th Congress, 3rd Session (Washington, D.C.: Government Printing Office, 1879).

10. The incoming correspondence of the American Colonization Society includes hundreds of letters from southern Blacks who were interested in emigration to Liberia. They discussed their current circumstances, the nature of their communities and religious lives, and often listed the names of individuals and families who wished to emigrate. The letters also offer a wrenching view of the challenges that prospective emigrants faced. The correspondence can be found in the Papers of the American Colonization Society in the Library of Congress in Washington, D.C. Interested readers may also consult *The African Repository,* the official journal of the American Colonization Society, which was published from 1825 to 1892.

THE TESTIMONY OF HENRY ADAMS, FREEDMAN

PART I

Testimony before the Senate Select Committee
to Investigate the Causes which have led to
the Emigration of Negroes from the Southern
to the Northern States, Washington, D.C.,
March 12–13, 1880

TESTIMONY OF HENRY ADAMS.

HENRY ADAMS (colored) sworn and examined.

By Mr. WINDOM:*

Question. State your full name.—Answer. Henry Adams.

Q. What is your residence?

A. Shreveport, Caddo Parish, Louisiana.

Q. How long have you lived there, Mr. Adams?

A. I first went there in 1865—the latter part of 1865.

Q. Where were you born?

A. In Georgia.

Q. Did you go from Georgia to this place in 1865?

A. No, sir.

Q. Where did you live?

A. In De Soto Parish, Louisiana.

Q. How long did you live there?

A. Well, I left Georgia—I don't exactly remember the date when I left Georgia—but I landed in Louisiana in 1850, when I was a little boy only seven years old.

Q. And you had lived in Georgia prior to that?

A. Yes, sir; ever since I was born I had lived in Georgia.

Q. Then your life has been spent in Georgia and Louisiana mainly?

A. I went to Texas and lived in Texas some, too.

Q. What is your business, Mr. Adams?

A. I am a laborer. I was raised on a farm and have been at hard work all my life.

Q. Now tell us, Mr. Adams, what, if anything, you know about the exodus of the colored people from the Southern to the Northern and Western States; and be good enough to tell us in the first place what

---

* William Windom (1827–1891), a lawyer, was a Republican congressman from Minnesota, 1859–69, and a senator, 1870–71, 1871–81, and 1881–83. He also served as secretary of the treasury, March–November 1881 and 1889–91.

you know about the organization of any committee or society among the colored people themselves for the purpose of bettering their condition, and why it was organized. Just give us a history of that as you understand it.

A. Well, in 1870, I believe it was, or about that year, after I had left the Army—I went into the Army in 1866 and came out the last of 1869—and went right back home again where I went from, Shreveport; I enlisted there, and went back there. I enlisted in the Regular Army, and then I went back after I came out of the Army. After we had come out a parcel of we men that was in the Army and other men thought that the way our people had been treated during the time we was in service—we heard so much talk of how they had been treated and opposed so much and there was no help for it—that caused me to go into the Army at first, the way our people was opposed. There was so much going on that I went off and left it; when I came back it was still going on, part of it, not quite so bad as at first. So a parcel of us got together and said that we would organize ourselves into a committee and look into affairs and see the true condition of our race, to see whether it was possible we could stay under a people who had held us under bondage or not. Then we did so and organized a committee.

Q. What did you call your committee?

A. We just called it a committee, that is all we called it, and it remained so; it increased to a large extent, and remained so. Some of the members of the committee was ordered by the committee to go into every State in the South where we had been slaves there, and post one another from time to time about the true condition of our race, and nothing but the truth.

Q. You mean some members of your committee?

A. That committee; yes, sir.

Q. They traveled over the other States?

A. Yes, sir; and we worked some of us, worked our way from place to place and went from State to State and worked—some of them did—amongst our people in the fields, everywhere, to see what sort of living our people lived; whether we could remain in the South amongst the people who had held us as slaves or not. We continued that on till 1874.

Q. Now, before you come to 1874, let me ask how extensive was the operation of your committee? Did they go into almost all the Southern States?

A. Nearly all of the States we could get reports from as to how our race was living there.

Q. Whom did you report to?

A. To the committee; we reported to the committee there.

Q. To the committee at Shreveport?

A. Yes. The reports were sent, and our committee met, so that they would be read at the meeting.

Q. Were they addressed to the committee or to some individual?

A. They were addressed to some individual of the committee—just addressed to the members or ones that we knowed belonged to the committee, and knowed would get the letters we would write to them.

Q. Was the object of that committee at that time to remove your people from the South, or what was it?

A. O, no, sir; not then; we just wanted to see whether there was any State in the South where we could get a living and enjoy our rights.

Q. The object, then, was to find out the best places in the South where you could live?

A. Yes, sir; where we could live and get along well there and to investigate our affairs—not to go nowhere till we saw whether we could stand it.

Q. How were the expenses of these men paid?

A. Every one paid his own expenses, except the one we sent to Louisiana and Mississippi. We took money out of our pockets and sent him, and said to him you must now go to work. You can't find out anything till you get amongst them. You can talk as much as you please, but you have got to go right into the field and work with them and sleep with them to know all about them.

Q. Have you any idea how many of your people went out in that way?

A. At one time there was five hundred of us.

Q. Do you mean five hundred belonging to your committee?

A. Yes, sir.

Q. I want to know how many traveled in that way to get at the condition of your people in the Southern States?

A. I think about one hundred or one hundred and fifty went from one place or another.

Q. And they went from one place to another, working their way and paying their expenses and reporting to the common center at Shreveport, do you mean?

A. Yes, sir.

Q. What was the character of the information that they gave you?

A. Well, the character of the information they brought to us was very bad, sir.

Q. In what respect?

A. They said that in other parts of the country where they traveled through, and what they saw they was comparing with what we saw and what we had seen in the part where we lived; we knowed what that was; and they cited several things that they saw in their travels; it was very bad.

Q. Do you remember any of these reports that you got from members of your committee?

A. Yes, sir; they said in several parts where they was that the land rent was still higher there in that part of the country than it was where we first organized it, and the people was still being whipped, some of them, by the old owners, the men that had owned them as slaves, and some of them was being cheated out of their crops just the same as they was there.

Q. Was anything said about their personal and political rights in these reports, as to how they were treated about these?

A. Yes; some of them stated that in some parts of the country where they voted they would be shot. Some of them stated that if they voted the Democratic ticket they would not be injured.

Q. But that they would be shot, or might be shot, if they voted the Republican ticket?

A. Yes, sir.

Q. State what was the general character of these reports—I have not yet got down to your organization of 1874—whether what you have given was the general character; were there some safer places found that seemed a little better?

A. Some of the places, of course, were a little better than others. Some men that owned some of the plantations would treat the people pretty well in some parts. We found that they would try to pay what they promised from time to time; some they didn't pay near what they promised; and in some places the families—some families—would make from five to a hundred bales of cotton to the family; then at the end of the year they would pay the owner of the land out of that amount at the end of the year, maybe one hundred dollars. Cotton was selling then at twenty-five cents a pound, and at the end of the year when they came to settle up with the owner of the land, they would not get one dollar sometimes, and sometimes they would get thirty dollars, and sometimes a hundred dollars out of a hundred bales of cotton.

Q. What were the best localities that you heard from, if you remember, where they were treated the best?

A. In Virginia was what they stated was the State that treated them best in the South; Virginia, and Missouri, and Kentucky, and Tennessee.

Q. There the treatment was better was it?

A. Yes, sir; it was better there.

Q. Had you any reports from North Carolina?

A. Some few from North Carolina.

Q. Do you remember anything about them; or is your knowledge of that State only general?

A. Well, they reported that some parts of North Carolina was very bad and other parts was very good.

BY MR. VANCE:*

Q. What year was that in?

A. When the reports was made, do you mean?

Q. Yes, sir.

A. From 1870 to 1874.

BY MR. WINDOM:

Q. During that period, from 1870 to 1874, was that what was known as the ku-klux period in the South?

A. The ku-klux was raging there in 1865, '66, '67, '68, and '69.†

Q. Well, what followed that—what organization as enemies of your race, as you regarded them, followed the ku-klux, as you remember?

A. The white league.

Q. Were there any other organizations of that kind?

A. Any other bull-dozing organization?

Q. Yes; any other white organizations that were abusing or murdering the colored people, that you know of?

A. I don't know of none, only the white league; still there was the same connection—they had other names besides the "white league," but they had so many kind of names.

Q. Do you remember any other names they went by?

---

* Zebulon B. Vance (1830–1894), a lawyer, was an American (Know Nothing) congressman from North Carolina, 1858–61. He served as a Confederate army officer, 1861–62, and as the Conservative governor of North Carolina under the Confederacy, 1862–65. After the Civil War Vance joined the Democratic Party and was governor of North Carolina, 1877–79, and a senator, 1879–94.
† The Ku Klux Klan was founded in Tennessee in 1866 and began expanding to other states in 1867.

A. Except ku-klux?

Q. Yes.

A. Well, since that time, of course it has passed as "bulldozing."

Q. I am speaking now of the period from 1870 to 1874, and you have given us the general character of the reports that you got from the South; what did you do in 1874?

A. Well, along in August sometime in 1874, after the white league sprung up, they organized and said this is a white man's government, and the colored men should not hold any offices; they were no good but to work in the fields and take what they would give them and vote the Democratic ticket. That's what they would make public speeches and say to us, and we would hear them. We then organized an organization called the colonization council.

Q. What was the difference between that organization and your committee, as to its objects?

A. Well, the committee was to investigate the condition of our race.

Q. And this organization was then to better your condition after you had found out what that condition was?

A. Yes, sir.

Q. The result of this investigation during these four years by your committee was the organization of this colonization council. Is that the way you wish me to understand it?

A. It caused it to be organized.

Q. It caused it to be organized. Now, what was the purpose of this colonization council?

A. Well, it was to better our condition.

Q. In what way did you propose to do it?

A. We first organized and adopted a plan to appeal to the President of the United States and to Congress to help us out of our distress, or protect us in our rights and privileges.

Q. Your council appealed first to the President and to Congress for protection and relief from this distressed condition in which you found yourselves, and to protect you in the enjoyment of your rights and privileges?

A. Yes, sir.

Q. Well, what other plan had you?

A. And if that failed our idea was then to ask them to set apart a territory in the United States for us, somewhere where we could go and live with our families.

Q. You preferred to go off somewhere by yourselves?

A. Yes.

Q. Well, what then?

A. If that failed, our other object was to ask for an appropriation of money to ship us all to Liberia, in Africa; somewhere where we could live in peace and quiet.

Q. Well, and what after that?

A. When that failed then our idea was to appeal to other governments outside of the United States to help us to get away from the United States and go there and live under their flag.

Q. Have you given us all the objects of this colonization council?

A. That is just what we was organized for, to better our condition one way or another.

Q. At the time you organized you had no idea of going into the Northern States, had you?

A. Yes, sir; we thought maybe the government would set apart a territory for us, or else say that we could go to some State or other and they would assist us in getting there.

Q. Then, if I understand you aright, your first object was to appeal to the President and to Congress for relief. Failing in that, you would then ask to have a territory set apart for you?

A. Yes.

Q. Failing in that, you would ask to be sent abroad under some other flag where you could be protected in your rights as men and citizens?

A. Yes.

Mr. BLAIR.* No; you have forgotten the proposition to Liberia.

Mr. WINDOM. Yes; it escaped me for the moment; that was the other proposition, to go to Liberia.

Q. Well, what did your council do now under these various modes of relief which they had marked out for themselves?

A. Well, we appealed, as we promised.

Q. Did you make any appeal to Congress and to the President?

A. Yes, sir.

Q. Who, in your association, authorized that appeal; how was it gotten up?

A. It was gotten up by resolution.

Q. By resolution?

A. Yes, sir; and just passed by the organization.

Q. Well, by "the organization," what do you mean?

A. I mean the members of it.

Q. Did they have meetings?

A. Yes, sir.

Q. How were these meetings held and where did they hold them?

A. We held them in rooms and houses.

Q. Were they secret meetings or public?

A. We didn't allow nobody in there but our friends. If he was not a member he couldn't get in until we came out in public. When we called a public meeting we came out to the park or anywhere, and didn't care who heard. Then anybody could participate who believed in our movement. There was no meetings held of our members that allowed anybody but our members unless it was somebody that wanted to give us some of their views.

---

* Henry W. Blair (1834–1920), a lawyer who had served as a Union army officer, was a Republican congressman from New Hampshire, 1875–79 and 1893–95, and a senator, 1879–91.

Q. Now, let us understand more distinctly, before we go any further, the kind of people who composed that association. The committee, as I understand you, was composed entirely of laboring people?

A. Yes, sir.

Q. Did it include any politicians of either color, white or black?

A. No politicianers didn't belong to it, because we didn't allow them to know nothing about it, because we was afraid that if we allowed the colored politicianer to belong to it he would tell it to the Republican politicianers, and from that the men that was doing all this to us would get hold of it, too, and then get after us.

Q. So you did not trust any politicians, white or black?

A. No; we didn't trust any of them.

Q. That was the condition of things during the time the committee were at work in 1870 to 1874?

A. Yes, that was the condition.

Q. Now, when you organized the council what kind of people were taken into it?

A. Nobody but laboring men.

Q. You did not extend the kind of membership; you did not take in the politicians?

A. Nobody that had held an office by the votes of the neighborhood could become a member.

Q. No one who held office could become a member?

A. No, sir; none of them.

Q. Did any prominent, active politician become a member of it?

A. No, sir; not if he was seeking an office he could not.

Q. Not if he was seeking office or had sought office?

A. No, sir; he could not.

Q. What kind of pledges did you make, if you are willing to state? Were you sworn?

A. Of course we was all sworn as members of the committee.

Q. You had then your formal initiation and pledges and forms as a secret society; was there any means of recognition? I am not asking you to tell your secrets, but when your men went out—the hundred or hundred and fifty men that went out from you all over the country as a sort of committee of investigation or inquiry—if one of these members met another, could he know it by any sign of recognition?

A. No, sir.

Q. They had no sign?

A. No, sir.

Q. And no means of recognizing each other?

A. No, sir; no sign.

Q. So that if one member should meet another he could not tell by any secret sign or password that he was a member?

A. No, sir. When we met in committee there was not any of us allowed to tell our name. I was chairman of it and I didn't dare to tell anything; I only had to perform my duty.

Q. You would not give to each other the name of any other one?

A. No, sir.

Q. Then you organized this council after you had made this investigation in the different States as to whether you could find any place where you thought you could be well treated under the present condition of things in the South?

A. Yes, sir.

Q. And this was a broader organization, which you called the colonization council?

A. Yes, sir.

Q. And you say you made your appeal to the President?

A. Yes, sir.

Q. To whom did you first appeal?

A. We first appealed to General Grant, when he was President.

Q. When was that; about what year?

A. That was in September, 1874. We told him our condition—
how we was living there; and told him, if there was no other chance,
why we wanted to leave. I will give you a little bit of a sketch of
some few things we said to him. I clipped it out of a Democratic
paper journal after it was published—after we sent the petition to
him.

Q. Well, just give us the facts.

By Mr. Vance:

Q. Was the matter correctly reported in the Democratic paper?

A. It was correct as far as I know. There is just a little bit of it
that is not correct. Some of it is correct and some of it is not.

Q. You had better not read it, then, if it is not all correct.

A. Well, it only sets forth the date and time, and what the origin
of the thing was.

Q. Well, go ahead and give it to us. [The witness searching but
failing to find the newspaper scrap.]

By Mr. Windom:

Q. If you cannot find it readily, you can tell us about the time
and what the nature of the appeal was. You may find it after a while,
and you can then give us the date.

The Witness. Very well.

Q. After you had appealed to General Grant, to whom did you
next appeal; did you send anything to Congress?

A. O, yes, sir; we sent something to Congress. I don't exactly
remember the date that we sent to Congress. It was some time in
1874; but I know at other times we sent to Congress.

Q. Well, what was the nature of the appeal?

A. We told them our condition, and asked Congress to help us
out of our distress and protect us in our lives and property, and pass
some law or provide some way that we might get our rights in the
South, and so forth.

Q. Well, you got no relief or any adequate protection, you say, under the appeal to the government, did you?

A. Yes, sir.

Q. Do you mean to say you did or did not?

A. We did not.

Q. You did not get any relief?

A. No, sir.

Q. Did you appeal again?

A. After the appeal in 1874, we appealed when the time got so hot down there they stopped our churches from having meetings after nine o'clock at night. They stopped them from sitting up and singing over the dead, and so forth, right in the little town where we lived, in Shreveport. I know that to be a fact; and after they did all this, and we saw it was getting so warm—killing our people all over the whole country—there was several of them killed right down in our parish—then we appealed.

Q. Do you, yourself, know of any who were killed there?

A. O, of course, I knowed some.

Q. How many, if you could state?

A. Heaps of them killed, of my friends.

Q. Could you give us the names of some of them?

A. Well, out there on the Buncombe road—well, it is about eighteen miles from Shreveport—a colored man I knowed very well, but I cannot think of his name now——

Q. Perhaps you will think of it after a while, and then you can give it to us. What were the circumstances of the case?

A. Well, he was killed on the public road.

Q. What was he killed for?

A. God Almighty knows; I don't. They had him arrested, and accused him of shooting an old white man that was shot down on the road, and he was accused of it by somebody, and they arrested him and started to bring him to Shreveport to jail, and they shot him.

Q. Shot him on the road?

A. Yes, sir; I saw him when he was shot.

Q. What sort of a man was he?

A. He was a colored man.

Q. Was he an active man in politics?

A. O, no, sir; he was a laborer.

Q. Well, you say that several were killed; do you remember the names of any who were killed about that time?

A. I don't remember the names by heart, but I think I have got them written down.

Q. Well, perhaps you can find some of them before we get through?

A. Yes.

Q. What was the condition of the people in that neighborhood as to the rights and privileges; had they any?

A. At that time, do you mean?

Q. Yes.

A. At that time it looked like it was almost dangerous for a colored man to say that he was a Republican.

Q. Well, was that the offense that caused the persecutions there, or was it some other offense? What was the chief complaint against the colored people, as they made it themselves, which caused this bulldozing and abuse?

A. Well, the Democrats would say to us, that "you all is trying to follow these carpet-baggers, scallawags, and negro leaders, and just as long as you try to follow them we are going just to kill you as we did them." They told us so to our teeth. They told me so many a time.

Q. Well, after you made your appeal to Congress and the President for relief, what next steps did your colonization council take, if you remember?

A. Well, after we seed that things got a little quieter, after along about the latter part of September——

Q. What year was that?

A. In 1874.

Q. Very well, go on.

A. When things got a little quieter then, and it looked like they were sort of talking friendlier to us than before—after September they commenced talking a little friendly with us then—so we knocked along and didn't say no more, and didn't hold any more meetings. We was scared to hold meetings then—afraid to meet— though we met on the sly sometimes, but we was afraid they would come across us and kill us, and sometimes we would have to go away off in the woods and hide ourselves.

Q. At the time you were doing that, was there anything political in your organization?

A. Nothing in the world.

Q. You were simply looking out for a better place in which you could get work and enjoy your freedom?

A. Yes, sir; that was all.

Q. When did the idea first enter your council to emigrate to the northern and northwestern States; if you remember, what were the first movements in that direction?

A. Well, in that petition we appealed there, if nothing could be done to stop the turmoil and strife, and give us our rights in the South, we appealed then, at that time, for a territory to be set apart for us to which we could go and take our families and live in peace and quiet.

Q. The design of your organization, then, as you understood it, was not so much to go north to live among the white people in the Northern and Western States as it was to have a territory somewhere that you could occupy in peace and quiet for yourselves?

A. That is what we wanted, provided we could not get our rights in the South, where we was. We had much rather staid there if we could have had our rights.

Q. You would have preferred to remain in the South?

A. Yes, sir.

Q. And your organization was not in favor of your moving, providing you could get your rights and be protected in the enjoyment of them as any other men?

A. No, sir; we had rather staid there than go anywhere else, though the organization was very careful about that, and we said so from the first; and then, if that could not be done under any circumstances, then we wanted to go to a territory by ourselves.

Q. Well, about what time did this idea of a territory first occur to you; did it occur at all during the organization of your committee, or after the council was organized?

A. After the committee had made their investigations.

Q. Well, what did you do after that?

A. We organized the council after that.

Q. About what time did you lose all hope and confidence that your condition could be tolerated in the Southern States?

A. Well, we never lost all hopes in the world till 1877.

Q. Not until 1877?

A. No, sir. In 1877 we lost all hopes.

Q. Why did you lose all hope in that year?

A. Well, we found ourselves in such condition that we looked around and we seed that there was no way on earth, it seemed, that we could better our condition there, and we discussed that thoroughly in our organization along in May. We said that the whole South—every State in the South—had got into the hands of the very men that held us slaves—from one thing to another—and we thought that the men that held us slaves was holding the reins of government over our heads in every respect almost, even the constable up to the governor. We felt we had almost as well be slaves under these men. In regard to the whole matter that was discussed, it came up in every council. Then we said there was no hope for us and we had better go.

Q. You say, then, that in 1877 you lost all hope of being able to remain in the South, and you began to think of moving somewhere else?

A. Yes; we said we was going if we had to run away and go into the woods.

Q. Well, what was the complaint after you failed to get the territory?

A. Then, in 1877 we appealed to President Hayes and to Congress, to both Houses. I am certain we sent papers there; if they didn't get them that is not our fault; we sent them.

Q. What did that petition ask for?

A. We asked for protection, to have our rights guaranteed to us, and at least if that could not be done, we asked that money should be provided to send us to Liberia.

Q. That was in 1877, was it?

A. Yes, sir; that was in 1877.

Q. Still, up to that time you did not think at all of going into the Northern States; at least you had taken no steps toward going into those States, had you?

A. No, sir.

Q. When did that idea first occur to your people?

A. In 1877, too, we declared that if we could not get a territory we would go anywhere on God's earth; we didn't care where.

By Mr. Vance:

Q. Even to the Northern States?

A. Yes; anywhere to leave them Southern States. We declared that in our council in 1877. We said we would go anywhere to get away.

Q. Well, when did the exodus to the Northern States from your locality, or from your country you are acquainted with best, begin?

A. Well, it didn't begin to any extent until just about a year ago.

Q. It didn't begin to any extent until 1879, you mean?

A. No, sir; not till the spring of 1879.

Q. But you had prior to that time been organized and ready to go somewhere, as I understand you?

A. Yes, sir; we had several organizations; there were many organizations; I can't tell you how many immigration associations, and so forth, all springing out of our colonization council. We had a large meeting, some five thousand people present, and made public speeches in 1877 on immigration.

Q. What was the character of those speeches as to what you intended to do?

A. We intended to go away, to leave the South, if Congress would not give us any relief; we were going away, for we knowed we could not get our rights.

Q. Where were these meetings held?

A. Some were held at Shreveport, in Caddo Parish, some were held in Madison, and some were held in Bossier Parish.

Q. Was there any opposition to these meetings in which you talked about going away?

A. No, sir. There didn't nobody say anything to us against our having our meetings, but I will tell you we had a terrible struggle with our own selves, our own people there; these ministers of these churches would not allow us to have any meeting of that kind, no way.

Q. They didn't want you to go?

A. No; they didn't want us to go.

Q. Why?

A. They wanted us to stay there to support them; I don't know what else. Mighty few ministers would allow us to have their churches; some few would in some of the parishes. There was one church, Zion, in Shreveport, that allowed us to talk there.

Q. Were the ministers opposed to it?

A. Yes, sir; they was opposed to it.

Q. How was it with politicians?

A. The politicians? When we held our meetings we would not allow the politicians to speak. We would not allow any one to speak but in our favor.

BY THE CHAIRMAN:*

Q. Are you speaking of colored men who were politicians?

A. Yes.

Q. And you would not allow the politicians among your people or the ministers to talk?

A. O, yes; we would allow them to talk in our favor.

Q. But not otherwise?

A. No, sir.

BY MR. WINDOM:

Q. Your meetings were composed, then, of men in favor of going away?

A. Yes, and of the laboring class.

Q. Others didn't participate with you?

A. No, sir.

Q. Why didn't the politicians want you to go?

A. They were against it from the beginning.

Q. Why?

A. They thought if we went somewhere else they would not get our votes. That is what we thought.

Q. Why were the ministers opposed to it?

A. Well, because they would not get our support; that is what we thought of them.

Q. They thought it might break up their churches?

A. Yes; that is what they thought; at least we supposed the ministers thought that.

Q. About how many did this committee consist of before you organized your council? Give us the number as near as you can tell.

---

* Daniel W. Voorhees (1827–1897), a lawyer, was a Democratic congressman from Indiana, 1861–66 and 1869–73, and a senator, 1877–97.

A. As many as five hundred in all.

Q. The committee, do you mean?

A. Yes; the committee has been that large.

Q. What was the largest number reached by your colonization council, in your best judgment?

A. Well, it is not exactly five hundred men belonging to the council, that we have in our council, but they all agreed to go with us and enroll their names with us from time to time, so that they have now got at this time 98,000 names enrolled.

Q. Women and men?

A. Yes, sir; women and men, and none under twelve years old.

Q. Well, the colonization council itself numbers about 500?

A. Its strength is about five hundred; it is not that strong at this time, for some has died.

Q. But that was the highest number it has reached?

A. Yes, sir; that is the highest it has reached.

Q. Then through that council, as sort of subscribers to its purpose and acts and for carrying out its objects, there were 98,000 names?

A. Yes; 98,000 names enrolled.

Q. In what parts of the country were these 98,000 people scattered?

A. Well, some in Louisiana—the majority of them in Louisiana, and some in Texas, and some in Arkansas. We joins Arkansas.

Q. Were there any in Mississippi?

A. Yes, sir; a few in Mississippi.

Q. And a few in Alabama?

A. Yes, sir; a few in Alabama, too.

Q. Did the organization extend at all into other States farther away?

A. O, yes, sir.

Q. Have you members in all the Southern States?

A. Not in every one, but in a great many of the others.

Q. Are these members of that colonization council in communication as to the condition of your race, and as to the best thing to be done to alleviate their troubles?

A. O, yes.

Q. So that is an organization for the purpose of giving direction to and managing the affair, and doing what it can to secure relief to your race from the oppressions of the South?

A. Yes, sir; that is what it is for—to try to get our rights some way or other.

Q. How many of your people have gone from that part of the country to the North, if you know?

A. I don't know exactly how many have gone.

Q. Of course you cannot tell us exactly, but as near as you know; give some idea of the number, if you can.

A. My reports from several members of the committee, in parts I have not been in and seen for myself—I take their words and put their words down as mine, because they are not allowed to lie on the subject. And so from what I have learned from them from time to time I think it is about five thousand and something.

Q. Do you mean from that section of country down there?

A. Yes, sir.

Q. From Louisiana?

A. Yes, sir.

Q. What do you know about inducements being held out from politicians of the North, or from politicians anywhere else, to induce these people to leave their section of country and go into the Northern or Western States?

A. There is nobody has written letters of that kind, individually—not no white persons, I know, not to me, to induce anybody to come.

Q. Well, to any of the other members of your council?

A. No, I don't think to any of the members. If they have, they haven't said nothing to me about it.

Q. Well, what inducements, if any, have been offered by railroad companies, speculators, or others, sending out representations of the advantages of Kansas or other States to the colored race; do you know anything about this?

A. No, sir; they ain't said nothing to me about such a thing.

Q. Have you heard of anything of that kind operating upon your people to induce them to leave?

A. They only told me, some members did, how cheap they would carry us, and how cheap they would let us have lands, provided we was going.

Q. That is, the government would let you have land cheap under the homestead law?

A. Yes, sir, and the railroads, too, would sell us land cheap if we wanted it.

Q. Now, Mr. Adams, you know, probably, more about the causes of the exodus from that country than any other man, from your connection with it; tell us in a few words what you believe to be the causes of these people going away.

A. Well, the cause is, in my judgment, and from what information I have received, and what I have seen with my own eyes—it is because the largest majority of the people, of the white people, that held us as slaves treats our people so bad in many respects that it is impossible for them to stand it. Now, in a great many parts of that country there our people most as well be slaves as to be free; because, in the first place, I will state this: that in some times, in times of politics, if they have any idea that the Republicans will carry a parish or ward, or something of that kind, why, they would do anything on God's earth. There ain't nothing too mean for them to do to prevent it; nothing I can make mention of is too mean for them to do. If I am working on his place, and he has been laughing and talking with me, and I do everything he tells me to, yet in times of election he will crush me down, and even kill me, or do anything to me to carry his point. If he can't carry his point without killing me, he will kill me; but if he can carry his point without killing me, he will do that.

Q. He would a little rather not kill you?

A. Yes; but if he cannot control my people just as he pleases, he will get us out of the way, or I can get out of the way, and he won't do nothing with me.

Q. You say that that occurs in times of election. Now you heard the examination yesterday, and the question that was asked the witness, how it was that in a population where there were five or six colored people to one white man, the white people could bulldoze the negro and prevent him from voting. Tell us the process by which that is done; how is that thing done by the Democrats of that country?

A. Well, I can tell you a little something about that. Now, in many instances, whenever they wants to do anything of that kind, they raise a little disturbment with some of the colored people to start on. They may not, perhaps, just come in with a rush and do anything that way to us, but they will come to a place where there is a kind of a little gathering. One will come down and take a drink, and after he takes a drink—he will not get drunk—he don't drink enough to get drunk——

By Mr. Vance:

Q. Whom are you speaking of?

A. Some of these bulldozers; some of these bad white men down there. Well, he goes and takes a drink, and then comes out and commences to meddle with one of the colored men; when he wants to, he will meddle with him; and maybe the colored man will say something sort of rash like, as he do to him. If he does, he will haul out a revolver and strike him on the head, and knock blood out of him, or something of that sort, and maybe, perhaps, shoot him. In many cases he will shoot him, or shoot at him—maybe he won't hit him, but shoot at him; and after he has shot at him, and as soon as they hear that firing, many will come with guns and revolvers, and the first colored man they see talking anything concerning this man that was shot at or struck, then they will commence on him and they will beat him or shoot him. Then there is a passel of them will commence firing on them colored men who haven't got anything to fight with. Now, if one of the colored men will show fight, if he shoots one or hurts one of them pretty bad, his life ain't no more than a chicken's. He may go home if he wants to, but he won't stay home, for a passel will come after him that night; and if they don't get him then they will come again. But they will get him; any one that done anything or said anything at the time this was first raised, they will get him. They won't get 'em all at once. They will come to their house and take one one time; then they will come and take another at another time, and so they will get all them that says or does anything to resist them.

Q. Suppose the colored men should resist these attacks; what would be the result?

A. Well, if the colored people think of showing any kind of resistance, or of making any stand against them, or come out like they were going to make a stand, they ain't going to come up boldly and fight.

Q. Who ain't?

A. The white men ain't; that is, if they think the colored men are prepared to make a fight, they ain't going to attack them. But they will do this: One kind of peaceable man amongst our people will come and say, "Don't have a fuss; don't be preparing to raise a riot or nothing; all this fuss is over, it is all settled, and settled good; it shan't come to no riot, and we want you all to be quiet." If there is any leader of that kind, he will say that, and he won't allow our men to raise a riot; and as all they ask is to have peace, they don't defend themselves against these men. Them men has done so to one after another, and they let them just go, and we will go on paying no attention and thinking no harm at all. But the white men will go around to this softhearted one who don't care for our race, and they will

find out from him all they can about who would have done something, who would have tackled them, and the first thing they know
here will come one or two white men in a field on the plantation
where one or two of them are working, and they will take them and
arrest them and take them to prison. Then they will go to another
plantation, and to another and another, and get them all arrested
after awhile, and maybe they will come to the jail in a little while
and take them out, and turn them loose, and tell them, "You had
better go such a course, because it is safer, and they might catch
you." They go, and a crowd meets them and catches them, and they
kill them in the woods. You never hear of them after that.

Q. Why do not the colored people arm themselves against these
outrages, and attempt to defend themselves? Cannot they get arms?

A. They can buy just as many arms as they want; if they have
money they can buy as many as they want to.

Q. Will they let them keep them?

A. Yes, till the riot come. I will tell you how that is. If there was
a riot started—for instance, this may be a little town here; if there
is a riot started somewhere about ten or fifteen miles from that town,
they would form themselves at that town and would go down there
by fifties and hundreds in a gang, which I have seen with these eyes
many a time—I have seen it many a time. And then they would go
there themselves, but would keep some one there at the place to
watch us, to see whether the colored men were going to that town
to buy arms or not. If the colored men are attacked they call it a
riot, because they are killing the colored men. You never hear of
the colored man raising the riot, because he never gets the chance.
If he shoots at a white man and strikes him, they kill fifty colored
men for the one white man that was shot.

Q. And the colored people understand that, do they?

A. O, yes, sir; and at the time, seeing there is a riot going on, the
colored man cannot buy any ammunition. If the riot is ten or fifteen
miles off he can't buy no ammunition.

Q. What is the process by which just before an election a large district is carried by these men? How do they prevent the colored man from voting?

A. In some particular districts, and districts where the colored people are in a large majority, there is the only places where they does such devilment. In parishes where the colored people are in the minority, they hardly ever raise up that way to prevent them.

Q. Do they visit them at night, or how do they manage that?

A. They go 'round to the houses at night.

Q. To individual houses?

A. Yes, sir.

Q. What do they do at these houses? We don't understand this, you see.

A. Well, in some instances they will come to our houses and ask us—well, if you are the president of a club, you know, they will call you out. The man will go out, and they will ask him is he going to—or, "Where's your tickets?" "What tickets?" he will say, and they will say, "The Republican tickets you are going to carry with you to the polls to-morrow." If he says he ain't going to carry none, they will say, "Why, you had some tickets to-day, hadn't you?" He will say "No," or will deny it, and then they will search him and search his house, and if he ain't got none they won't do anything to him; but if they find any tickets on him, or in his house, they will perhaps whip him or knock him about a little. They won't kill him then, without he says he is determined to issue his tickets and go to the polls and vote them. They won't kill him at all, but just beat him and knock him about a little and let him go. That scares him from going. Then they will tell him, "If you go to the polls to-morrow, and carry them tickets to your club and vote against us, we will fix *you*. You had better not do it." And to save his life he won't do it. Some will undertake it, but in some instances they have to run off during election day. They have to leave the polls, or else they will be killed; many of the presidents of the clubs have to do so.

Q. How many colored people would vote the Democratic ticket if they had the chance—if you would just let them have the privilege?

A. Well, not but a few sets of men will do that. All the ones I ever seed vote the Democratic ticket down there is men, some of them barbers, in the stores, some few draymen that dray for the houses when they can get it. If the boss men know they vote the Republican ticket they won't employ them.

Q. Well, that is not what I mean; that is not voting from choice.

A. Well, otherwise I don't believe there is over a hundred, to my knowledge, that would do it, unless it was something about theories of working, or something of that kind it would have to be to combine them to make them do it. I recollect I used to run a plantation; I used to boss a plantation for a man in Shreveport, in 1872, and boss a wood-yard. I was a wood-chopper myself, and managed the affairs of the wood-yard for a part of the time for him. Then, in 1873, I had charge of his plantation and used to boss on his plantation for him, and attend to all the business on his plantation, and made my reports to him each month. It was about twelve or thirteen miles from the town of Shreveport, in Caddo Parish; and in 1874, the time when the white league raised up so, and said this was a white man's government, and nobody who voted the Republican ticket should not have no more employment, and anybody who employed such a man as that he should be denounced by the white men, and they called it the white man's party. Well, then, me and him was very friendly till that time. He is a large farmer, and he owns twelve plantations, and I had been his agent, buying cotton seeds and corn to run his plantation, and attended to his oil-mill; he owns an oil-mill, and he thought a heap of me. In March and April I worked for him, and when I went back to get employment, and told him that I wanted him to employ me, he said, "I cannot do it." I never had anything to do with politics any more than going to vote; or when my men who belonged to the society that I belonged to would come to me and ask me what I thought best as to the way they should vote, I would tell them, of course, and I would issue them tickets—all my members; I would issue tickets to them and tell them how I thought they ought to vote. To a great extent our organization would not vote there unless I issued an order to them telling them how I thought they ought to vote, and they would not prepare to do so unless I would tell them. Well, I went back to my old employer and told him that I wanted employment. He said to me, "Adams, I think a heap of you as a man; I know you are a true man, and that you will do what you promise to do, but under this order I cannot employ you."

Q. What was his name?

A. Hambleton—W. C. Hambleton, of Hambleton & Company.

Q. Is his residence at Shreveport?

A. Yes, sir; at Shreveport. Well, Mr. Hambleton said to me, "Adams, you are a good old Republican, and I cannot employ you because you are a Republican. I cannot employ you no more." I says to him, "Why, Mr. Hambleton, you votes as you please, and acts as you please, and why not me?" "Well, I have no objection to that whatever, but you know I cannot employ you, because I said I would not employ no more Republicans, and I cannot do it. That is all the reason. I've got nothing against you—nothing in the world against you but that, and I cannot employ you nohow on that account." Now, him and me had been good friends. He gave me four hundred and fifty dollars a year the first year I done business for him, and I have made off'n him one hundred dollars a month chopping wood."

Q. By what?

A. By chopping wood; with these hands and a maul and axe, chopping and cording wood, I made a hundred dollars a month off of him, that same man, and he knows it.

Mr. VANCE. That is equal to wages in Indiana, Mr. Chairman.

By Mr. Windom:

Q. Did he allow you by the cord?

A. Yes; so much by the cord. I got $1.25 a cord, and I can cut from three to seven cords a day, and cord them up; and I can split from three to five hundred rails a day.

Q. Well, Mr. Adams, you regard this organization to which you have referred as the first movement in this country on the subject of this emigration of your people, do you not?

A. Yes, sir; the first I have known anything about.

Q. I will ask you, Mr. Adams, what you think of the probabilities of this exodus in the future; is it going to be large or small; is it increasing or decreasing?

A. Well, it is increasing to a great extent.

Q. Do you think it is likely to reach much larger proportions?

A. O, yes, sir; I believe it will.

Q. In any event, do you mean?

A. I believe it will unless there are some steps taken to prevent it.

Q. What kind of steps?

A. Well, by extending to my race their rights, in every respect.

Q. You think, as you said awhile ago, that your people lost all hope of securing these rights in 1877, and have not recovered any confidence in that matter since?

A. Yes, sir; we have lost all hope of securing our rights where we are, and we are preparing to leave.

Q. What would be the effect, do you think, of the election of a Democratic President upon this movement of your people?

A. I could hardly tell what effect it would have upon them.

Q. Would it increase the confidence of the colored people that their rights as freedmen and their privileges would be secured to them?

A. My own candid opinion is that if a Democratic President was elected—I, myself, believe—I give that as my belief, that if a

Democratic President was elected, that we would not be able to come out of there, unless we come through the woods as we did when we run away in the slave times.

Q. Is not that fear operating now, to some extent, in hurrying your people away at this time?

A. Yes, sir; that is making them feel like going now.

Q. You want to get away before a Democratic President is elected?

A. We don't know who is going to be elected.

Q. That is what I think.

A. That is what I tell them, and what I believe.

Q. You believe that would be the effect if such an evil were to befall the country?

A. Yes, that is what I believe.

Q. Do you know whether they are interfering with any one's going away now?

A. There has been many reports to me, individually, of that kind, that they have been interfered with in getting away.

Q. Tell us in what way this interference has been shown, from the reports you have heard and from what you have seen and know yourself.

A. Well, I belong to that emigration committee that was created by that convention in New Orleans last April. There was a committee of fifteen appointed by that convention, and in that committee of fifteen I was one of them that was appointed. The convention appointed it to consider the matter of emigration.

Q. Were you a member of that convention?

A. Yes, sir; and I was appointed on the committee there; and that committee of fifteen that was created by the convention appointed me as a member of the committee on arrangements and transportation. I served as a member of that committee, and was not chairman of that committee of arrangements and transportation, but only a member of it; but I did my duty which I was instructed to do by that committee what time I was about there. I was there in part of May, about four or five days in May, when I went away into the country and country parishes, and never came back till along about the 7th of June, and then I staid there then for two or three months. And the people, whilst I was there on that committee, several of them came from the country, some of them from Mississippi, and some from Alabama, and some from several parts of Louisiana, and would report to me this: Two men reported that, one of them, he left a place where he was living at in Mississippi, and whilst being in the field plowing alone, that he saw a large crowd of white men coming to him with guns, and he said that he didn't know what they was coming for, but somebody, some colored person, got to him before they did, and said that these men was going to kill him. "What for?" he asked. "Wasn't he out on the river that night with a lot of colored people going to Kansas?" "Yes, he was," he said, "Well, that man is going to kill the man that was leading them." And sure enough he had been. So he whirled right out and they captured his horse; his horse was plowing; and he run that night to his house and expected to get his things, as fifteen others was going away with him; but when he went back to his house he found that they had been there and took his trunk and all his clothes, and everything he had, and carried them up to the boss-man's house, and they had his horse too. I asked, "Did he owe the man anything?" and he said, "He didn't owe the man five cents in the world." He said this was his own crop and everything. And this man took his horse and his plow, and everything he had, and put his horse in his own stable and put his things up there in his own store-room, and told him that he could not have anything. And he had $125 in his trunk that he was going away with, and he took that too; and he had to run away himself to save his life.

Mr. VANCE. Perhaps that man borrowed some money of you?

The WITNESS. Not a cent, sir. He was trying to get away, and to save up enough to take the boat that evening, but they took all he had from him; but the next Saturday I gave him something to get away with.

Mr. Vance. Then you did help him?

The Witness. O, yes; I paid his fare myself, out of my own pocket.

Q. Have you heard of any other difficulties in your people getting away?

A. O, yes, sir; another man with him that run off from the same place was in the same condition, though he didn't have as much as that other left behind; and then there was some come from Red River that said the captain of the boat would not take him and his family because they said he was going to Kansas, and they would not take them down to the mouth of the river.

By Mr. Blair:

Q. Did he offer to pay the captain?

A. O, yes, sir.

Mr. Vance. Give me the name of the man from whom this horse and property was taken?

The Witness. I can't remember the name in either case at this time, but I know 'em, and I knew at the time the man told me. I wrote it down on a piece of paper, because that was some part of my duty; as being a member of the colonization council, it was part of my duty to do so, and I did do it, though I don't remember where it is now, but I know it is written down. Not only his case is writ down, but those who came to me in these circumstances I wrote down, and I have got them somewhere now.

By Mr. Windom:

Q. Were there many cases like that?

A. Several come to me and said during the time that I was performing that duty, that they had to slip out and run away; and while I was absent from there off of the duty I don't know how many people had taken the boat there during the time I was absent, but I was informed that there was six hundred; but I had taken the account of those that had taken the boat during the time I was there, and I had a conversation with the majority of them.

Q. What was generally the reason they gave for going away?

A. A great many of them stated that "I have been working ever since I pretended to be free"—some would say "pretended to be free," and others would say "ever since I have been free"—"and I never have got nothing of any account, but every year I come out in debt," and he says that sometimes I may come out, this year may be, perhaps, he says, with about twenty dollars—and again I would come out with nothing, and if I attempt to go away from the place where I live and on which I have a horse, and I have a cow, and I have hogs, and I have a wagon, and I have a team—some of them would state—and if I attempted to leave the place, everything that I have would be taken away from me, and I would go off with nothing.

Q. Was that to go off from one place, from one plantation, to another?

A. Yes, to go off to any other plantation.

Q. This is what some of these people told you who were ready to leave their homes and were waiting to take the boat at Shreveport?

A. Yes, sir; these facts—the people that took the boat there told me this, and I took them down at the time, and I can state facts that I seen with my own eyes, where they did do it.

Q. What were they?

A. In the parish of Caddo, on Red River, there is Reuben White, a well-known farmer there.

Q. Is he a colored man?

A. No, he is a white man, and a rich man. He have two plantations on Red River, to my knowing. And I knowed the man that knowed him in slave times, that belonged to him, and have been with him, and been working on the plantation ever since he was there—the old man Logan Low. He has a son named Tim; and then an old man named Dickson, if I recollect the names right now, and many more that knowed their names personally, but I cannot call their names personally. They went to go off of his place, and some of them made—the men and their families—and they were working their families in conjunction. I have known them to make a hundred bales of cotton to the family; and when they went away, year before last, they swept the last thing from them, and never allowed them to carry away nothing, nothing more than their wearing clothes.

Q. Where were they going—to Kansas?

A. No; only from his place to another place.

By Mr. Vance:

Q. Can you recollect the name of the man who took their property?

A. Yes; his name is Reuben White.

Q. What is the name of the colored man?

A. Logan Low is one, and Dickson is one.

By the Chairman:

Q. Does Reuben White live at Shreveport?

A. Yes, sir; he is one of my friends.

By Mr. Blair:

Q. Have you heard any reports from the men who have emigrated with their families and made this exodus?

A. Yes.

Q. As to how they were received in the places where they went, and how they are doing?

A. Yes.

Q. What reports came back to the organization from these people?

A. They all gave good reports—every letter I have received is encouraging for them to come.

Q. What do they say of their condition in the localities where they now are as compared with what it was in the places which they left?

A. They say that when they work for a man there in Kansas and Nebraska, and some of them that has gone to Colorado—they says that when they work for a man there he pays them, he has no trouble to get his money whatever. They says there is no such thing as whipping him, there is no such thing as shooting him, there is no such thing as running him off from his club meeting, or any thing of that sort, when he is holding his meetings. They says there is no such thing as an order to close the churches at nine o'clock at night, and there is no such thing as arresting them if they sets up over their dead after nine o'clock, as it has been in some parts of Louisiana where he had lived. They says everybody is free there, and everybody has free intercourse there every way. And they says that wages is—some stated that they got nine dollars a week for their work, and some of them stated—that is the men—and some of them stated that their wives got from three to four dollars a week for work in Kansas, Nebraska, and Colorado.

Q. Did they say anything about their advantages for schooling?

A. Yes; they said that they had public schools there, and they had the same privilege to send their children as anybody else had that was there before.

Q. What did they say, if anything, as to the climate, whether it was hard on them, or otherwise?

A. They says that is a little colder there, than where they come from, but they said that the cold didn't hurt them anything; they was all satisfied to stand the cold; they can stand it.

Q. What did they say, if anything, about the sickness and suffering amongst them as they were going to Kansas, and getting settled there?

A. Well, they say they have had some little hard times in that way, of sickness in traveling, before they got to the places and got settled; some of them says that, but some of them says they had no trouble in that way.

Q. Some had more strength and were in better spirits, and so were a little more jolly?

A. Yes, sir.

Q. Did they say anything as to the disposition of the people to receive them in a friendly way, and to assist them in getting places, or otherwise?

A. Yes; everybody seems willing to help them in every respect; everybody, men and women, was ready to help them and was kind to them, and they could find a friend most anywhere who would be ready to do something for them.

Q. These people that you mention as having heard from went to Kansas, Colorado, and Nebraska; have you heard anything from those who have gone to other States in the North?

A. Not directly I haven't; I have received letters only from Kansas, and Nebraska, and Colorado—these three States.

Q. Have you had any correspondence with the colored men that have been interested in the movement at any time in Missouri?

A. O, yes; we have heard from them.

Q. Mention any names that occur to you of colored men who have corresponded with you in reference to that?

A. I have had correspondence with the leaders of the organizations there.

Q. Can you mention the names of any of these men?

A. Yes; two of them were Turners—two different Turners. I don't know just their names; I know both of them started with J's—they were two Turners anyway.*

---

* A mass meeting held in March 1879 at St. Paul African Methodist Episcopal in St. Louis resulted in the formation of a Committee of Twenty-five to aid the Exodusters arriving in St. Louis. The next month the committee split into two rival organizations: the Colored Immigrant Aid Association, founded by James Milton Turner (1839/1840–1915), who had served as U.S. minister to Liberia, 1871–78, and the Colored Refugee Relief Board, led by Moses Dickson (1824–1901) and John Dickson, both ministers of the A.M.E. Church.

Q. Well, tell about these two Turners, each of them, what correspondence you had with them?

A. They wrote to me and sent me their pamphlets.

Q. From what parts of Missouri did they write to you?

A. Both of them from Saint Louis.

Q. What did they represent themselves to be; what connection did they say they had with the movement?

A. They were leaders of the Emigrant Aid Associations there in Saint Louis. One was the Emigrant Aid Association there, and one was the Emigrant Relief Association there. I think that was it. One was, I think, called the Colored Emigrant Aid Association, and one of them was president of the Colored Emigration Relief Association—that was it—or Relief Board perhaps.

Q. Now were these two associations organized for the same purpose—that is, to relieve the colored people who were going North?

A. I do not know what was their purpose more than what they said.

Q. Well, what did they say their object was?

A. One of them said the object was to help all those which came; the other said the object was to help them and encourage them when they did come.

Q. Did either of them write anything to discourage the emigration?

A. O, nobody didn't write nothing to discourage us at all; only in this light, they would tell me when the money was nearly exhausted, you know—they would tell me that, and when they didn't think they would be able to help us and when they would be able.

Q. Well, what was this correspondence about; what else did they say?

A. Well, when they first wrote to me I didn't know anything about it—they wrote to me first.

Q. Have you any of these letters, any of this correspondence, with you?

A. I have got one of these Turner letters or pamphlets with me. I have one of the others, too, which I can bring.

Q. Go on.

A. Well, when they first wrote to me they sent me some of the pamphlets of the organizations. I didn't know them, but supposed that there was some men that had went from our place up there which gave them my name, and they sent them to me; I didn't know nothing about them till then; or they may have seen my name in some printing of the organization in the papers, or something of that sort; I don't know how they got my name.

Q. Well, what did you do when you got these pamphlets or circulars?

A. When they wrote me I answered them, and then kept a regular correspondence with one of the associations.

Q. With which one of the associations did you keep up a regular correspondence?

A. I kept up a regular correspondence with John Turner, I think it was—his name started with "J"; some time he would put it John Turner.

Q. Was that the Aid Association or the Relief Association?

A. That was the relief.

Q. And the other was the Aid Association?

A. Yes; that was the other, the aid.

Q. What became of your correspondence with the Emigration Aid Association, the other Turner?

A. Well, it busted up somehow or other. I didn't receive no more than one letter from him, I think; I got the pamphlet.

Q. He sent you a circular or pamphlet?

A. Yes, sir; he sent me his pamphlet about the organization.

Q. Have you got it with you?

A. Well, I have got one of them here, and I can get the other.

Q. Was that circular to encourage or discourage your people from emigrating?

A. The letter was to encourage I know; the pamphlet I hardly know about now; I did not get no more letters about that.

Q. Have you the circulars or pamphlets from both of them?

A. I have one of them here, I know. (Searching.) Here is one from the first Turner. (Handing to Mr. Blair the circular of the Emigration Aid Association.) This is the one that busted.

Q. You mean the one whom you ceased to have correspondence with?

A. Yes, sir; this is the one that the correspondence busted with.

Q. I would like to know further about it. This man, you say, wrote you a letter?

A. Yes, sir.

Q. He was the president. (Reading:) "Hon. J. Milton Turner, president."

A. Yes, sir; and he wrote me a letter.

Q. Yes; and in that letter he wrote you, what did he say with regard to the exodus?

A. Well, I don't remember all that he said; I remember a few words.

Q. Well, what few words do you remember, or the substance of them; I don't expect you to give the words—just give us the impression made upon you as to what its meaning was, and whether it was for or against the exodus?

A. Well, it was for the exodus, because you know that he wrote it altogether for the exodus, so that our people could get out of their distress, he said; he said he was glad to see them trying to get out of their distress.

Q. He said he was glad to see them trying to get out of their distress?

A. Yes, sir.

By the Chairman:

Q. You say you have not got the letter?

A. No, sir; not here, I haven't. (Producing the circular of the Colored Immigration Aid Association.) I did not know I had this till I found it in my pocket here.

Mr. Blair. I will read this, as I understand Mr. Turner* is a man who has changed position on this subject. (Reading the circular.) On the first page is—

An appeal to the humane and philanthropic.

THE COLORED IMMIGRATION AID ASSOCIATION.

Hon. J. Milton Turner, president.

Albert Burgess, secretary.

W. H. Scudder, acting treasurer.

Board of directors: Chas. H. Tyler, Jas. W. Wilson, Matthew Richardson, John J. Harris, James P. Thomas, Richard Smith.

Board of managers: Chas. H. Tyler, Jas. W. Wilson.

The citizens of Saint Louis are in no way instrumental to instigate this migration of colored people. Their work is alone that of humanity.

Then follows the appeal, in these words:

THE COLORED IMMIGRATION ASSOCIATION.

Saint Louis, Mo., *April* 22, 1879.

The colored men of this city, who have been active in the organization of the above-named society to assist the colored immigrants from the South in finding a local habitation in the rich and growing West, have just perfected that organization, with the above named as president, secretary, treasurer, and directors. These names include some of the leading colored men of the place and an advisory

---

* James Milton Turner.

board, to be composed of some of the most public spirited and benevolent of our citizens, and these are a guaranty to all who know them
of perfect good faith, integrity, and trustworthiness in the distribu-
tion of such funds as may be contributed to them for the purposes
indicated.

The articles of the society have already been incorporated, and the
object is set forth in the following:

The object of the association shall be to raise funds for the
establishment of colored settlements and to aid the colored immigrants who may reach our city while fleeing from the Southern
States.

Aid will only be extended to the colored immigrant on his way *bona
fide* to his own home.

The exorbitant rent he has been compelled to pay the land-
owner in the South, and the annual bills to the storekeeper, eat
up the entire fruits of his labor, while murder, rapine, arson, and
most barbarous outlawry have prevailed to persecute the negro,
and now that a general exodus of those poor afflicted people is
upon us, we recognize in that only the legitimate result of the per-
sistent plunderings and exactions of the haughty planters of that
section.

Saint Louis is the first objective point of all these exiles, and is
the place where aid can be most effectively and economically ren-
dered them, and where sound judgment and friendly counsel can be
best employed to so distribute them in their desire to form settlements in Kansas and other parts as to avoid their becoming paupers
in the land whither they journey.

Our streets are crowded almost daily with men, women, and
children without sufficient clothing, shelter, or food. The tireless
charity of our citizens has responded liberally to the appeal of suffering humanity in this case until we find it necessary to ask for
help.

This appeal is made to the charitable, the philanthropic, the bene-
factors of the race of all localities who desire to assist the lowly and
the down-trodden in establishing homes where he and his family can
enjoy in peace and security all the fruits of his labor.

Contributions to the cause can be sent through Charles Parsons, president of the State Savings Association, Saint Louis, Mo., and will be thankfully received.

Respectfully,

ALBERT BURGESS, *Secretary.*

By order of—

Hon. J. MILTON TURNER, *President.*

[Following is the text of the other "Turner circular," referred to by witness as the "J. Turner pamphlet," and made a part of his statement, ordered on the following day to go in the record, but which is inserted here as in proper place:]

COLORED REFUGEE RELIEF BOARD, OFFICE
903 MORGAN STREET, SAINT LOUIS, MO.

Directors: Rev. Edgar Pitts, C. H. Tandy, P. H. Murray, J. W. Wheeler, Sandy Mix, James W. Grant, Wm. H. Stanton, John Casey, Golden Worthington, Rev. G. W. Wright, Rev. J. Washington.

Committee on transportation: Daniel Prince, C. E. Parker, C. W. Prentice, chairman.

Committee on commissary: Wm. R. Lawton, chairman.

The frequent and continued arrival of colored emigrants from the South, in a majority of cases utterly destitute, and the information received from credible sources that thousands are assembled at steamboat landings along the Mississippi ready to embark, and that tens of thousands in the interior of Mississippi and Louisiana are preparing to join the exodus at the first convenient opportunity, has made it necessary for the relief committee of twenty-five, originally appointed and approved by mass meetings of the citizens of Saint Louis, to assume a form more perfectly adapted to meet the increasing demands and facilitate its operations.

They have organized under the title of the Colored People's Emigration Relief Board of Saint Louis, Mo., with the following officers, directors, and committees:

Rev. Moses Dickson, president; Wm. R. Lawton, vice-president; John H. Johnson, secretary; Rev. John Turner, treasurer.

Work of the committee: The committee found 2,000 emigrants half clad, without food or means, filling the colored churches, halls, and houses, and began at once an active canvass for funds, and for weeks liberal hands administered to their every want, and boxes of clothing and baskets of food were given without stint; but still they came upon every boat from the Lower Mississippi, until the movement assumed stupendous proportions, and the original committee felt the necessity of extending their appeal.

Already the committee, through solicitations, have issued 50,000 rations and clothing and transportation for 4,004 persons, with the following

Financial exhibit: By Rev. Moses Dickson the committee on finance made its report as follows:

Received by the committee up to April 1	$374 00
Mullanphy board*	287 00
Charles Starks	206 95
By Rev. John Turner, through Globe-Democrat	1, 220 85
By Rev. John Turner, from other sources.	523 47
By the chairman, through Indianapolis Journal	85 00
From other sources, of which notices have been	
published in the Globe-Democrat	257 15
Sarah O. Farrar, Newton Centre, Mass	20 00
Good Samaritan, Boston, Mass	250 00
Joseph Hale, Boston, Mass.	5 00
Christopher Wey, Portland, Maine	2 00
L. W. String, Saville, Ohio	5 00
J. R. Parkins, Brookline, Mass	6 00
From refugees.	97 00
	———
Total	3, 341 42

---

* The Mullanphy Board managed the fund established by Bryan Mullanphy (1809–1851), the heir to a mercantile fortune, to "furnish relief to all poor emigrants and travelers coming to St. Louis, on their way bona-fide to settle in the West."

Amount paid out ending April 22: . . . .
To Missouri River Packet Company for refugees
  and freight 2, 607 50
For transportation on railroad 30 00
Groceries and provisions. 247 99
Telegrams, stationery, and stamps. 10 40
House rent and cartage. 74 00

      Total 2, 973 89

In treasury 367 53

When they arrive in Kansas their wants are still pressing. Governor St. John,* of that State, through representations made by delegates sent from our board, has organized a State central board, with auxiliaries throughout the State, to afford them relief.

We earnestly beseech the friends of humanity everywhere to send money, food, clothing, and grants for land if possible, to help us in this arduous but laudable undertaking.

Contributions may be sent to the following persons: Rev. Moses Dickson, No. 903 Morgan street; Rev. John Turner, 1512 Morgan street; John H. Johnson, customhouse; Dr. B. St. J. Fry, Central Christian Advocate; and office of the Globe-Democrat, Saint Louis, Mo.

Adjourned to Saturday, March 13, 1880.

TWENTY- FOURTH DAY.

WASHINGTON, *Saturday, March,* 13, 1880.
Committee met this day at 10 o'clock a. m. Present, Messrs. Voorhees (chairman), Vance, Windom, and Blair.

---

* John Pierce St. John (1833–1916), a lawyer and former Union officer, was the Republican governor of Kansas, 1879–83.

TESTIMONY OF HENRY ADAMS CONTINUED.

HENRY ADAMS's direct examination continued:

By MR. WINDOM:

Q. Mr. Adams, how long were you a soldier?

A. I enlisted in September, 1866, and I was discharged September, 1869. I have my papers in my pocket if it is necessary to show them.

Q. You were in the Regular Army, I think you said?

A. Yes, sir.

Q. Where were you stationed during these years?

A. Part of the time I was stationed at Shreveport, part of the time at Greenville, near New Orleans, and part of the time at Fort Jackson.

Q. State whether you have been through the country a great deal or not during the last ten years.

A. I have, sir; I have traveled a great deal on horseback, on the steamboat, and on the cars.

Q. In what capacity were you traveling?

A. Well, part of the time I traveled on my own hook, sometimes going to a place to attend to my own business; at other times I traveled as a government scout to gain all the information I could.

Q. In the interest of your organization?

A. Yes, sir; in the interest of our organization.

Q. Well, during these travels through the last ten years have you kept any memoranda of occurrences which you observed?

A. Yes, sir; I have kept a memorandum of a great deal.

Q. State whether you have prepared a succinct statement of these facts which you can swear to?

A. Yes, sir; I have got some drawed up which I ascertained in traveling from 1865 up to 1876; and then there is times that I have got some that is written out in lead pencil, writing from time to time since that time up to the date of 1879; but I haven't got that in good shape, not written off in ink.

Q. I will ask you in a few moments to give us that statement, but in the mean time, and before I ask you that, I will ask you whether you have ever been attacked yourself—whether any attempt has been made to injure you in any way, or to do anything to your detriment, by reason of what you were doing?

A. Yes, sir; in some instances; but I will explain that. In De Soto Parish, where my mother and father have lived for many years—my mother is now dead, she died since I left Shreveport, or about the time that I left, and I have not seen any of my people since she died—and in going down there to see them late in 1865, or in 1866, I was shot at in December, 1865, twenty times by a crowd of white men, and in running from them trying to make my escape, dodging behind trees and one thing or other, they never struck me, but I was shot through the coat tail once or twice, and through my hat once.

Q. What was the cause of their shooting at you?

A. Well, they said that I had left De Soto Parish, in one instance, and was trying to come down there to get others to leave of my friends; and then, besides that, there was some robbers of 'em who was trying to rob me. I had a little wagon and plenty of produce, and I was going back to Shreveport, and they robbed me of all that—everything I had—to about $500 in all. I called it $250, but it was about $500. And then at another time in 1866 I was down there, and going on back I was met up by about five men, and they asked me who I belonged to. I told them I belonged to nobody. "You don't belong to nobody?" I said "No." "Well, by God," they says, "negroes can't travel through here that don't belong to somebody, and we will fix you up right here." I was on a good horse—a pretty good horse—and I made a break and ran. They tried to kill me but I got off; they shot four or five times at me, but never hit me. I ran and got away.

Q. I will call your attention to the condensed statement that you will swear to of outrages which have fallen under your observation; do you recognize that as your paper (handing paper to witness)?

A. Yes, sir; that is my statement.

Q. Are you prepared to swear to that statement?

A. Yes; I can swear to that.

Q. It is a pretty long statement and we will have to have it read, or at least parts of it. You say this statement was prepared by yourself and copied by your clerk or secretary?

A. Yes, sir.

Mr. WINDOM reading portions of the statement.

The CHAIRMAN. (To the witness.) Do you write yourself, Mr. Adams?

The WITNESS. Yes, sir; but I am not a good reader of anybody else's writing than my own.

The CHAIRMAN. Well, Mr. Windom, we will just consider this statement as presented, and will not require it to be read through at present.

By MR. BLAIR:

Q. What are the other papers you have there?

A. (Handing papers.)

Q. Is this also a statement of things that have occurred?

A. Yes, sir.

Q. How came you by these, Mr. Adams?

A. They gave me them statements when I was part of the times in my travels in every direction. I traveled to gain information of what had been transacted concerning them.

Q. Are these from memoranda made by yourself of statements made by these parties?

A. They made the statements and I wrote them down as they made them. They signed some of them, and they were told me what they knowed by others.

Q. And here are two sheets marked "affidavits"?

A. Yes, sir.

Q. Were these made in your presence?

A. Yes, sir.

Q. And signed in your presence?

A. Yes, sir.

Q. And they were read over in your hearing before they signed them?

A. Yes; as they made them I wrote them out and they signed them.

Q. These are not the writing as made by them are they?

A. No, sir; these are copies.

Q. They are correct copies are they?

A. Yes, sir; I know that they are correct. I wish to say, Mr. Chairman, that none of these papers that I have got here I didn't prepare to meet any committee whatever with; I didn't know I would be called on to swear to anything concerning these things.

By Mr. Windom:

Q. Why did you prepare them, how did you come to prepare them?

A. In keeping a statement of the true condition of our race in the South and others that I ascertained when I was a scout for the government—some of them.

(The statements and affidavits were admitted as evidence and are inserted at the close of witness's examination.)

Q. You speak of being a scout for the government; when were you employed in that capacity?

A. I commenced in April or March.

Q. Of what year?

A. 1875.

Q. You were employed by whom?

A. When I made my reports I always reported to the adjutant of the Seventh Cavalry at Shreveport.

Q. That was while you were in the Army?

A. No, sir; in 1875.

Q. After you went out?

A. Yes, sir.

By Mr. Blair:

Q. You said you had some memoranda in pencil?

A. Yes, sir.

Mr. Windom. He left that with me.

(Mr. Windom was referring here to another lead-pencil document—the petition to President Grant—not to the papers in question.)

Q. What have you there?

A. (Handing some printed matter to Mr. Blair.)

Mr. Blair. (Reading.) It is entitled "The White League in Louisiana; examined by the Light of White League Testimony: the occasion of its Organization, its Object, and the Design of its Originators and Leaders."

Mr. Blair. We will look it over and see whether it is pertinent.

(Admitted afterwards, and portions, as marked by Mr. Windom, inserted at close of witness's examination.)

Mr. Windom. (To the witness.) That is all.

Cross-examination of witness:

By the Chairman:

Q. Mr. Adams, were you born a freeman?

A. No, sir. I was born a slave, and was a slave till June 16, 1865.

Q. You were born in Georgia, I think you said?

A. Yes, sir, I was born in Georgia.

Q. What time did you go to Louisiana?

A. If I mistake not, it was in March, 1850.

Q. How old were you when you first went to Louisiana?

A. They told me that I was seven years old that month.

Q. When you went to Louisiana?

A. Yes, sir.

Q. You say you wrote this paper that I hold in my hand?

A. That is the copy of it that I wrote from memorandums that I made at the time.

Q. Do you know that it is a correct copy?

A. I believe it is a correct copy, because I sat by my clerk when he was writing it.

Q. In one place you say: "Whilst traveling on my way to De Soto Parish a large body of armed white men met me and asked me who I belonged to. I answered them and told them that I belonged to God, but not to any man." Is that right?

A. Yes, that is correct.

Q. "They then asked me where was my master, and I told them the one I used to have was dead, and I have not had none since 1858." Is that right?

A. Yes, that is correct.

Q. You were not a slave at that time?

A. Well, that was when my master died, in 1858, and I belonged to one of his little children, a girl.

Q. So that you were not a freeman then, and were not until 1865?

A. No, sir.

Q. And you went to Louisiana in March, 1850?

A. Yes, sir; if I don't make no mistake I think that was the month I got there; I always heard my mother say so.

Q. Tell us more about this secret organization you belonged to; when was it first organized?

A. The committee was organized in 1870.

Q. You call it a "committee."

A. Yes, it was a committee.

Q. Well, it was a committee, if you choose to call it such, that extended its influence among your people there?

A. Yes, and to other States too.

Q. Some of its members traveled to the other States, too?

A. Yes, sir.

Q. And you took in a certain class of your own people?

A. Yes, sir; those who would keep their work secret amongst themselves.

Q. But you said you did not take in preachers or politicians?

A. Yes, I said that; we just took in laboring men that worked on the plantations.

Q. Then you said you sent out traveling agents through your State and through other States?

A. Yes, sir; you can call it "agents" if you see proper.

Q. Well, you may call it what you choose.

A. I call it men of the committee.

Q. Well, they were agents of the committee, were they not?

A. They might be called agents, perhaps. When one of them leaves here he may be going to go to one or the other of these States, and before he start he would have a kind of consultation, and they would give him instructions what he must do.

Q. Very well, he went then as your agent?

A. Yes; agent of the committee.

Q. That is all I wanted to get at, simply that fact.

A. Yes, sir.

Q. What are you doing now, Mr. Adams?

A. When I am at home, do you mean?

Q. Yes.

A. Working.

Q. What at?

A. I was working on the levee at New Orleans when I was subpœnaed here.

Q. Do you live at New Orleans?

A. No; my home is in Shreveport, but I have been in New Orleans off and on.

Q. For whom were you working when you were subpœnaed here?

A. Who for?

Q. Yes.

A. O, I was working for anybody that I could get work from.

Q. Well, for whom were you working?

A. At the very moment I was subpœnaed I was just working for anybody I could get a job from.

Q. Well, what was the last job you were working on?

A. The last job I had was working on the levee with the weigher.

Q. How long since you were employed in the custom-house?

A. I was employed there some six weeks, I think, by Mr. Smith.

Q. How long ago was that?

A. In March or April, last year.

Q. Six weeks; was that all the time you ever spent in the custom-house?

A. I worked five weeks there since.

Q. Is that all?

A. Yes, that is all, regularly. Twice I got a job from a weigher on the levee who would hire me, and I took jobs from any one who would hire me.

Q. How long has it been since you were in Shreveport?

A. The last time I was in Shreveport was the 4th day of December, 1878.

Q. Why have you not gone back since?

A. I was afraid to go back; I didn't expect to go back to Shreveport until them cases were decided.

Q. What cases?

A. Them men that went down before the United States court as witnesses. I was subpœnaed there.

Q. Haven't these cases been dismissed long ago?

A. No, sir; not them in Caddo.

Q. Where are they pending now?

A. The district attorney told me there was no appropriation to have any witnesses brought there.

Q. Where are the suits pending?

A. Before the United States court at New Orleans.

Q. How many of them are there?

A. Of Caddo? I don't know how many there is.

Q. You left in December, 1878?

A. Yes, sir; then is when I left.

Q. And you have not been back since?

A. No; not in Caddo.

Q. And you say you will not go back until those cases are decided?

A. No; not in Caddo.

Q. When they are decided are you going back?

A. If they turn them loose and don't do nothing to them I will go back, and if they put them in prison I will go back, but if they fine them a big pile of money I won't go back.

Q. How many are prosecuted, if you know?

A. I don't know how many.

Q. They are the only ones you are afraid of, are they?

A. The ones I testified against.

Q. What were they indicted for?

A. There were some armed forces going through the country the day and night before the election, and we was afraid to go to the ballot-boxes.

Q. You had been driven away from Caddo by violence, had you?

A. No, sir; nobody come to me and told me to leave.

Q. You have not left Louisiana to settle anywhere else, have you?

A. Because they were going to do anything to me?

Q. Well, for that or any other reason?

A. Well, I am going to leave.

Q. When are you going to leave?

A. Just as soon as I can get my business fixed.

Q. Where do you think of settling?

A. I am making arrangements for that purpose. I allow to go there to fix up my business.

Q. Where is your family?

A. I haven't got no family now but one child.

Q. There is a large majority of colored people in Caddo Parish, is there not?

A. Yes, sir.

Q. But you think that whenever white people ride around—that when they meet free colored people, the colored people just give up their arms and do not resist?

A. Yes; I have known it in several cases. In 1874, I will say, the time when I had a little office at Caddo, when they killed a parcel of colored people, that the white men went around and took the guns away from them, and after everything was over, they gave them back to them—in some cases they gave them back.

Q. Now, you say that this secret society of yours was for the purpose of appealing first to Congress and then to the President, and, if necessary, to a foreign government?

A. Yes, sir; that was the object of the council.

Q. I think I understood you to say that you did appeal to Congress?

A. Yes, sir.

Q. When you made your appeal to Congress, was not the Republican party in the majority in both houses in 1874?

A. The first time we made an appeal it was.

Q. Did they pay any attention to your appeal?

A. Not that I heard of.

Q. If they did would you not have heard of it; you would be likely to hear of it, would you not?

A. It looked like we ought to.

Q. Whom did you send your appeal to?

A. In 1874, do you mean?

Q. At any time that you appealed to Congress?

A. In 1874 we sent to General Grant.

Q. But you appealed first to Congress, you say. When was that?

A. Yes, to Congress, in 1874; we first appealed to General Grant.

Q. You mean, I suppose, that you appealed to Congress through General Grant?

A. O, yes.

Q. You did not appeal directly to Congress, but you appealed to General Grant?

A. Yes, sir.

Q. How did you send the appeal, through General Grant?

A. By the petition itself.

Q. Did he ever answer you?

A. Well, I told you that I had a little sketch about that that I saw in the newspapers.

Q. Well, you know that would not be a respectful answer, would it?

A. No, sir.

Q. He never paid any attention to it, did he, so far as you know?

A. So far as the appeal was concerned to him individually, why we saw a change down there pretty shortly afterwards.

Q. What did he do?

A. Well, troops came down there and they stopped killing our people as much as they had been; the White Leagues stopped raging about with their guns so much as we had seen them rage about.

Q. Do you mean that when you appealed to General Grant as a secret society, in 1874, he sent the Army there then?

A. No, sir; I don't say he did on that account, but we see'd after that there wasn't so much killing done.

Q. Were the troops there when you made your appeal?

A. Not in our part.

Q. You say there were no troops at Shreveport after the war closed, in 1874?

A. I didn't say that; there was none at Shreveport in 1874, when we made our appeal.

Q. Directly after you made your appeal, you say, troops came there?

A. Yes, sir.

Q. What troops came there?

A. Some part of the Seventh Cavalry.

Q. A portion of the Seventh United States Cavalry?

A. Yes, sir.

Q. That was Colonel Sturgis's regiment—Custer's command.*
Were they down there?

A. Major Merrill†was in command of the Seventh Cavalry.

Q. You may be mistaken about its being the Seventh Cavalry.

A. No, sir; I do not think I am mistaken.

Q. You think the Seventh Cavalry was at Shreveport in 1874?

A. Some of it was.

Q. How many companies?

A. I cannot say exactly how many companies.

Q. Who was in command of the regiment?

A. Major Merrill—Merrill—I think that is his name.

Q. Now you say you were a scout in March and April, 1875?

A. Yes, sir; and in May and June of that year.

Q. You were a government scout during those months?

A. Yes, sir; I was.

Q. And reported to whom?

A. To the adjutant.

Q. Who was the adjutant?

---

* Colonel Samuel D. Sturgis (1822–1886) was given command of the 7th U.S.
Cavalry in 1869, but was on detached recruiting and depot duty at St. Louis from
October 1874 to October 1876. In his absence the regiment was led by his second
in command, Lieutenant Colonel George A. Custer (1839–1876), until Custer's
death in the battle of the Little Bighorn on June 25, 1876.
† Major Lewis Merrill (1834–1896) was assigned to the 7th Cavalry in 1868 and
led a detachment from the regiment in South Carolina from 1871 to 1873 that
helped suppress the local Ku Klux Klan. Merrill commanded several companies
of the 7th Cavalry and a small infantry force at Shreveport from October 1874 to
January 1876. Assigned as the military representative to the Centennial Exhibi-
tion at Philadelphia, he was not present at the Little Bighorn.

A. He was Lieutenant Wallace.*

Q. Who employed you to go as a scout?

A. Some of the Army officers.

Q. Well, who were they?

A. Lieutenant Wallace was in command, and he had more to do with it, I suppose.

Q. You were sent out as a scout to find out what was going on?

A. Yes, sir.

Q. What did they pay you as a scout?

A. He gave me fifty dollars a month.

Q. He did?

A. Yes.

Q. You were not in the Army then, were you?

A. No, sir.

Q. How long were you in this business at fifty dollars a month?

A. I named the months.

Q. Very well; when did you first engage in that service?

A. I commenced about the 20th of March.

Q. And continued through April, May, and June?

A. Yes, sir.

Q. A pretty good business, was it not?

A. No, sir; a very dangerous business. I had ten times rather have been employed splitting rails. We daren't let nobody know what we was up to.

Q. Did you quit after that and go to splitting rails?

A. Yes, sir; after that I went to splitting rails.

Q. You say that you entered the Army in 1866, and remained in it until September, 1869?—

A. Yes.

---

* Lieutenant George D. Wallace (1849–1890) served as Merrill's adjutant at Shreveport. He fought at the Little Bighorn and was later killed at Wounded Knee.

Q. Were you a private or an officer?

A. I was a private until—I don't know the very day of March; but I was a private till March, 1867; then I was promoted quartermaster-sergeant, and remained till I was discharged a quartermaster-sergeant.

Q. How did you come to be discharged?

A. My time was out. I only enlisted for three years.

Q. Did they take an enlistment of privates in the Regular Army for only three years?

A. At that time they did, but before I came out they would not— they would not take for less than five years.

Q. You are sure of that, are you?

A. Yes.

Q. Now, you say you lost all hope in 1876 and 1877?

A. In 1877 we lost all hope; yes, sir.

Q. In 1877; that was after the State had been counted for Mr. Hayes over Mr. Tilden, was it not?

A. Yes, sir.

Q. And that was the reason you lost all hope, was it?

A. No, sir.

Q. What was the matter then?

A. Because States in the South had officers that had held us as slaves; that is the reason we lost all hope.

Q. Why did you not appeal to Mr. Hayes?

A. We did appeal to him.

Q. Did you appeal more than once?

A. Several times; ten to one more than we did to General Grant.

Q. What did he do?

A. Nothing yet.

Q. He has done nothing?

A. No, sir; but I seen a bill was introduced in Congress in 1878, by somebody, I don't remember the name of the gentleman who introduced it—he was from Pittsburgh, Pennsylvania—I suppose you know more about it than I do; we seen it in the papers,* we did; we then made out a petition backing up this bill that he presented to Congress in regards of the poor people of our country for the government land to be set apart for them, and so much money to be aided to them, and for them to pay the amount back at some length of time. And after we sent it we whirled in this petition then to Congress through him to urge that bill to be passed by Congress, so that we could get lands and protection given to us, so that we could stay there. This was in 1878 after we had been rallied so in 1877 to get away; we thought if that could be done, if that bill could be passed, we would stay there.

Q. Do you know that the Constitution of the United States authorizes Congress to pass laws to protect your people in their rights?

A. I have heard people say so, and I have read so.

Q. Have you seen any bill introduced within the last five, six, seven, or eight years by anybody in Congress to carry out the power of the Constitution?

A. Well, I don't know, sir. I think I have seen a sketch of some bills.

Q. How do you account for the fact that your friends, the Republican party—I do not speak disrespectfully—that your friends here, and they are your friends no doubt, have taken no steps under the Constitution to protect your people, if your condition is what you have described it to be, and you have made known your appeal; how do you account for that, and what do you think of that?

A. I can't tell what I do think of that, really. I think, in the first place, that they thought—I think they thought—if they was to

---

* In March 1878 the Louisiana press reported that Russell Errett had recently introduced a bill in the House of Representatives "to aid and protect colonies forming for the purpose of emigrating and settling upon the public lands." Errett (1817–1891) was a Republican congressman from Pennsylvania, 1877–83.

undertake to do that they would not be successful in that, and on that account they have failed to do so.

Q. Therefore they have just allowed you to suffer all these wrongs that you were undergoing?

A. Yes, sir; just because we are colored and have been slaves.

Q. Don't you know this, that the Republican party has the administration of this government now, and that President Hayes is commander-in-chief of the Army and Navy, and can use them for the purpose of suppressing insurrections and putting down riots? How do your people regard the course of the President and leaders of the Republican party on this question?

A. I have heard some of them talk, and they look at it this way: Since Mr. Hayes has been President both Houses of Congress have been Democratic, and President Hayes, he can't do nothing without they agreed to it.

Q. But that has been only a little more than a year, and President Hayes has been President three years. You know the Senate of the United States became Democratic just a year ago, and two years before that the Senate was Republican and the President was Republican, and the President has the power to use the troops to put down insurrection; and yet it seems you did not hold them to any responsibility?

Mr. BLAIR. I think the chairman ought to make that statement fairly and in full. I would suggest that he incorporate in it the further statement that the President cannot use the troops, except at the call of the governor of the State, who in this case happens to be Democratic.

The CHAIRMAN. Mr. Adams, Mr. Blair did not know, but you do, of course, that for four years there was a Republican governor in Louisiana, or he would not have made the remark he did.

Mr. BLAIR. I think the chairman will bear me out that I was suggesting a modification of his question which related to the last two or three years.

By the Chairman:

Mr. Adams, are you aware that you had a Republican governor in Louisiana for four years during this period that you speak of?

A. Yes, sir.

Q. Well, did he do anything for you—did you appeal to him?

A. No, sir.

Q. Did he do anything at all for you?

A. No, sir.

Q. He did not?

A. Who are you speaking of now?

Q. I am speaking of Mr. Kellogg.*

A. Yes.

Q. He did not try to help you, did he?

A. He did not do it.

Q. Well, do not you know the further fact that you have had several Republican legislatures in Louisiana during this time?

A. Yes.

Q. Have they done anything for you?

A. They passed laws that would do so if they were enforced, but they have never been enforced.

Q. Do not you know that the United States courts are in the hands of Republicans, that the judges are Republicans, the district attorneys are Republicans, and the marshals are Republicans, and that they select the juries; don't you know that?

A. Well, I know that all these men goes by the name of Republicans.

Q. But you do not have much faith in them?

A. No, not in them.

Q. You do not have much faith in Kellogg?

---

* William P. Kellogg (1830–1918), a lawyer from Illinois, was appointed collector of customs at New Orleans in 1865. Kellogg was a Republican senator from Louisiana, 1868–72 and 1877–83, governor, 1873–77, and a congressman, 1883–85.

A. I think he was not brave enough; that is my opinion.

Q. You thought he was a little cowardly?

A. Yes, I always thought so.

Q. What do you think of the courts, are they cowardly too?

A. Well, I don't think they are all good staunchest Republicans.

Q. No? And the legislatures you say made the laws?

A. Yes, they made the laws.

Q. Well, do you remember any particular legislation that they enacted to put down these troubles?

A. Well, I have seen little sketches of bills and resolutions that was introduced giving the government power to enroll as many men as they wanted for State marshals, &c., to put down insurrection.

Q. You do not know whether they passed and became laws?

A. I do not know.

Q. Now, Mr. Adams, during four years of this time that Mr. Kellogg was governor and you had a Republican legislature, did Mr. Kellogg, or did your legislature either, ever call on the President of the United States, either on Grant or on Hayes, for assistance to put down these troubles in your State?

A. Well, I have seen sketches in the newspapers where he did.

Q. Where he called for troops?

A. Yes, sir; where Governor Kellogg did in—1874 he did.

Q. You say that Governor Kellogg called for troops in 1874?

A. Yes, I seen in the newspapers that he did.

Q. Was that the time you made your appeal?

A. Yes, at that time we did.

Q. What did you mean, then, by saying that Governor Kellogg did not do anything to help you?

A. I do not call that doing anything to help us, individually, but I say that we made an appeal one time and he helped us because we was being treated so mean; that was the only time I seed it.

Q. Was not that at the time he was about to lose his own office?

A. Yes [laughing], and we thought that was the reason he done it.

Q. I think so.

Mr. VANCE. It was coming home.

The CHAIRMAN. Things were getting too close to him.

Q. You spoke yesterday, Mr. Adams, about a man by the name of Reuben White, of Shreveport. What did you state about him?

A. I stated that he had a colored man on his place that had belonged to him before the war, and many others, too, and many of them had lived with him ever since they got to be free, and some of them had went there since their freedom and had made a great deal on his place and had horses, and cows, and hogs, and wagons, and teams; I know when they went to leave his plantation he swept the last thing they had away from them. He even took their hogs, and turkeys off the roosts. I was right there on the place at the time.

Q. How long have you known him?

A. Reuben White?

Q. Yes.

A. I have known Reuben White since 1864.

Q. Has he ever been a member of the legislature?

A. I heard that he was before I knowed him. I never saw it.

Q. Do not you know that he has been a member of the Republican legislature?*

A. No, sir.

Q. Do not you know that he is a Republican?

A. No, sir; I don't—Reuben White—he ain't no Republican.

Q. Do you know Major Riley, sitting there?

A. Yes, sir; I know him; I have known him before.

Q. Do you think Reuben White is a Democrat?

---

* White (1810–1886) had served in the Louisiana legislature before the Civil War. He was elected to the state senate as a Democrat in April 1868, but lost his seat in September when he was disqualified because of his previous support of the Confederacy. White would support the Republican ticket in 1872 and later ran for police juror (parish commissioner) in Caddo Parish as a Democrat in 1876 and as a Republican in 1878, in both cases unsuccessfully.

A. I think he is a Whig.

Q. O, you have Whigs down there?

Mr. VANCE. I protest against that in the name of the Whig party.*
[Laughter.]

Q. Has he held any office since you have been down there, or
run for any office?

A. O, yes; he run for office in the State.

Q. Did he run on the ticket opposed to the Democratic party?

A. O, yes.

Q. Are you certain?

A. Yes; he will tell the colored people he is their friend.

Q. Yes; and take their last turkey?

A. Yes; he tells them he is a great friend of theirs.

Q. You elected him at one time to the State convention?

A. That's what we thought; but after the ticket was nominated
he would say he will see that we have peace on his plantations, and
we then put such a man in to protect us.

Q. He says he is a Whig and a friend of the colored people?

A. Yes; but it don't look like he was the way he is taking away
their property from them when they leave his plantation.

Q. Well, you think he is a great humbug, don't you?

A. Yes, sir; I do.

Q. He always pretends to be a Republican with you folks and a
great friend of yours?

A. He says he is a Whig.

Q. Has the Whig party got down into that corner of Louisiana?

A. I never heard no one talk much about it but him.

Q. Well, you colored people voted for him, didn't you?

A. Yes; we voted for him because he said he would see that we
got our rights.

Q. And he took away your turkeys?

* Vance began his political career in antebellum North Carolina as a Whig.

A. Yes; and our other goods and property.

Mr. VANCE. That is Whig profession and Democratic practice. [Laughing.]

Mr. WINDOM. That is true.

Q. What was it, Mr. Adams, you said about Hambleton? You worked for him and you thought he was a pretty good man?

A. Yes, sir; I worked for him and thought he was a pretty good man.

Q. The only trouble with him was that after you took a prominent part in politics, he didn't want to employ you as before?

A. Yes; that is what he said.

Q. Did you ever hear of such things up in New England where the folks work in big factories?

A. No, sir.

Q. You never heard of any of the rich men in the North walking up to the polls and showing their hired hands how to vote?

A. No; I never knowed anything about that.

Q. You say, Adams, that you could make one hundred dollars a month chopping wood.

A. I did do it, sir.

Q. How many cords did you chop in a day?

A. Three to seven cords a day, and corded them up.

Q. What kind of timber did you work in, to enable you to cut that much?

A. Wood.

Q. I never heard of such a thing; I was brought up on a farm myself, and I never heard of as much wood as that cut in a day. What kind of wood was it?

A. Ash, box elder, red oak, and post oak.

Q. And you say you cut from three to seven cords of that kind of wood in a day and put it up?

A. Yes, sir; I done it with these hands.

Mr. BLAIR. I will say right here, that I knew a man in my State who chopped five cords a day for a week.

Q. And you say, Adams, that you cut and split from three hundred to five hundred rails a day?

A. I didn't say I could cut and split them; I say I have did it.

Q. You have cut that many rails in a day?

A. Yes, sir; I have cut and split from three hundred to five hundred in a day, and good timber too; pine timber.

Q. And you made a hundred dollars a month at it?

A. Yes, sir; I did.

Q. Well, don't you think that is pretty good wages for a laboring man?

A. Yes, sir; it was pretty good wages at that time. It was when a man could get it.

Q. When was that?

A. In 1870 and 1871.

Q. Now, Adams, you have been very active in politics and in the affairs of your people, haven't you?

A. Yes; I took the part of the laboring classes.

Q. I am not complaining of your doing it, but merely want to know the fact. You took a leading part in your committee business, and stood up for what you thought were your rights, did you?

A. Yes.

Q. And with the exception of the two or three times you speak of, you have not been molested in any way, have you?

A. No, sir.

Q. You held public meetings, you say; when did you generally hold public meetings of your committee?

A. We never did hold no public meetings of the committee.

Q. Well, when then did you hold public meetings?

A. Of the council, do you mean?

Q. Public meetings of any kind among your people?

A. In 1877 and 1878.

Q. Why was it that your preachers and ministers would not allow you to hold your meetings in their meeting-houses?

A. A great many of the ministers was opposed to the movement.

Q. Which movement do you speak of?

A. The movement of our race leaving the South, and going anywhere.

Q. They thought you could do as well there as any place else, did they?

A. No, sir; they could not have thought that.

Q. Did they say they thought it?

A. No, sir.

Q. Well, what reason did they give for not wanting you to go away?

A. They told us to wait a while longer and see; the government would maybe give us our rights after a while.

Q. Have you not in your statement said that the preachers were not allowed to preach the gospel as they wanted to; that is the black preachers?

A. Yes, sir; and that is what they said to me at that time.

Q. You say here in your statement, Mr. Adams, that [reading] "During the time I was passing through the parish a black man was not allowed to preach the gospel anywhere any more than he was about 1865." Is that true?

A. I didn't state that in that connection.

Q. That is what you give here in your written statement?

A. I didn't know any more than what they would say and explain to me; the ministers told me these things.

Q. Well, would the ministers want to stay if they were not allowed to preach the gospel?

A. Well, at that time; you see they are different dates.

Q. Well, this was in the year 1866; I believe you have got it here?

A. Not at that time; they was not allowed to.

Q. And again you say, "As he was, he daren't to preach such doctrines as was suitable to the congregation, and a truth from the holy bible, but he had to preach just what they (the white men) wanted and what they told him to preach." What have you to say to that?

A. That is what they told me.

Q. Who told you?

A. Five or six ministers told me that.

Q. And you say further on "My father was a preacher, and he is even until this day, and they all, or at least the most of them, says they cannot preach the gospel as they wish for the white people didn't nor don't allow them to do it; for the white man says the preachers make meaner niggers, and that they cannot rule the niggers." Do you think they told you that?

A. Yes, several of them told me that.

Q. Did he tell you that?

A. My father?

Q. Yes.

A. Yes, sir.

Q. Do you know whether that is true?

A. It is only what the preachers told me.

Q. Still your preachers would not let you hold your meetings in their meeting-houses?

A. No, sir; they would not. This was in 1866; and this was in 1877 when we was trying to hold meetings in the churches, and they refused; since then they have changed, and they allow them to preach more now than before.

Q. Exactly; things have improved for the preachers since 1866, and the preachers are allowed now to preach the gospel as they please, are they?

A. At this time, in a great many cases, as they please.

Q. And the preachers now have the liberty to preach the gospel, and they don't want their congregations to leave them?

A. Yes, that is the way they stated it to me in several instances.

Q. Then so far as the preacher is concerned the white people allow freedom of speech down there?

A. Yes, sir; so far as the preachers is concerned.

Q. And so much so that the preachers do not want the people to go away from there; they are not in favor of the exodus, and they tell the people so; is that right?

A. They are not in favor of their going on account of the fact that if their people go away they would not get their support.

Q. Are you a member of the church, Mr. Adams?

A. Yes, sir; I am attached to the Methodists.

Q. At Caddo Parish?

A. No, sir.

Q. Where?

A. At the city, since I have been down there.

Q. New Orleans?

A. I joins there lately.

Q. Did you belong to the church in Caddo?

A. Yes; I professed religion just before I left.

Q. Well, was your preacher in Caddo against the exodus?

A. Some say he was and some say he was not.

Q. Your preacher, then, was opposed to the exodus?

A. Yes, sir.

Q. In Caddo, you mean?

A. No, sir; I never joined in Caddo.

Q. You never joined in Caddo?

A. No, sir.

Q. You mean that you made a profession of joining in Caddo, but did not join the church there?

A. Yes.

Q. But after you went to New Orleans you became attached to the Methodist Church there?

A. Yes.

Q. And the minister in New Orleans was opposed to this exodus?

A. No, sir; he ain't.

Q. He is in favor of it, then?

A. Yes; he is for our going anywhere where we can get our privileges.

Q. Does he advise you to go away from New Orleans?

A. Yes, sir; he says we should go anywhere on God's earth that we can get our rights.

Q. He thinks you do not have your rights at New Orleans, does he?

A. I don't call that my home.

Q. Well, let us go back to Shreveport, in Caddo Parish; do you know of any exception there to the preachers who are opposed to this exodus?

A. Yes.

Q. Some of them are in favor of it, are they?

A. Yes; some of them are in favor of it.

Q. Who are they?

A. I consider all them is for it that allows us to hold meetings in their churches.

Q. Do you take that as evidence that they are in favor of your going?

A. Yes.

Q. But, as I understand you, the body of the preachers there are against it?

A. Yes; two denominations of the churches allow us to hold our meetings.

Q. Who are they?

A. One organization that allows us is A. M. E. (African Methodist Episcopal), and, I think, another organization that allows us to preach in the churches is the M. E.'s (Methodist Episcopals) of America. They allow us to hold our meetings in their churches, and they is the only ones that allow us.

Q. Another class you speak of as being opposed to your people going away is the politicians; how is it about them?

A. Well, they is opposed to it, and always have been opposed to it; if I was to get up on this stand and make a speech, and was going to mention to the congregation to leave, why, the politicians would not allow me to make a speech if I was going to say anything about that.

Q. What politicians do you speak of?

A. The colored men and white Republicans.

Q. The colored and white Republican politicians?

A. Yes.

Q. They would not even allow you to speak on the subject?

A. No; if I was going to make a speech, or mention to our people to leave, they would not let me make a speech; they would not even do it in 1874—not until 1877. Until then I did not get but one public speech to make in regards to our people leaving before 1877; and I made one speech in October, 1874, in the court-house in Shreveport concerning our people going away. I did it to back up the petition which we had sent to the President.

Q. Who are the most prominent Republican politicians in Caddo Parish?

A. Harper; he is the leading politician there.*

Q. Well, what about him?

A. He has always been opposed to our going away.

Q. Has he been in office?

A. O, yes, he has been in office off and on since 1870.

Q. Mr. Adams, have you ever had any office except the one you were in in the custom-house?

A. No; I didn't have no office then but as a laborer, not only what I was doing in the Army and at the ballot-boxes in election. I have been a supervisor of election some time, and been a marshal at election, but that didn't last more than two or three days.

---

* William Harper (d. 1909), a freedman, served in the Louisiana house of representatives, 1870–72, and in the state senate, 1872–80.

Q. You say that when your committee met in its secret council, you allowed nobody to speak except those who were in favor of the exodus?

A. No; not in our secret rooms we would not.

Q. But even in public you didn't do it?

A. No, sir.

Q. When you met outside, the colored Republican politicians and white Republican politicians and ministers would not allow you to speak in favor of it?

A. No, sir; but in the meetings with ourselves everybody was allowed to express his opinion.

Q. I understand that. Whose district is Caddo Parish in?

A. In the fourth district.

Q. Who represents it in Congress?

A. At this time?

Q. Yes.

A. Mr. Elam.*

Q. You spoke of discontent in Arkansas; what do you know about that?

A. In what way?

Q. Didn't you speak of the colored people being discontented with affairs in Arkansas, and of their wanting to leave there?

A. I did not say there was discontent there; I said that some one in Arkansas had signed the roll to leave.

Q. You know nothing about that, then, except what you have told us; you have never been in Arkansas yourself, have you?

A. Yes; I have been in Arkansas, in Pratt County.

Q. When?

A. In 1875 and 1877.

Q. How many did you get to sign the roll to leave?

---

* Joseph B. Elam (1821–1885), a lawyer who had voted for secession in the Louisiana convention of 1861, served in the U.S. House of Representatives as a Democrat.

A. Up there?

Q. Yes.

A. I don't know exactly how many; when I was up there I never got nobody till 1877 to leave.

Q. How many did you get to sign the roll then?

A. About two hundred and fifty the time I was up there.

Q. What other States did you go into besides Arkansas?

A. I went into Texas.

Q. Whereabouts did you go in Texas?

A. I went away out to Limestone County; then I went to Houston, and to Galveston, and to Marshall and several other places.

Q. What year was that?

A. 1875, 1876, 1877.

Q. What were you doing there?

A. I was up there on business.

Q. What business?

A. Business belonging to my organization.

Q. What was the nature of it?

A. I don't want to tell everything about it.

Q. Still, Mr. Adams, we will have to get what we can about it?

A. Well, I expect to be killed for what I am telling you here; I don't expect to live no more after making mention of these places; I won't be allowed no show. If I was to tell you all, why, good gracious——

Q. How did you come to be subpœnaed?

A. I don't know.

Q. Didn't you tell anybody to have you subpœnaed?

A. No.

Q. Mr. Windom and Mr. Blair just heard of you then?

A. I reckon so; my name being connected with the Emigration Association.

Q. Didn't you tell Mr. Ruby* to write and have you subpœnaed?

---

* George T. Ruby (1841–1882) was born in New York City and raised in Maine. Ruby administered and taught in freedmen's schools in Louisiana, 1864–66, then

A. No, sir; I never spoke such a word to Mr. Ruby in my life.

Q. Do you mean to be understood as declining to answer what you did in Texas?

A. I told you I didn't care to tell you all my business that I was doing there.

Q. You said you were on business of the committee, and I asked you the character of the business.

A. The character of the business was to find out the condition of our people, and also to enroll names of who was willing to go away.

Q. Did you find your people were whipped and murdered and deprived of their rights in Texas also?

A. Yes, sir, according to the reports of the people.

Q. Reports of all of them?

A. Reports from heaps of them.

Q. What points did you visit in Texas?

A. In Harrison County, in Panola, in Saint Augustine, in Shelby, and I have been in Houston, Galveston, Jefferson, and in Limestone.

Q. Is that a county?

A. Yes.

Q. Go on.

A. That and several other counties.

Q. Were you in Grimes County and in Brazos?

A. I passed over the Brazos River, but I don't remember all the counties I went into nohow.

Q. You were in a town called Navasota, were you not?

A. I have been there, but not on this business.

---

moved to Galveston, Texas, where he taught school and became one of the few Black agents working for the Freedmen's Bureau. He later served as a delegate to the Texas constitutional convention, 1868–69, and as a Radical Republican in the state senate, 1869–73, before returning to New Orleans, where he worked as a customs clerk and edited the *New Orleans Observer*. A strong supporter of the Exodus movement, Ruby testified before the Senate select committee for three days in March 1880, preceding Henry Adams.

Q. What year was this in?

A. Some of these visits I made in 1871; some of them I was there in 1875; some of them I was there in 1876; and some of them I was there in 1877.

Q. You have not been there since 1877?

A. Let's see; O, I may have went in some portion of Texas in 1878; I don't exactly remember; I am always more or less crossing the line; it is not far to go into Texas from Louisiana any time; but I never staid in Texas long at a time.

Q. Well, then, were you in Mississippi?

A. Yes, sir; I have been in Mississippi.

Q. Were you in Mississippi on this business?

A. Yes, sir; on this business.

Q. When were you in Mississippi on this business?

A. I was in Mississippi last year.

Q. In 1879?

A. Yes, sir.

Q. Well, were you there the year before?

A. No, sir; not on this business.

Q. At no time before 1879 were you in Mississippi on this business?

A. No, sir.

Q. What parts of Mississippi were you in when you were there last year?

A. In the eastern part.

Q. Will you name the counties, please?

A. I don't know the names of none of the counties I was in.

Q. Were you in any of the towns?

A. Yes; I was in Coomb's City and several other places up there.

Q. How long a time did you spend in Mississippi?

A. About four or five days.

Q. Did you go down into Alabama?

A. Never. I was not ever there.

Q. You were in Mississippi only four or five days?

A. O, I forgot; I went into Mississippi twice last year.

Q. Did you go into any other States beside Mississippi?

A. At that time?

Q. At any time, on this business.

A. (Reflecting)——

Q. Were you in Tennessee?

A. No, sir; I never went to Tennessee.

Q. Did you visit any other States besides Arkansas, Texas, and Mississippi?

A. No, sir; I don't think I did.

Q. Now when you visited Texas in 1871, 1875, 1876, and 1877, and Mississippi last year, and Arkansas at a previous date, who bore your expenses?

A. I bore them myself.

Q. You did?

A. Yes, sir; I did.

Q. In all that traveling you paid your own expenses?

A. The time I was in them places I bore my own expenses.

Q. You didn't raise any money out of your committee for that purpose?

A. No, sir; I never asked the committee for a cent.

Q. And they never paid you anything for that work?

A. No, sir; they did not.

Q. You had the money yourself?

A. Yes, sir; I makes money outside at hard labor.

Q. What at?

A. I am a faith doctor.

Q. A what?

A. A faith doctor. Sometimes I get a hundred dollars to cure one case, sometimes two hundred.

Q. I think, perhaps, that is as good as some other kinds of doctors. How long have you been a faith doctor?

A. From when I was nine years of age.

Q. Do they call you doctor?

A. A great many of them does what knows me.

By Mr. Vance:

Q. Can you explain to us the theory of that kind of medical practice?

A. I make all my medicine myself, more or less, what I do use.

By the Chairman:

Q. Now, doctor, you say you make money outside of your labor in practicing your profession?

A. Yes.

Q. Did you get a good deal of employment among your own people?

A. More than I can attend to.

Q. You did?

A. Yes.

Q. Your style of doctoring is what is called doctoring by faith, is it?

A. Yes.

Q. And you have cured diseases by that system since you were nine years old?

A. Yes, sir. I recollect curing the toothache when I was nine years old, and I have been following it ever since then.

Q. You have acquired quite a reputation amongst your people for it, have you?

A. Yes.

Q. And in that way you got money more freely and easily than you did as a mere laborer, did you not?

A. O, yes, sir; a good deal more easily.

Q. You spoke of your doctor bills as being sometimes pretty large?

A. Yes, sir.

Q. Did you make a regular charge at such rates?

A. I never make no charges; they always make it themselves and give it to me.

Q. Sometimes they would give you one or two hundred dollars, you say?

A. Yes.

Q. Those cases must be pretty stubborn cases?

A. Yes; such as other doctors can't mend up, and they get me to work on them and I cures them.

Q. Well, when you leave Louisiana, will you follow your profession and practice as a faith doctor?

A. If anybody calls on me I will. If they find I am a doctor and they send for me I tend to them; if not, I won't; I never go to them without it's a case of necessity.

Q. Were these large fees paid to you voluntarily by the people of your own color?

A. By white as well as colored people I was employed.

Q. You attended white folks then?

A. O, yes; I have had white people many a time.

Q. I will only ask one question about your practice; I don't want to pry into your mysteries, but this question of faith, is it faith in God or faith in you that the patient has to have?

A. Well, if they have faith to believe that I can cure them, that is their faith; of course my faith comes from God.

Q. Yes; so that the patient looks to you, and you look above?

A. If the patient believes that I can cure them, of course I can cure them, and I looks to God for my faith.

Q. How old are you?

A. I will be thirty-seven years old if I can recollect the day. I think my mother said I was born March 16, 1843. I think that is what she gave me my age at.

Q. Are you a pretty good stump speaker among your people, doctor?

A. O, yes, sir; I can speak to them in my language.

Q. Pretty freely, too, can't you?

A. Well, they hear me and believe what I tell them; and I aim to tell the truth under all circumstances.

Q. And yet you lived at Shreveport twenty years?

A. No, sir; not twenty years.

Q. Well, pretty nearly, and you never got killed?

A. No, I ain't been killed yet; but it ain't by the will of them people that tried.

Q. Now, about this robbery you speak of, of five hundred dollars out of a little wagon?

A. I said I would say, to make myself clear, two hundred and fifty dollars, but I know it was five hundred.

Q. Did you have to get out and leave the wagon?

A. O, yes, sir; I got out and they captured the wagon and everything.

Q. Well, robberies are committed in other counties as well as there, are they not?

A. O, yes, sir.

Q. You don't think anybody has been bulldozing you on account of your faith doctoring, do you?

A. No, sir; they have not bothered me about that; I always thought I got along so well among them because they knowed me, and because I could cure them when their doctors gave them up; and heaps of them would speak for me in times of trouble, and that would cause them to let me alone.

Q. You can hold over these college doctors when it comes to curing old troubles can't you?

A. I goes over medical doctors for I takes cases they can't cure. I rather take them kind than any other kind.

Q. Do you know a colored man by the name of Wash Walker, at Shreveport?

A. Wash Walker? No, sir; I don't remember him.

Q. Do you know a colored man by the name of Alexander there?

A. I know several by the name of Alexander.

Q. Well, here is a little item in the Shreveport Standard; that is a Democratic paper, is it?

A. Yes.

Q. It says, "Wash. Walker and another colored man named Alexander, with their families, some ten persons in all, who worked last year on Capt. J. M. Foster's plantation across the river, and who took the Kansas fever and emigrated to that State about the 10th of January last, returned here bag and baggage on the train Friday night, and left yesterday evening for their old home"?

A. Yes, I know Alexander on Foster's plantation.

Q. Did you know he had gone?

A. Yes.

Q. Did you know he had come back?

A. No, sir; I had not heard that.

Q. The account says further: "When they took their departure for the promised land, they carried with them a two-horse wagon, four good mules, and nine hundred dollars between them. When they returned they brought back the wagon and mules, but were minus eight hundred dollars of their cash." Did you ever hear of that fact?

A. No, sir; I had not heard they had come back.

Q. Well, it seems, according to this item, that "they went to Clark County, Kansas, where they designed purchasing land, but they became so thoroughly disgusted with the country that they gave it out. The only kind of work they could get was husking corn, and the wages paid to a grown hand was only twenty-five cents for a day's work." Is that the kind of information these people send you?

A. No, sir.

Q. They write you that they get two and a half to three dollars a day in Kansas, do they not?

A. Not that much.

Q. How much?

A. Nine dollars a week for men; they tell me that.

Q. Nine dollars a week, that is one dollar and a half a day?

A. Yes, sir; but some of them gets trades, they say, and makes more.

Q. Well, this account goes on to say that "they became homesick, and concluded to pull up stakes and return to their old quarters in Louisiana before their means were all exhausted. They said that some of the colored people who had emigrated from this section had purchased land upon their first arrival, but afterwards deeply regretted that they had done so; and that nearly all of the emigrants they met would gladly return to their former homes if they possessed the means to do so. They complain of the bitter cold weather they encountered, and the scarcity of fire-wood, which they had to haul ten miles, and say that Kansas is no place for a southern darkey to go. For their part, now that they have been and seen for themselves, they candidly confess the folly of the step they took in leaving homes where they were comfortably situated, plentifully supplied with provisions and clothing, and where they were enabled to lay by at the end of the year a handsome surplus from the proceeds of their labor."

Q. Now, what kind of a man is Alexander?

A. He is a pretty good man, a hard worker, and always lives well about his house.

Q. Had he ever been molested that you know of?

A. I don't know particularly whether he had or not; but he always told me he wanted to get away from Louisiana on account of his children; he didn't think his children would ever be raised there as men and women with good education, and he wanted to go where he could have them educated and give them a trade.

Q. This account proceeds to say that they "would advise the colored people everywhere to let well enough alone, and not go penniless to cast their fortunes in a strange land and among strangers, who have neither aid nor sympathy to offer them, and where they are ultimately bound to starve or freeze to death. Walker said that he never wanted to go again where he couldn't see cotton-stalks and gin-houses; and that Marsee Jeems Foster was just as good a man as he ever wanted to work for again. He was completely cured." Did Alexander or Walker ever tell you that?

A. Alexander never told me that, and if he made any such statement as you have read there, I am sure he will tell me.

Q. You don't know anything about that?

A. No, sir; I do not.

The WITNESS. You asked me a while ago about whether our organization sent a petition to President Hayes. I have got a copy of one petition we sent to him here in my pocket, if you desire to read it.

The CHAIRMAN. Your statement is sufficient on that point.

Mr. BLAIR. Let me see it; and if you have any other papers you would like to introduce let me see them.

The WITNESS. You asked me yesterday for the pamphlet that came from Mr. Turner, the other Turner, from Saint Louis. (Handing it to Mr. Blair.)

Mr. BLAIR. (Glancing over it.) Well, we will put this with the other Turner circular.

[Printed in connection with the Saint Louis circular, before submitted.]

The WITNESS. I was asked whether I had been encouraged by anybody concerning our going to some territory that we made application for in our petition. I wish the chairman would read that.

The CHAIRMAN. (Reading.) Well, this is a communication from the secretary of the Territory of Arizona, J. J. Gosper, inviting colored immigration to his Territory. That is all right if he wanted them there. (Reading.)

Some time in June, 1877, The Inter-Ocean, of Chicago, published the following letter of J. J. Gosper, secretary of the Territory of

Arizona. The original communication of which The Inter-Ocean speaks was sent to that paper about the 1st of June. It was signed by the colonization council, by the president of the council, and by others.

TERRITORY OF ARIZONA, OFFICE OF THE SECRETARY,

Prescott, June 20, 1877.

To the Editor of The Inter-Ocean:

Can you place me in correspondence with any of the more intelligent and leading men of that class of colored people who wish to colonize in some Territory? If they have means with which to pay their expenses to this country and a little left upon which to live for a time, and are willing to work, we can furnish them thousands of acres of good, rich land, which can be made to produce the regular Louisiana sugar-cane, or any kind of grain, fruit, and vegetables. The land would have to be irrigated, however, but that can easily be done. The sugar-cane in question has already been raised in the valley of the Gila, in the south part of the Territory. Under a recent act of Congress any citizen of the United States can select one section of land anywhere in the Territory which is not mineral, timber, or land that will produce without irrigation, occupy and own the same by paying at the time of selecting the land twenty-five cents per acre, and any time within three years thereafter he can procure a patent by proving by two witnesses that he has reclaimed said land by running water upon it, and paying an additional sum of one dollar per acre. I am willing to assist so far as I can in aiding a colony of industrious colored people in this Territory. I served with the colored troops during the late war, and know something of their habits and character. You have permission to make public notice of the above facts if you see fit.

Yours, &c.,

J. J. GOSPER,*
Secretary of Territory.

---

* John Jay Gosper (1842–1913) was the secretary of Arizona Territory, 1877–82. During the Civil War he served as the quartermaster of the 29th U.S. Colored Infantry Regiment.

The above letter is called out by a communication in The Inter-
Ocean of a late date said to represent the sentiments of 2,000 colored men of Louisiana who, tired of the wrongs heaped upon them,
desire to emigrate to some of the Territories. The original communication has been mislaid, and we are unable to give any of the
names attached, as they were not published. The letter, however,
came from the region of Shreveport, and the parties wishing can no
doubt obtain the information they desire by opening correspondence with the secretary of Arizona, whose letter is published
above.

Q. Do you state in this paper you have submitted as your account
of affairs among your people anything about your skill as a faith
doctor?

A. I don't exactly remember. If I did it is all correct. Whatever it
says is correct.

Q. Very well?

A. I may have made some little mistakes in putting a word or a
number down in its proper place, but it is all so; it is correct.

Q. Now, in point of fact, you had about as much trouble with
your own people on the subject of the exodus, so far as the people
from Shreveport were concerned, as with anybody else, had
you not?

A. There was no trouble with anybody but the ministers, as I have
said, and the politicians; we had had more trouble with the politicians than with anybody else.

Q. They are rather against you as a general thing, aren't they?

A. Yes, and always have been. They spoke against it last year and
year before last they spoke against it; they told me not to say anything about it at these club meetings; that is what they told me.
This is what they would say: "For God's sake, don't stir up the people
to go away; wait until next year and we'll elect somebody that'll give
us our rights." Why, when we done got ready to vote, and done registering, they would not give us registration papers, you know. They

would just write our names down on a book, and when we would go to the polls and want to vote they would say, "What is your name?" and I would say, "Henry Adams." Then they would say they would look over the book. And after they would look over the book they would say, "Your name ain't on this book." "It ain't?" "No." "Well, it was put on there." And they would say, "It don't make no difference; your name ain't on the book and you can't vote." Well, there was many of us was used that way, and several of us went to the man that was supervisor of registration and told him that they would not allow us to vote, and he would go and tell that man that did register our names; but he would say, "Your name is not on the book and you can't vote." They didn't let me vote in '78; they refused to let me vote, although they knowed me, and who I was, very well.

Q. Now, you said that if a Democratic President is elected next time you would all start and take to the woods, now I know that Mr. Blair wants to know whom you would prefer for the Presidency, and I will ask you?

A. You desire me to give my sentiments?

Q. Yes, and the sentiments of your people, if you know what those sentiments are.

A. Well, what I wants and what I know the laboring classes wants—for I speak for them as much as for myself, for I am in amongst them there, and I am considered a leading man among them there——

Q. You consider yourself a leading man among them, do you?

A. No; I am considered a leading man with the people there. Well, the laboring class of people down there wants General Grant. I do, myself.

Q. Yes; you differ from Mr. Ruby on that question?*

A. O, yes, sir.

---

* In his testimony Ruby had expressed doubt that the election of Grant to a third term would improve political conditions in the South.

Q. Colored people will differ in politics as well as white people, won't they?

A. Yes, sir; and the largest amount of ministers—I have heard them when they talked generally throughout the county—says General Grant.

Q. The ministers?

A. Yes.

Q. How are the politicians?

A. O, well, the politicianers, you know—a great many politicianers will say Sherman.*

Q. They will, hey?

A. That's what they say; I have heard them say that.

Q. That is the way with some politicians up here.

A. But the politicianers ain't holding any position at this time, and where they have been holding office by the votes cast by colored people, why the majority of them says Grant or Blaine.† That is the way they speak. I just say it as it is, and no other way.

By Mr. Vance:

Q. The most of your testimony has been concerning the political condition of your people in Louisiana and Mississippi. I want to ask you something about their industrial condition. What is the average wages of good hands on the cotton plantations?

A. At this time you mean?

---

* John Sherman (1823–1900), the younger brother of General William Tecumseh Sherman, was secretary of the treasury, 1877–81. He also served as a Republican congressman from Ohio, 1855–61, as a senator, 1861–77 and 1881–97, and as secretary of state, 1897–98.

† James G. Blaine (1830–1893) was a Republican congressman from Maine, 1863–76, and speaker of the house, 1869–75. He also served as a senator, 1876–81, and as secretary of state in 1881 and 1889–92. An unsuccessful candidate for the Republican nomination in 1876, Blaine was the party's candidate in 1884 but was defeated by Grover Cleveland. At the convention held in June 1880, Grant, Blaine, and Sherman led the voting for thirty-five ballots before the anti-Grant delegates nominated Ohio congressman James A. Garfield on the thirty-sixth ballot.

Q. Well, say for the last year or two?

A. For the past three years. I will explain that.

Q. Well, for the past three years and up to now?

A. For the past three years labor on plantations, by the month I mean, is from—well, I will commence at five dollars; it is from five to fifteen dollars a month.

Q. For what kind of hands?

A. Some women hands, they only give them five dollars a month, and boys about ten and twelve and fifteen years old they gives them five dollars a month.

Q. You say the women and boys from ten to fifteen years old get five dollars per month. What do the next higher class get?

A. The next class hands gets ten to twelve dollars a month.

Q. Ten to twelve dollars; and the first-class hands, you say, get fifteen dollars?

A. Yes, sir.

Q. And that has been the case for the last two or three years?

A. Yes, sir.

Q. Well, does that include rations?

A. Yes, sir; with that they get rations.

Q. And do they get a house to live in?

A. Yes; a house to live in besides.

Q. And firewood?

A. Yes.

Q. And garden patches or something of that sort to raise sweet potatoes and garden stuff?

A. Well, they don't give garden patches to such as that; if any of them wants that they get it.

Q. How is the labor done; by the day?

A. Well, the general run of them now ain't giving them more than that, and haven't for the past two or three years; they haven't been giving more than fifty cents and a dollar a day.

Q. Fifty cents and a dollar a day; that is, according to the hand?

A. Yes; and that is in the field. A great many is giving seventy-five cents, and makes them board themselves at a dollar a day.

Q. You say a great many of them do that, but that is not the universal rule, is it?

A. Yes, sir; they makes them board themselves at that price.

Q. Now, when they are hired by the month at this price you have mentioned, that means for the year round, does it not?

A. For the year round; and at that time they only pay half the money at the end of the month when they pays by the year.

Q. They keep half the money back till the end of the year. Is that what you mean?

A. Yes.

Q. Well, now, is there any one season of the year when labor is worth more than it is at another season? What is it worth, for instance, in cotton-picking time?

A. In cotton-picking time they don't give them no more by the month.

Q. That is when they are hired by the year?

A. Yes; when they are hired by the year round.

Q. But it is customary to hire to pick cotton by the hundred, is it not?

A. Yes; that is often done.

Q. What do they pay a good man for picking cotton by the hundred?

A. They pays all, good and bad, the same price.

Q. Well, what do they pay by the hundred?

A. From fifty cents to seventy-five cents a hundred.

Q. How much can a skilled hand pick in a day?

A. A real good hand—cotton-picker—can pick from one hundred and fifty on up to three hundred and four hundred.

Q. Three hundred pounds is not an extraordinary amount for a good hand to pick in a day, is it?

A. No, sir.

Q. How long does that cotton picking season last?

A. It lasts from August sometimes up till December; but the very blooming of the time is in September and October.

Q. The cotton-picking season, then, runs from August until the last of December?

A. No; to the first of December.

Q. Now cotton-picking depends more on skill than on strength, don't it?

A. Yes.

Q. A woman or a boy, then, who is skilled at it can make as much as a man, can he not?

A. O, yes.

Q. You say he can make from one dollar and a half to two dollars a day during the bloom of the season?

A. In many cases they have some trouble to get it; there is few men that pays what they promises.

Q. How does that happen?

A. You know he is figuring it down; he keeps the account and reckons it up at the end of the week—a hundred or three hundred he puts down for this one and so much for another one; but some good man that has good sense can figure it down for himself, and he will keep the account and will settle up with him just as the count is, and keep him from cutting.

Q. You mean that the owners cheat them?

A. Yes, sir; they cheats them that can't understand—that can't count up for themselves.

Q. Exactly; but how does it follow, if they can't understand, that they know they are cheated?

A. The way he knows this is by getting some friend who does know to put down the figures in secret from the man that is keeping the account. I have did it myself.

Q. Do not they ever have this thing tried in the courts?

A. No, sir; it would be foolish in us to go to the courts about it.

Q. Why would it be foolish to take it to the courts?

A. Because they always comes out behind.

Q. The judges, justices of the peace, jurors, and planters, then, are all dishonest?

A. I don't say that they are all dishonest, but I say the one that's got the money will gain the suit.

Q. Those that have the money will gain the suit?

A. Yes; it don't matter how honest a case is, they gains the suit.

Q. Well that is the result of dishonesty, of a want of integrity?

A. Yes, sir.

Q. Exactly; let us inquire now a little about the renting; how many ways of renting do you have down there; you rent for cash and for part of the crop, and so on, do you not?

A. Yes, sir; some rents for money and some for a portion of the crop.

Q. What is the ordinary price when a man rents for money?

A. Well, on the hills it is from a dollar to three dollars an acre—the hill land—where they can make about one-quarter of a bale to the acre, and about fifteen or twenty bushels of corn to the acre, it is from one dollar to three dollars an acre.

Q. Land that will produce twenty bushels of corn will produce more than a quarter of a bale of cotton, will it not?

A. I don't know as it will; it makes about half a bale in my county; if the land brings sixty bushels of corn to the acre it only makes a bale to the acre.

Q. But the best corn land is not the best cotton land?

A. No, sir; not always.

Q. The biggest stalk does not always produce the best cotton?

A. No, sir.

Q. How is it with the bottom land?

A. The bottom land rents from five to fifteen dollars per acre.

Q. According to quality?

A. Yes, sir; the river bottom brings a bale to the acre and sixty bushels of corn.

Q. Is that the highest rent for land that produces a bale of cotton to the acre—fifteen dollars?

A. It depends upon the number of years the land has been in cultivation; now about the fifth, or fourth and fifth or maybe the sixth, year of cultivation the land will sometimes make a bale and a half to the acre sometimes, but mighty seldom. Taking the land through, it won't average more than a bale to the acre. If you plant ten acres it won't make more than ten bales. I have planted sixteen acres and only got ten bales of cotton, but four acres and a quarter in one place I made four bales and a quarter out of it.

Q. How much can one strong man cultivate?

A. On the hills he can cultivate twenty-five acres of land.

Q. In cotton?

A. No, sir; half cotton, half corn.

Q. Twelve and a half acres of one and twelve and a half acres of the other?

A. Yes, sir; he can cultivate that on the hill land.

Q. Can he make off of that land sixty bushels of corn to the acre?

A. No, sir; that is on the hills.

Q. I thought you were talking about the bottom land.

A. No; I am talking about the hill land, and twenty-five acres that one man can cultivate.

Q. On that land how many bales of cotton and how many bushels of corn can he produce?

A. About a quarter of a bale to the acre. He will put twelve and a half acres in corn and twelve and a half in cotton, and you can add that up yourself.

Q. That will make about two hundred and fifty bushels of corn and about three and a half bales of cotton. Now, cotton was worth about fifty dollars a bale last fall?

A. Yes, sir; about ten cents a pound.

Q. What was corn worth?

A. Generally, for these times, along in gathering corn time, you can buy it at fifty cents a bushel.

Q. Well, say fifty cents a bushel; that would make one hundred and twenty-five dollars' worth of corn and one hundred and seventy-five dollars' worth of cotton, besides his fodder, peas, sweet potatoes, and garden patches?

A. Yes, sir.

Q. That is what a renter can make on the hills?

A. Yes, sir.

Q. Now, on this bottom land that will make sixty bushels of corn and a bale or a bale and a half of cotton to the acre, how many acres can a man cultivate?

A. Ten acres in cotton and corn, with a good mule.

Q. Can he not cultivate more than ten acres?

A. Some of them plants ten acres, but they has to hire all the time that they cultivate that.

Q. That would be five bales of cotton and three hundred bushels of corn?

A. He don't plant half and half; he would plant in ten acres about three acres in corn and the balance in cotton.

Q. Well, that would be seven bales of cotton, or more if the land was good?

A. Yes, sir.

Q. And one hundred and twenty bushels of corn?

A. Yes.

Q. That cotton is worth three hundred and fifty dollars—seven bales or more, if he made more—and the corn would be worth about sixty to sixty-two and a half dollars?

A. Yes, sir.

Q. That is what one man could do?

A. Yes.

Q. And if he had children big enough to help him, he could do still more?

A. He could take twenty or twenty-five acres when he had help.

Q. Now, sometimes, you said a family would make one hundred bales?

A. Yes, sir, they would; a man or wife, maybe, with two or three sons and some daughters, or some connections of his, maybe his wife's sister or brother, all connected with that family, would work together and in that way one family could make one hundred bales of cotton.

Q. And what proportion of that would they make in corn?

A. They would plant what they thought would do; a wagon should hold, say forty bushels to the load; then they would make from twelve to thirteen loads of corn.

Q. They would produce corn enough to do them?

A. Yes, sir.

Q. Well, that hundred bales of cotton would be worth five thousand dollars, and twelve loads of corn—448 wagon-loads—would be about two hundred and twenty dollars; now, you say that in such cases they frequently came out at the end of the year without a cent.

A. Yes; come out without a cent, and then have to borrow money to buy provisions.

Q. What do they do with the five thousand dollars?

A. What do the men do that takes possession of their cotton?

Q. He and his family don't eat that much up?

A. No, sir; they don't eat it up.

Q. So, if the landlord and the merchant had been honest, they would have heaps of money left?

A. Yes, they would have heaps of money left.

Q. You say it is nothing but the dishonesty of the landlords and merchants there that keeps your people from making money?

A. Yes, sir; they keeps our people from making money.

Q. You described to us yesterday this White League, and filed a paper here this morning in reference to them; were there any other kind of leagues in that country?

A. White men?

Q. Yes, or colored men.

A. Not that I knows of.

Q. Did you ever have an institution there called the Union League?*

A. If they did, I didn't belong to it.

Q. You never heard of it before?

A. I seen a Democratic paper speak of it once or twice—about the Union League there.

Q. Why, Mr. Adams, don't you know of colored people in the South that belonged to it—that were sworn into it?

A. Well, I don't know.

Q. But don't you know that fact—that it existed among your people?

A. No, sir, I don't; because none of these men communicated with me in regards of our movement and didn't have nothing to do with it. I know that much, because they would not have did it without consulting with us about it; so I don't know none that belonged to it.

Q. You deny, then, so far as your knowledge goes, that any such thing as a political Union League that your people belonged to was in existence?

A. I don't deny nothing for the politicians, but for the laboring classes of people in my section where I had dealings in that line, I say that they did not.

Q. You don't deny that a Union League was there, and that the politicians may have belonged to it?

---

* A political secret society allied with the Republican Party. Originally formed in the North to support the Lincoln administration, the League expanded into the South after 1865. Its members included freedmen, freeborn people of color, and wartime white Unionists.

A. They may have.

Q. And that was a sworn organization?

A. I don't know nothing about that.

Q. You told us that in 1877, when the State of Louisiana went Democratic, you colored people gave up hope?

A. Yes, sir; we gave up all hope then.

Q. Now, Adams, I want to ask you if you know it to be a fact in all the States that you have any knowledge of, that after the government passed into the hands of the Democrats there was less of disturbance and more of peace between the blacks and the whites— that everybody got along better than they did while it was under the control of the Republicans?

A. No, sir; I don't know that.

Q. You don't know that?

A. No, sir; I don't know that; because just as soon as the election came it was raging the same, where I was, as it did before, only worser.

Q. New Orleans went into the hands of the Democrats in 1877 when Nicholls* was inaugurated governor. You had an election for another governor, legislature, &c., last December; was not that the most peaceful election you have had in the State since the war? Was there not less opposition and violence between the races?

A. That was in the first election we had under Governor Nicholls's administration.

Q. But you heard my question?

A. Yes.

Q. Well, answer it, if you can. I will repeat it. Was not the election in last December the most peaceful election you have had in Louisiana since the war?

---

* Francis T. Nicholls (1834–1912), a former brigadier general in the Confederate army, was the Democratic governor of Louisiana, 1877–80 and 1888–92. He later served on the Louisiana Supreme Court as its chief justice, 1892–1904, and as an associate justice, 1904–11.

A. In regards to that I was not any where during that election but at New Orleans, and I didn't participate because I was not at my home to vote.

Q. Well, from what you heard of the election in different parts of the State, was it not a peaceful election, and was not there less violence and opposition?

A. I heard from several parts of the State that nobody was hurt at their elections; that I heard; but I heard from some other parts of the State that they was hurt; so I don't know anything but what I seed with my own eyes in New Orleans. In New Orleans it was peaceable—what I saw of it.

Q. Well, in New Orleans, on the day of the election, was it not as quiet as any election you ever saw?

A. Yes, I think it was quiet there.

Q. And were not the reports from parishes, as to people being hung, contradicted; that the men who had been so reported were alive and had not been touched?

A. Yes, sir.

Q. Well, don't you know that in Georgia, Alabama, and Mississippi, since the State governments there have been under the control of the Democrats,* there has been peace between the blacks and whites?

A. I have heard so; and it ought to be that way.

Q. Certainly.

A. It ought to be so, because at that time when the Republicans had it—I will say this much as my own judgment of it: When the Republicans had it and had their ticket running, and the Democrats

---

* In elections marked by widespread violence and intimidation directed against Republican voters, the Democrats gained control of the Georgia legislature in 1870, the Alabama governorship and legislature in 1874, and the Mississippi legislature in 1875. The Republican governor of Georgia resigned in 1871 to avoid impeachment by the new legislature, as did the Republican governor of Mississippi in 1876.

knowed that the colored people was in the majority, they knowed that if they let them vote just as they pleased, the colored men or the Republicans was going to be elected. Now, the Democrats in Louisiana has the count of the ballot, and it don't matter who is elected, they will count him in if he is a Democrat.

Q. Just as the Republicans counted Mr. Hayes in?

A. I know the Democrats counted them in.

Q. Well, that returning board down there in Louisiana started with your folks, didn't it? The Democrats never had any returning board there before that, had they?

A. I say I don't know what they did do there before the Republicans got in, for I was in the Army and didn't know. I never seen a ballot-box till 1870.

Q. But you have heard all about that, haven't you?

A. Yes; I have heard the Democrats didn't have none.

Q. Now, tell me, Adams, as an honest man, which I believe you to be, didn't the Republicans, when they had the control of Louisiana and Mississippi, and these carpet-bag fellows were down there, didn't they have a pretty bad government, and didn't they plunder the State and oppress the people by taxation most outrageously?

A. Well, I will say this: that in many cases the white people had to pay a great many taxes, a great deal of taxes, but I will tell you this much, I will tell you the truth and nothing but the truth, that the colored people didn't have to pay as much taxes as they do now.

Q. No?

A. No; it was better on our side, I know, than it is now under the Democrats.

Q. They don't have much property to pay taxes on, do they?

A. O, yes; they have a good deal of property that they has to pay taxes on.

Q. How did they get it?

A. They worked hard for it and earned it all.

Q. Yes, but your people were just out of slavery, and you have been accumulating more and more since the war, haven't you?

A. Up to '77 we did, but we have not bought so much property after that time as before, you know.

Q. I don't know that.

A. Well, we have not bought so much since that time as up to that time.

Q. I thought the property of your people in that State had been increasing slowly; that you had been acquiring horses, mules, land, &c.?

A. Up to 1877, to my knowledge, in many cases it was so; but not after that.

Q. Well, what is your explanation in regard to that?

A. You know that many of the colored people that had lands at that time they got it before; that is, they have not got it now. If you get the last census, you will see that they have not got as much land now as before, because they have been expecting that they would have either to leave, or something would happen, so that the land would be no use to them.

Q. You say that the black people did not pay as much taxes under the Republican rule as they have paid since?

A. Yes, sir; not so much as they pay now under the Democrats.

Q. How does that happen? The taxes are laid the same upon the black man and the white man, are they not?

A. Yes, sir.

Q. How does it happen, then, that you paid less under the one administration than you do under the other?

A. In that part of the country there is a man goes round collecting taxes on colored men, and the colored man don't know the difference. He brings a paper, and the colored people thinks he comes from the right place, and they respond to it; and they have collected down there a tax for his horse, and made him pay fifteen dollars for one old horse. A man showed me a receipt that he gave of his tax for an old gray horse of fifteen dollars; and then sometimes they tax him for his wagon; some of them had to pay four bits for a wheel and two dollars for the wagon. Then some pays a poll tax for the head. When the Republicans had it, we know we didn't pay that.

Q. You did not pay a poll tax under the Republican administration?

A. No, sir.

Q. This fifteen-dollar tax on an old horse was not levied by the law, was it?

A. No, sir; but that is what they do now.

Q. Some fellow has imposed upon you in that matter. Who did that?

A. Some of them white folks about there; I don't know who.

Q. He wasn't a carpet-bagger, was he?

A. I don't think he was; he was a man that lives there, somewhere in that part of the country. They said he was a collector.

Q. Was it Reuben White?

A. No, sir; it was not Reuben White; it wasn't him.

Q. Where was this case that you speak of?

A. This case I speak of was down right in De Soto Parish, near my own relations. I have ten people, relations of mine, that live in De Soto Parish, and some of them in Bossier, and some in Texas.

Q. And that is what they told you in reference to these taxes?

A. I saw the receipt.

Q. You saw the receipt?

A. Yes, I saw several receipts where they had to pay taxes, and I know I wasn't taxed for any such foolishness myself.

Q. Well, Mr. Adams, you mentioned, as one of the kinds of oppression, that your people were subjected to the fact that your churches had to be shut up at nine o'clock?

A. Yes, sir.

Q. Where was that done in any case?

A. That was done at Shreveport.

Q. When?

A. In 1874.

Q. In the city, or was it in the district around?

A. In the town.

Q. What was the reason assigned for it; did they give any excuse for such action?

A. They didn't give no excuse at all for it. They just said that the nigger shouldn't have no meetings after nine o'clock. These men, that called themselves police, walked about with guns at night, and would go around to the churches, and tell 'em they must all close up at nine o'clock; and if they didn't, their pastor would be arrested.

Q. Was not the excuse given that the colored people in these churches disturbed the citizens in the neighborhood by singing and shouting at night?

A. Yes, that's the excuse they give; they said the churches was disturbing the peace at night.

Q. There was no such order as that given in reference to any churches in the country, where they were off by themselves, was there?

A. Well, they followed the same movement if there was no orders issued; they would follow the same movement in the country places.

Q. But no orders of this kind were issued to country churches, were they?

A. Not as I know of.

Q. Now, in reference to these people getting away from your country, how did they mostly go, on the railroad or on the steamboat?

A. By steamboat, more or less, in the river parishes; but up in my part of the country more by cars and land.

Q. You say that you went over the country a good deal, for the purpose of getting the names of colored people enrolled who were about moving off?

A. Yes, sir.

Q. Did you get any pay for that service?

A. No, sir; not a nickel.

Q. Not a nickel?

A. No, sir. It was the duty of every member of the organization to do this work, and he would do it if he was fulfilling his duty.

Q. Who made the rates with the railroads and steamboats for them?

A. We could not make special rates in hardly any cases for the colored people who was going away.

Q. Did they not get special rates?

A. No, sir.

Q. They were required to pay full fare?

A. They made them pay full fare.

Q. Have you attended to the transportation of any these emigrants?

A. At New Orleans, last year, I have been appointed on the committee of arrangements and transportation. The reason why I was appointed was this: we heard there was a parcel of our people on the river bank—the Mississippi—that was not allowed to take the boats; they was prevented from getting on 'em, and in some places the boats wouldn't carry 'em. Then we appointed a committee of arrangements and transportation to seek into these matters, with the captains of the steamboats. I went to the captains of the steamboats as they come to the city of New Orleans, in June, July, August, and September, along there, and then they told me—the captains of two of the boats that was running to Saint Louis, told me—"Look here," they would say, "I don't refuse to take colored people at all that wants to go. I am running my boat for the money, and any of 'em that wants to go can make their way to my boat and I will take them on if they have got the money to pay their fare. But," they would say, "there is two places on the river"—on the Mississippi river, it is—"which I refuse to land my boat at." I asked, "which was them?" and they said "Vidalia on the Louisiana side, and at Natchez on the Mississippi side"; and another place above that he said he wouldn't land his boat for all the money in Louisiana. I asked him why; and he said "why, by God! they have armed every white man there to mob the first captain that lands a boat there with colored people on board; and he would not land there for anything, or take any colored people there; but they should go on his boat to Saint Louis, if they wanted to go to Kansas or anywhere else." "Well, captain, if they come to your boat here or at any other landing on the river but those you mention, will you take them on board?" "Yes," he said, "I will take them on board if they have got the money to pay their fare with." "Well, what will you charge?" "Our rates we have been taking them for generally is $2.50 and up to $4; but now they has got to be such a terrible rage by the people about carrying the labor off the river, that we won't take them at that now; our charge is five dollars a head." Said I, "supposing I was to say I could have a hundred here to take the boat this evening, would you take them then for three hundred dollars?" And he says "No, I would not do that. They must pay me, all over five years old and up to fifteen must pay me half price, two dollars and a half; and all that is over that age must pay me five dollars; and all under five years may go free; that is all I can do about that."

Q. What is that captain's name?

A. I can't give his name, because if I was to give his name or the name of the boat, he might lose heaps of freight; so he said he didn't want it exposed; and I won't do it under them circumstances.

Q. Suppose we were to admit what you have said; how are we to disprove it, if you won't give the man's name?

A. I could give his name or the name of the boat he run, but I would rather not be doing it; but if you insist upon my doing it I will do it and let the blame fall upon him.

Q. Well, it don't matter.

A. No, sir.

Q. Did the railroads or steamboats pay you any commission for selling tickets for them?

A. I never sold a ticket on the railroad or steamboat in my life. I tried to get the fare as low as I could. I got two or three men to go on the boat and the men to pay the captain a dollar apiece to go and then they would agree to help scrub on the way up for their rations.

Q. You say you never got a commission from the railroads or steamboats for bringing these people to them?

A. I never did.

Q. You never got any money at all, for doing this work, from the railroads or from any one else?

A. Not five cents.

Q. By the way, do you know what the price of labor is on those steamboats—for deck-hands and working hands on those boats?

A. The price awhile back was thirty dollars a month. I think they have struck and raised now to sixty dollars—forty cents an hour, and sixty dollars a month. I am not quite certain; but I know it was forty cents an hour on the levee.

Q. Well, ain't it seventy dollars a month now?

A. It did get up to seventy one month.

Q. It was seventy dollars a month in December, when I was in New Orleans.

A. I know it was; but I think when they struck last, the steamboat association gave them forty cents an hour and sixty dollars a month on the levee; I am not quite sure.

Q. That is pretty good wages, is it not?

A. Yes, sir.

Q. About four dollars a day?

A. Yes, sir; but he ought to have it, because rent is so high in New Orleans.

Q. Of course he ought to have it; I am not finding any fault with that.

A. No, sir.

Q. You have considerable property yourself about Shreveport, have you not?

A. Yes, sir.

Q. May I ask how you acquired it?

A. When I first went out of the service I went up there, in December, 1869. Me and my cousin up there, Moses Bartlett, we bought some property from a man named Pith there, in Shreveport.

Q. Real estate?

A. Yes, sir.

Q. How much did you pay for it?

A. We gave him fourteen hundred and twenty dollars for it; I think that was what we paid him; with the interest it amounted to fifteen hundred and twenty-five dollars.

Q. Do you own that now?

A. I don't own it all myself, I said me and my cousin bought it.

Q. You and your cousin own it together, now, do you?

A. Part of it we do.

Q. Your cousin is farming it?

A. It is town property, in the city of Shreveport.

Q. Do you rent it?

A. No; it ain't rented.

Q. Why not?

A. When I left home I locked it up and gave a gentleman the keys, as I didn't expect to be gone more than a few weeks; but when I got to the city and heard the decision of them men that I had testified against, and seen they was determined to do something to me when I got back, I haven't gone back yet.

Q. Is your cousin there?

A. My cousin lives on George Simpson's place, twelve miles from town; and I understand that George Simpson has closed a mortgage on him for about one hundred and twenty-five dollars—so my cousin said, about a month before I left.

Q. Could you not raise that one hundred and twenty-five dollars?

A. He might have raised it if he had tried hard to do it.

Q. Could not you have raised it?

A. Not at that time I could not.

Q. Did you try to raise it?

A. He did not notify me of it at that time.

Q. You say you have been an election supervisor?

A. At election time, you mean?

Q. Yes; I mean one of those fellows who stand at the polls at election time and challenge other people.

A. It means to stand at the polls and protect the interests of candidates for Congress, &c.?

Q. Yes.

A. I have been one of them.

Q. How often?

A. Once.

Q. When?

A. In 1874.

Q. Did you say you had been a marshal?

A. Yes, sir; a deputy United States marshal.

Q. Yes; and you served writs?

A. No, sir; I never served no writs.

Q. What did you do when you were deputy United States marshal at Shreveport?

A. I never served as a deputy marshal at Shreveport.

Q. Where did you serve?

A. In Bienville Parish.

Q. That is near Caddo?

A. No, sir; you have to go through Bossier and Webster, and then comes Bienville.

Q. Did you live in Bienville Parish then?

A. No, sir.

Q. What were you doing as deputy marshal there?

A. I was in one of the districts of Louisiana.

Q. You were deputized while at Shreveport, were you?

A. No; I was deputized in Bossier; I was working in Bossier at the time.

Q. Deputized as United States marshal there?

A. Yes, sir; deputized as marshal there.

Q. What did they deputize you to do?

A. To go down and be around the polls on election day, and see that everything went on fair.

Q. Down at Bienville, where you did not live?

A. I lived in that district.

Q. You lived in that district?

A. Yes.

Q. Were you acquainted in Bienville?

A. A great deal; I had relations there.

Q. You say you were deputized as United States marshal to go down to Bienville?

A. Yes, sir.

Q. You had been election supervisor in Caddo Parish, had you?

A. Yes, sir.

Q. When?

A. In 1874.

Q. And deputy United States marshal in Bienville in what year?

A. In 1876.

Q. In 1876; and you were in the custom-house what year?

A. In 1879 that was.

Q. For how long?

A. I staid about six weeks one time and five weeks another time.

Q. Well, how was it that you could get such a prominent place on this committee you speak of, if no politicians were allowed in it?

A. That was not being a politician, necessarily.

Q. Well, aren't you looked upon as a politician by your people?

A. I will tell you how that came about. The committee always say they could not control a great many people of the laboring class without I spoke to them and told them how they ought to vote, or something of that sort in behalf of their own interests, to better their own condition, and so I would speak to them and tell them how I thought it would be best for them to vote. And I would have to tell a great many of them whether they ought to take part in politics, and in regards to their voting.

Q. You have said that you were a "faith doctor." Did the fact that you were a faith doctor help you with your people?

A. Yes, sir; they have more confidence in me in every way on that account.

Q. In this practice of faith doctoring you put on hands and go through certain forms, do you not?

A. Yes, sir; I rub the patient.

Q. Do you make these little hair balls?

A. No, sir; nothing like that.

Q. You do not believe in voudou?

A. No, sir; I never use anything of that kind.

Q. You never did?

A. No, sir.

Q. Didn't you now just a little, doctor, before you joined the Methodist church?

A. No, sir; I never did use anything of that kind in my life, never!

Q. Were you present in Shreveport when Mr. Allston, the Republican candidate for sheriff killed Mr. Flanagan, one of the Democratic candidates for commissioner last fall?*

---

* James Alston, the defeated Republican candidate for Caddo Parish sheriff, shot Charles Flanagan (1828–1878) outside a store in Shreveport on the afternoon of November 26, 1878. Flanagan, who was unarmed, died on December 2. In the recent election he had served as a Democratic commissioner for the First Ward, where the only polling place was set up in the remote Black Bayou region of the parish. After more than two hundred Back citizens walked for twenty miles through woods, swamps, and bayous to reach the polls and vote for the Republican ticket,

A. Yes, sir; but it was not last fall.

Q. Was it in 1878?

A. Yes, sir.

Q. Well, that did happen, did it?

A. Yes, sir; that did take place there.

Q. He shot him?

A. Yes, sir.

Q. And killed him?

A. He shot him and he died.

Q. Yes; that is generally the way. Well, doctor, that is all.

Redirect examination of witness:

By Mr. Blair:

Q. Doctor, you seem to have acquired a professional title in the course of your examination here, and your professional method seems to have interested the committee considerably; I want you to explain what you mean by being a faith doctor, and your method of treatment—something of what you have done in your practice, the class of patients you have had, what your success has been, and so on. I do not wish you to make a very long story of it, but make it as intelligible as you can to the committee.

A. You mean the sort of diseases I have cured?

Q. Yes; and the method of your practice, the class of patients you have had, &c.

A. Well, any kind of risings and swellings coming on people, I rub them with my hands and blow my breath on them and take 'em away. And you find these wens on people, I take that away; and these old sores on the legs of people that are hard to cure, I make a kind of salve myself and cure it. I have studied it myself; it came to me natu-

---

a group of armed white men that reportedly included Flanagan seized and destroyed the ballots. A divided grand jury failed to indict Alston for murder in March 1879, as did a second grand jury in June.

rally; it always was with me. And then other diseases, a great many kinds of diseases I could name, backache, toothache, jawache, earache, rheumatism, white swellings, and such things as that I cure.

Q. The gout?

A. And phthisic, dyspepsia, fits, spasms, and so forth, I cure naturally.

Q. How do you treat them?

A. In some cases I make a medicine to give them, and in a great many cases to rub with, but I don't propose to give any of the instruments.

Q. O, no; I don't want any of the secrets of the profession.

A. I could not give them.

Q. What class of patients have you had—some white and some colored?

A. Yes; and all classes I have had, from the lowest to the highest.

Q. You may mention some of the more reputable among the "highest" as you call them?

A. Well, I could mention a lady in Texas by the name of Mrs. Ashton.

Q. Is she a white lady?

A. Yes, sir; and her husband is a lieutenant, and had the rank of captain in the rebel army.

Q. Any others?

A. She is one of the highest I have had; and then her husband's mother—I worked on her; and her husband's brother-in-law, Mr. Ashton, too; I worked on him; and from that to the lowest.

Q. You have never taken any fees for your services, I believe you said, except such as patients chose to give you and offered to give you?

A. No, sir; I would not make a price on nobody under no circumstances, because I didn't pay for my practice.

Q. You mean you didn't pay for acquiring the skill you have?

A. My learning—I didn't pay for it; it come to me naturally, so I wouldn't make no price for curing them. Them that says they are not able to pay, I says to 'em, "all right, may be you will some day"; but if they pays me and gives me a thousand dollars, I would take it—that is, rich people—but if a poor person was going to pay me more than he ought, I would say, "Don't do it; that is too much; you are not able to spare it"; but if a rich person was to give me a thousand dollars I would take it, in pay for curing him.

Q. You never did receive so large a fee as that, did you?

A. O, no, sir.

Q. What is the largest fee you ever received?

A. The largest was two hundred dollars.

Q. You say you didn't pay for your medical knowledge—how did you come by it?

A. I came by it naturally.

Q. You spoke of having cured the toothache when you were nine years old?

A. Yes, sir; I did.

Q. How did you cure the toothache?

A. I just blew my breath in the mouth and rubbed my hands over the jaws.

Q. Was the pain relieved at once?

A. Yes, sir.

Q. When you were how old, did you effect such cures?

A. When I was nine years old.

Q. Now, as I understand you, the chief purpose of your life during the last ten years or so, has been to ascertain if possible, and to make better, the condition of your race in the South?

A. Yes, sir; that has been my purpose.

Q. And you have given your time and efforts principally to this organization?

A. Yes, sir.

Q. And to carrying out the purposes I have indicated?

A. Yes, sir; to better the condition of my people in the Southern States in every way I could.

Q. You say you were in the Army at one time?

A. Yes, sir; I was in the United States Army.

Q. When did you enter the Army?

A. I entered the Army on the 10th day of September, 1866. I have got my papers here with me, and you can read them if you wish.

Q. No; nobody questions that. How long were you in the service?

A. Three years.

Q. In the regular service?

A. Yes.

Q. What regiment was it?

A. The 39th.

Q. The 39th what?

A. 39th Infantry. When I first enlisted I was attached on to the 80th Volunteers. Then from that I was sent on to New Orleans to be attached on to the 39th Infantry. Then I served in the 39th Infantry till April, 1869. Then the 40th and 39th was consolidated together and made the 25th. Then I remained in the 25th till my time expired in September.

Q. September of that year?

A. September of 1869.

Q. That was three years and a little over?

A. About three years; yes, sir.

Q. What was your position in the regiment?

A. When I first enlisted I was a private, of course. I remained a private until March, 1867. I do not suppose I would have remained a private that long, but I was taken sick and was sick for sixty-five days, and a promotion was ready for me, but I was not ready to receive it. Then I was promoted.

Q. To what?

A. I was promoted to quartermaster-sergeant from the ranks.

Q. And you remained a quartermaster-sergeant during the rest of the time you were in the service?

A. Yes.

Q. Could you read and write when you entered the Army?

A. I could not read a bit. I knowed the letters and figures when I seed them, but I could not put them together under no circumstances.

Q. How did you learn to read and write?

A. We had a teacher when we were stationed at Fort Jackson, in Louisiana. She was a white lady, Mrs. Bentine, and we had a school for the soldiers, and we had three hours a day to go to the school. I never went all that time, but only part of the time; and I learned to read and write a little in one month's time; and after I quit her I never went only two weeks more.

Q. The rest you acquired yourself?

A. Yes, sir; I acquired all the rest myself.

Q. That is all the schooling you ever had, was it?

A. Yes; I never had no more schooling but that.

Q. Well, I think that is a pretty good showing even for a white man. Now, I will read a few pages from this statement of yours which you have submitted in writing and offer here as evidence. (Reading:) "Statement of affairs and outrages in the South, 1866. Compiled by Henry Adams," is the heading you have given it. You then say—

In the year 1866, in the parish of Caddo, State of Louisiana, I seen hanging to a limb of an oak tree, about six miles south from Shreveport, the body of a colored man. He was dead when I seen him. About six miles north from Keachie I saw a wagon belonging to a colored man burning, with all his things; even his mules were burned to death. While on my way to Sunny Grove I seen the head of a colored man lying on the side of the road. Whilst traveling on my way to De Soto Parish a large body of armed white men met me and asked me who I belonged to. I answered them and told them that

I belonged to God, but not to any man. They then asked me where was my master, and I told them the one I used to have was dead, and I have not had none since 1858, but worked for those who would hire me and pay the largest price.

Mr. VANCE. What year is that (addressing Mr. Blair)?

Mr. BLAIR. 1866. This is an account of things that came under the witness's personal observation.

Mr. VANCE. Well, I have no objection to going back in the account to the discovery of America.

Mr. BLAIR. I suppose it is necessary to go back to these occurrences, for the purposes of the witness's statement and this investigation.

Mr. VANCE. Perhaps it is; if Columbus had not discovered this country there would have been no exodus.

Mr. BLAIR (Continuing to read a few moments longer.)

Q. (To the witness.) Are these statements contained here true, to the best of your knowledge and belief?

A. Yes, sir; they are.

Q. Are the parts I have read substantially the same in character with what is here given in the statement throughout?

A. That statement is just like I received it, the facts just like I seen it.

Q. Now, here is another document, in continuation of your statement, headed "Statements of individuals" (colored), and beginning with De Soto Parish, and going on to detail the specific cases of outrage to the number of 683, each case occupying a line or two—the last one being as follows: "683d. James Metimes (colored), beaten by Billy Willfort, a white man on Dr. Shempa's place, because he did not get out to work as soon as he wanted him to go. Done in 1868"; and these instances occurring as I see in the different years from 1866 to 1876. You say that these statements of colored people are statements as made to you and you jotted them down as they were given?

A. Yes, they are as they were told to me, and I would set it down as they say.

Q. These statements, then, are given here as they were given to you in this course of your travels—these 683 cases, and noted down by you?

A. Yes, sir.

Q. Here are also eleven affidavits of colored men, with their signatures where they have signed them, and "marks" of those who could not write their names. Are these true copies of those affidavits?

A. Yes, sir; they are.

Mr. BLAIR. Well, we will receive them without taking the time to read them.

Mr. VANCE. But we ought to have the opportunity to cross-examine the witness on these statements. You wish these statements to go in as testimony (addressing Mr. Blair)?

Mr. BLAIR. Yes, sir; they are statements such as we have been receiving and admitting into the testimony. We have had any amount of such testimony in the examination.

The CHAIRMAN. I would suggest that they be allowed to go in the record.

Mr. VANCE. I see the statement says a colored man's head was seen lying by the roadside. For all we know to the contrary, the body might have been lying there attached to the head. And it says a wagon belonging to a colored man was burning, and the mules were burned to death. How do we know but the mules set the wagon on fire!

Mr. BLAIR. The witness testifies to the event; it is a simple and brief record of the occurrence, that is all.

Mr. VANCE. I know that; but if the thing is filed in bulk, we can have no opportunity of cross-examination.

Mr. BLAIR. I have no objection to the cross-examination whatever, if required.

Mr. VANCE. But it would take six months to go over it in any kind of cross-examination.

Mr. BLAIR. I know that, but that is no reason for excluding testimony that is pertinent, and it is such as we have been receiving.

Mr. VANCE. Very well.

[These statements, with the affidavits, are printed at the close of the witness's examination.]

Mr. BLAIR (To the witness.) And here is a copy of your petition or appeal to the President—the one you addressed to President Hayes, dated Shreveport, Caddo Parish, Louisiana, September 15, 1877. Is this a true copy of one of the petitions or memorials that you sent to President Hayes?

A. Yes, sir.

Q. What was the occasion of your sending it?

A. It was at the time of the large meeting we held there, of over five thousand persons.

Mr. BLAIR (Reading):

SHREVEPORT, CADDO PARISH, LA.,
September 15, 1877.

To his Excellency R. B. HAYES,
President of the United States:

At a meeting of the National Colored Colonization Society, held in Shreveport, Caddo Parish, State of Louisiana, held on September 15, 1877, there being at said meeting representatives representing 29,000 colored people of the South, the following preambles and resolutions were unanimously adopted:

Whereas the Constitution of the United States guarantees to us equal civil and political rights and protection in the exercise of those rights, and as we the colored people of the South have been debarred from exercising those rights, the right to vote, hold office, and the privilege of education without molestation, and it being a well-established fact that we have been oppressed, murdered, and disfranchised on account of our race and color, and have not received that protection in the exercise of our rights guaranteed to us by the Constitution; and

Whereas we feel that the blood of the martyrs of freedom—John Brown and Abraham Lincoln—and the thousands that fell upon the battle-field have been shed in vain, having failed to awaken that interest as to demand in unmistaken language the enforcement of the Constitution relative to the amendments that guarantees protection to our race and color in the exercise of our rights, and after twelve years we find the colored race of the South in a worse condition than they were before those constitutional guarantees were extended, and we find our race in a worse state of slavery than before, being denied those rights that belong to us, and we feel that that passage in Lamentations, chapter 5th, of the Holy Scriptures, fully cover our grievances, and we cry out with a full heart that we have suffered all that and even more in the maintenance of our rights, and we feel and know that unless some protection is guaranteed to our race that we will cease to be a race or people and that we cannot live in the South in peace, harmony, and happiness, and we feel that our only hope and preservation of our race is the exodus of our people to some country where they can make themselves a name and nation and be happy and prosperous; and

Whereas we, the down-trodden race of Ham residing in the South, feeling that we can no longer dwell in the South in peace, harmony, and happiness, call on you as the President, and Congress of the United States, to assist us in our exodus by using your power and influence to aid us either by appropriating some Territory in which we may colonize our race, or, if that cannot be done, appropriate means whereby we can colonize in Liberia or some other country, as we feel that for us to remain in the South will be the destruction of our race. We therefore ask the Government of the United States, with full confidence that the same will be granted, an appropriation to enable us to colonize, knowing full well that we are more worthy than the Indians who return the favors of the government by murder, war, and rapine, while we return neglect by cotton and sugar. We as a race can point back to the robberies perpetrated on us by the

Freedman's Bank, whereby thousands of our race were plunged from affluence to poverty;* we also look back to the battle-field where thousands of our race shed their blood in defense of that government who guaranteed rights to us and have failed to perform them. We look at our soldiers faithfully fighting in defense of that government who neglects them. We look back to those lost victories gained at the ballot-box, lost lives in vain. We look to the future where in case of war we would feel compelled to fight for that government that looks coolly on our sufferings and see our rights one by one taken away from us, and we cry out with a full heart, the cup is full and running over, and with a loud voice cry to God, O, how long?

Therefore be it resolved, That we, the colored race of the South, do call upon the President and Congress of the United States to look back upon the blood shed on the battle-field by our race in defense of the government; to look back on the cotton and sugar raised by our labor; and we, in view of those facts that the rights guaranteed to us by the Constitution be restored to us, and ample protection be given to us in the maintenance of those rights. If that protection cannot be given and our lost rights restored, we would respectfully ask that some Territory be assigned to us in which we can colonize our race; and if that cannot be done, to appropriate means so that we can colonize in Liberia or some other country, for we feel and know that unless full and ample protection is guaranteed to us we cannot live in the South, and will and must colonize under some other government, and we put our full trust in God that our prayers and petition will be speedily answered.

Be it further resolved, That we respectfully and earnestly call upon Congress to restore back to us the savings of years that our race was

---

* The Freedman's Savings and Trust Company was chartered by Congress in 1865 as a mutual savings bank investing in federal securities. Although the bank was a private company, it often shared offices with the Freedman's Bureau and many depositors believed it was a government institution. After its charter was revised in 1870, the bank began speculating in railroad securities and real estate. Severely impacted by the Panic of 1873, the company collapsed on June 28, 1874. Only about half of its 61,000 depositors received any funds when the bank was liquidated, and none of them received full value.

robbed of by the failure of the Freedman's Bank, feeling that it is only an act of justice due us.

Be it further resolved, That we as a race will abstain from voting on all national questions and at the elections for national officers unless we have full protection and our own officers to guard our interests and rights.

By Mr. Blair:

Q. This, you say, you adopted at the convention and forwarded to the President?

A. Yes, sir; forwarded a copy to the President, and a copy to both Houses of Congress.

Q. Have you ever had any response whatever to this appeal?

A. None whatever.

Q. Well, Republican or Democrat, whichever may be responsible, I coincide with you in saying it is an infernal outrage.

By the Chairman:

Q. What is the date of the appeal?

A. It is dated September 15, 1877.

Mr. Blair. Here is the document introduced by witness in his direct examination, in relation to the White League organization in Louisiana, that he came in contact with. It appears to be extracted from the reports of the Congressional committee consisting of Messrs. Hoar, Wheeler, and Frye,* and gives the history of the organization mainly in extracts from the Democratic press of Louisiana.

Mr. Vance. I submit that we ought not to republish anything that we have published before in a Congressional report.

---

* In December 1874 the House of Representatives appointed a seven-man select committee to investigate the recent election in Louisiana. Three Republican members, George F. Hoar (1826–1904) of Massachusetts, William A. Wheeler (1819–1887) of New York, and William P. Frye (1830–1911) of Maine, submitted a minority report on February 23, 1875.

Mr. BLAIR. No, that would be unnecessary; but a good deal is here that has never been in testimony. We will go over it and mark for insertion such extracts as may be pertinent.

(Inserted at close of witness's examination.)

Mr. BLAIR. Here is a document in pencil. (Reading.) It appears to be another appeal to President Hayes, from witnesses who were summoned before the United States court, in New Orleans, last winter, to testify against the murderers of colored men.

Q. (To witness.) Is that the occasion and purport of this document in lead-pencil writing?

A. Yes, sir. It is a petition that we men who was summoned to testify in the court at New Orleans appealed to the President for. We was in the city, and after we had testified was afraid to go to our homes, and we appealed to the President of the United States to give us either protection at home, or employment under the United States Government.

Q. Was this ever acted upon?

A. We never heard that nobody acted on it.

Q. You never received any response to it from the President or anybody else?

A. None whatever.

Mr. BLAIR. (Reading portions of the appeal.) We will have it go in the record.

The petition follows:

NEW ORLEANS, *March* 10, 1879.

To His Excellency R. B. HAYES,

  President of the United States of America:

  SIR: We, the undersigned citizens of the State of Louisiana, from the several bulldozing parishes of this State, do now appeal to you as the Chief Executive of the nation who now presides over the millions who have placed you at their head.

  We are a few of the four million who were made free by the Proclamation of Emancipation, and the Constitution of the United States has granted to us equal, civil, and political rights, and protection in

the exercise of those inalienable rights given by God. And as we, the
several witnesses who have been summoned from the bulldozing
regions of this State to appear before the United States court in this
city to testify against the murderers of men whose blood now cries
from the ground in the language of Zachariah, "Oh, Lord, how long!"
dare we not return to our homes and families for fear of being murdered by the very men against whom we were summoned by the
United States court to testify.*

Time after time we have received letters and threats against our
lives even here in this city, the metropolis of the South. Threats on
our lives have been made without fear even in the custom-house,
and within the vicinity of the United States court now sitting to try
the murderers of men of color on account of politics, and yet the
proud banner, the stars and stripes, waves over us here, which, as it
floats upon the breeze above the United States custom-house, seems
as a hollow mockery; yet, as an emblem of freedom, here it waves,
while we are driven from home, and are now out of employment,
pressed hard to procure the necessities of life, and dare not go home;
yet this free America, and colored men are free according to the
Proclamation and constitutional amendments. And inasmuch as you
have in charge, as the Chief Executive of the nation, not only the
States, but the Territories, and can, by request or demand made on
any of the government officials at this or any other port, cause men,
especially men in our condition, to be employed even at levee work,
laboring for the government in any capacity, hence we appeal to you
in good faith, and hope, as President of the United States, believing
that you will lend a listening ear to the cries of and the appeal of a
portion of the citizens of the United States whose wrongs would make

---

* After the 1878 election Adams and a number of other witnesses were subpoenaed by the U.S. district court in New Orleans as part of an investigation into
the use of violence, intimidation, and fraud to suppress the Republican vote in
Caddo, Natchitoches, and Tensas parishes. Although a grand jury handed down
120 indictments for conspiracy to deny the right to vote in a congressional election, none of the accused were convicted. On March 6, 1879, a jury acquitted
forty-eight defendants from Natchitoches Parish, and on March 12 another jury
deadlocked in the case of the first three defendants from Caddo Parish. The
remaining cases were eventually dismissed.

angels weep and almost shake man's belief in the existence of a just God. We ask you to give us employment of some kind, or cause those under your command to aid us in that direction, for we cannot go home; yet, our families are there in want in North Louisiana; yet we cannot ever hope to return to them, for to return is but to be *murdered* for daring to be free, and to exercise that right, yet this freedom was given us by a nation's council, and we have dared to persist in its enjoyment; yet we are a part of the millions of voters; yet we dare not stay at home; still we are here in God's free country, and have been led to believe that we were free. Your petitioners pray, in the name of the God of liberty and justice, that you will hear the cry of the following distressed colored citizens.

By Mr. Blair:

Q. I understand that in addition to the statements of outrages in 1866, and the specific cases covering the period from 1866 to 1876 you had prepared a statement in pencil covering the time from 1876 up to the present?

A. Yes, sir.

Q. Where is that statement?

A. I thought I had it with me, but I have not got it.

Q. We want it in your testimony if you have it, or can furnish it. Have you any other matter you wish to put in the record as your evidence?

A. Yes, sir. (Handing a newspaper extract.)

Mr. Blair. This appears to be an extract from "the New York Herald of the 19th," containing "a dispatch from Washington dated the 18th," and it says, "The President to-day received a petition signed by one thousand colored citizens of Caddo Parish, Louisiana, asking to be removed to a Territory where they could live by themselves" &c. What is the date of this?

The Witness. That was in 1874.

Mr. Blair. I do not see anything on it to indicate the date. You say it is offered as proof that a petition was sent to President Grant?

The WITNESS. Yes, sir.

Mr. BLAIR. I do not see the date.

The WITNESS. It is on the back somewhere. It was September 9, 1874, when the petition was preferred. That was September 18th, 1874, when the President received it. You will see on the back that the slip is taken from the Shreveport Times, a Democratic paper, of some time in September, 1874.*

Mr. BLAIR. Very well.

It is as follows:

A NEW DEVELOPMENT IN THE RADICAL PROGRAMME; THE NEGROES TO BE COLONIZED IN AFRICA.

The New York Herald of the 19th instant contains the following dispatch from Washington, dated the 18th:

"The President to-day received a petition signed by one thousand colored citizens of Caddo Parish, La., asking to be removed to a territory where they could live by themselves, as it was utterly impossible to live with the whites of Louisiana. They were willing to be sent to Liberia, if no better place could be given them."

That such a petition has been laid before the President we have not the least doubt; but we emphatically and unequivocally declare that it is a base forgery. Neither one thousand nor any other number of the colored citizens of Caddo Parish signed or know anything of it. The petition was undoubtedly concocted in New Orleans, and the names of negroes in this parish signed to it by George L. Smith, C. W. Keeting,† and other carpet-baggers who had access, for that purpose, to the old registration-lists of the parish.

---

* The extract was taken from the *Shreveport Times* of September 25, 1874.

† George L. Smith (1837–1884), a native of New Hampshire, moved to Shreveport after the Civil War. A banker and newspaper proprietor, Smith served as a Republican in the state house of representatives, 1871–72, and in Congress, 1873–75. He later served as collector of customs at New Orleans, 1878–79, before moving to Arkansas. Charles Wellington Keeting (1841–1906), a former Union officer from Massachusetts, became a merchant in Shreveport after the war. Keeting

The WITNESS. Here is something with regard to our people that was published in a Texas paper, that caused us to leave.

Mr. BLAIR. (Reading.) It is an extract republished in the New Orleans Louisianian of the date of May 26, 1877, under the heading of "sound sentiments," and taken from the Comanche Chief, a Democratic journal published in Texas.

It is as follows:

SOUND SENTIMENTS.

The Comanche Chief, a Democratic journal published in Texas, has the following:

"It is now, as it has been for ten years past. The entire people of Texas have to bear all the slander and abuse for the crimes of the desperadoes and villains who have cursed the State by making her soil the scene of their crimes. Just at a time when the national administration is offering us peace and liberty, and protection in the exercise of self-government by the States, comes the news of the destruction of a negro colony in Lee County, by a band of drunken villains. The negroes had purchased the property upon which they were living, and were, as the letter detailing the outrage informs us, honest and industrious citizens. They had constructed their rude cabins far from the neighborhood of the white people, and were laboring to make themselves comfortable homes, that they need not become thieving vagrants, and thus receive, as such characters deserve, death or confinement. But their prospects were too fair. They were too fortunate. A blood-thirsty mob came and undertook to lynch one of their number, but the friends of the victim interfered to rescue and save him from the horrible doom. But not to be baffled thus, the brutes waited but a few nights before returning to consummate what they had undertaken. This time they were more successful; and after burning the house of a prominent member of the colony, notified the balance to

_____

served as the city's postmaster, 1869–72, and as a Republican in the state house of representatives, 1872–78. He then moved to New Orleans, where he worked in the customs service from 1878 until his death.

leave the country, which command was promptly obeyed. When asked why they did not appeal to the civil authorities, one of the negroes replied that it would do no good, because it would be dangerous for any of their number to appear as witnesses against men who did it.

"There is sufficient power in the government of Texas to protect every citizen of the State. If such be not true let the people call upon the national government for such protection as it can afford."

That a Democratic journal condemns such outrages in such emphatic terms, and proposes even to call in Federal bayonets if necessary to put an end to them, is evidence of a revulsion of public sentiment that must eventually produce beneficial results. We believe that the traditional opinion which prevailed in the days of slavery, that the negro must be kept in ignorance and poverty in order to fulfill the design of his creation, has long since been discarded by the progressive white men of the South, and that such persecutions as are narrated above are, as stated, the work of "desperadoes and villains" who care nothing for the fair fame of the State, and whose idea of "self-government" is immunity for the crimes which their ignorance and malicious nature prompts them to commit. It may be an unfortunate thing for "the entire people of Texas" that they have to bear the responsibility for the evil deeds of such characters, but it is one which they share in common with all who are free to manage their own affairs in their own way. In other words, it is one of the responsibilities which must accompany such freedom, and it becomes at once the duty and the interest of "the entire people of Texas" to show their capacity for self-government by ridding their State of desperadoes and villains, or at least securing protection for "honest and industrious citizens," whether they are white or black. Many politicians of our day have adopted the theory that a government which is unable to sustain itself and perform its proper functions has no right to exist, and if the theory is applicable in any one instance it must be true in all cases. It is not at all likely that an appeal for Federal interference, even coming from a Democratic journal, would procure a single bayonet from President Hayes; and, in any case, such a way of meeting the difficulty would be extremely objectionable to the public sentiment of the nation. Hence Texas must rely solely upon her own citizens for the preservation of peace within her borders. If she cannot protect "honest and industrious citizens in making for themselves" comfortable homes, they must flee from her borders or become "thieving vagrants," and Texas must bear the loss. Every honest, industrious citizen is a gain, every "band of drunken villains" a loss, and the State has her own election to enjoy the one or suffer the other. One plan of reconstruction of which the Republican party was the author, and for which it was held accountable, has failed; it remains to be seen whether the party now in power will achieve greater success in dealing with our great national problem: How to secure for the South the blessings of good government and the protection of the law for every citizen who deserves such protection. The carpet-baggers of the South have been hurled from power, loaded with the maledictions of all parties, but those who have succeeded them in power have to pass through the same ordeal to which they were subjected, without, however, having the same difficulties with which they had to contend. Every true friend of the South, of whatever party he may be or whatever color, has become wearied out with the repetition of such outrages as occurred in Lee County, and they are highly detrimental to the interests of all classes. No political party can afford to accept the responsibility for them. Hence it becomes the duty of all good citizens to give a hearty support to a State administration that will vigorously repress them and to condemn one that will not.

Mr. BLAIR. Here is something in relation to a difficulty at Shreveport.

The WITNESS. Yes, sir; that happened in Shreveport, and caused our people to raise up with excitement. It is from a Democratic paper there.

Mr. BLAIR. What is the paper?

The WITNESS. It is from the Shreveport Times or Standard, I don't know which.

Mr. BLAIR. (Examining.) It is from the Shreveport Times, and is headed, "Nearly a difficulty." Is that the extract you wish to put in? It appears to be published some time in October, 1878.*

---

* The story appeared in the *Shreveport Times* on October 20, 1878.

The WITNESS. Yes, sir; that was in the last campaign. I knowed
the man that kept the ferry-boat, and I saw the thing myself.

Mr. BLAIR. That was in the campaign of 1878?

The WITNESS. Yes, sir; in October, 1878.

The extract is as follows:

NEARLY A DIFFICULTY.

Quite a sensation was created yesterday morning on board the
ferry-boat, which came near terminating in a serious difficulty
between the whites and blacks. The circumstances, as we have
them from those present, are, that early yesterday morning a negro
man by the name of Ben Smith came aboard the ferry-boat in a
beastly state of intoxication, and fell asleep before the departure of
the boat for this side of the river. He was put on the dock and a stick
of wood placed under his head, where he slept two hours, when he
came aboard the boat and asserted that he had lost fifty cents, and
believed some one on the boat had robbed him, at the same time
using very insolent and abusive language, and continued to be abusive until the boat had nearly reached this side of the river, when
he was approached by Mr. William King, special police officer, and
told to keep quiet. He became more violent and demonstrative than
ever, threatening to knock King down with the whip-stalk which he
held in his hand, and went so far as to execute his threat, when the
officer dealt him two heavy blows on the head, knocking him down.
This action on King's part excited the indignation of a large number
of negroes who had gathered at the landing, attracted by the blow-
ing of the whistle of the Stirling White* signaling assistance, and
they were loud and bitter in their threats against King and the white
people generally, but, fortunately for them, they made no effort to
carry out their threats.

Policeman Henry Weinstock arrived, and took charge of the prisoner, and marched him to the lock-up, followed by a large crowd of
negroes, where he is now, and where he is likely to remain for several
days.

---

* A steamboat used as a ferry on the Red River.

The conduct of this turbulent negro, and the sympathy he received, is the effect of the teachings of a few bad white men, and shows to what excess their unbridled passions would lead them to if not restrained by fear.

It was a most fortunate thing for the blacks that they did not provoke a difficulty, for just as certain as cause follows effect, if one drop of white man's blood had been shed the lives of nearly every negro present would have paid the penalty of their folly.

Mr. BLAIR: And here is a call for a convention to be held at Shreveport.

The WITNESS. Yes, an address to the freedmen of Louisiana, calling a convention on Thursday, December 5, 1878, with the names of the officers signing it, and called by the president of the Negro Union Co-operative Aid Association, and signed by me as president of the Colonization Council.

Mr. BLAIR. Very well, we will receive it.

Following is the call:

CONVENTION.

To the Freedmen of Louisiana:

FELLOW-CITIZENS: In order that we may unite in a common band of brotherly love and union, I, as president of the Negro Union Co-operative Aid Association, appeal to the freedmen without regard to sex, religion, or politics, to immediately assemble in their respective religious bodies, and all other societies as may choose to send delegates to a convention which will meet in Shreveport, at 12 m. on Thursday, December 5, 1878. To the discouraged we have but one remark to make. Join with us and try by one mighty effort to elevate ourselves morally and socially, and to aid each other in getting lands and homes, that we may not give all we make every year to stay on somebody's plantation. The foregoing is presented to you as a plan for coming together in council to devise a general plan whereby we may become united as a race.

APPORTIONMENT FOR DELEGATES.

Any organized religious body, one delegate; any benevolent society, one delegate; any secret organization, one delegate; any plantation with fifty persons, one delegate; any organization composed
exclusively of negro people, one delegate. Each delegate is requested
to come prepared to pay the sum of two dollars towards paying the
expenses of the convention.

Officers and directors.—R. J. Cromwell, president; E. Allen, vice-
president; C. Morris, secretary; J. Cleaveland, treasurer; P. James,
ass't treasurer; H. Human, ag't; J. Alexander, E. Johnson, Aaron
Williams, J. M. Mitchell, R. L. Cook, Chas. Wilson, L. High. H.
Adams, president of the council.

Mr. BLAIR. Have you any other matters you wish to present as
evidence?

The WITNESS. Only these two or three. One is a list of the steam-
ers and prices they charged for passage of our people up the river,
and the letter I wrote about it to the committee on relief and immigration. The letter is on the back.

The following are the letter and list:

NEW ORLEANS, LA., *June 27,* 1879.
To the Chairman and Members of Committee on Relief and
Immigration:

GENTLEMEN: I went on board of steamer James Howard this
morning, bound from this port to St. Louis, Mo., to ascertain the
lowest figure that they would carry immigrants from this city to
St. Louis, Mo. The clerk informed me that he would carry them as
follows, viz: Grown people, deck passage and feed themselves, $4;
grown people, cabin passage and feed you, $20; children from three
years up to ten, half price, and all over ten years full fare. On deck
they will charge nothing for bedstead, trunk, and mattress, and your
grub or provision. But when an over excess of plunder, they will

Steamer.	No.	Date.	Charges per head.
James Howard	121	June 7, 1879	$4 (and four delegates).
John A. Scudder	146	June 14, 1879	$4
City of Alton	154	June 21, 1879	5
Centennial	12	June 25, 1879	5
E. O. Stanard	3	June 26, 1879	3
James Howard	97	June 28, 1879	4
W. P. Halliday	13	July 2, 1879	5
Jno. A. Scudder	175	July 5, 1879	4
Belle of Shreveport	14	July 9, 1879	5
City of Alton	126	July 12, 1879	5
Centennial	18	July 16, 1879	5
James Howard	112	July 19, 1879	5
W. P. Halliday	25	July 23, 1879	5
John A. Scudder	28	July 26, 1879	$5 deck, $10 cabin.
City of Alton	20	Aug. 2, 1879	$5
Belle of Shreveport	12	Aug. 6, 1879	$5, $15 cabin.
W. P. Halliday	15	Aug. 16, 1879	$5
Golden City	5	Aug. 20, 1879	5
City of Alton	5	Aug. 23, 1879	5
E. O. Stanard	10	Sept. 6, 1879	5
City of Alton	29	Sept. 13, 1879	5
Commonwealth	20	Sept. 21, 1879	5
Centennial	6	Sept. 27, 1879	5
W. P. Halliday	9	Oct. 2, 1879	5
City of Alton	19	Oct. 4, 1879	5
Belle of Shreveport	8	Oct. 21, 1879	5
Centennial	5	Oct. 22, 1879	5
W. P. Halliday	9	Oct. 26, 1879	5
City of Alton	3	Nov. 1, 1879	5

charge for it, but very cheap; making through trips to St. Louis in six days and a half.

Respectfully submitted.

HENRY ADAMS,
Member Committee on Arrangements and Transportation.

Mr. BLAIR. Have you anything else?

The WITNESS. This circular, addressed by the Migration Society to colored people desiring to emigrate.

It follows:

CIRCULAR.

ROOMS MIGRATION AND RELIEF ASSOCIATION.

To the Colored People desiring to migrate:

The Migration and Relief Association, at a meeting held April 28, 1879, decided that the wisest plan for our people to pursue is to remain quietly at home and at work until such time as this committee shall be able to assist you by such advice and means, if necessary, as will enable you to depart decently and in order.

This committee is doing all in its power to prepare for your departure with safety to yourselves and families.

Committee: Geo. H. Fayerweather (chairman), A. R. Blount, J. G. Lewis (secretary), who desire all information relative to this movement.

BY MR. BLAIR:

Q. That statement in lead pencil of occurrences from 1876 to 1879, what do you say as to that?

A. I have not got that with me.

Q. Where is it?

A. At home.

Q. What is the nature of it?

A. It is a statement of outrages that happened from 1876 to 1879. I have not got them written out yet with ink, just in lead pencil. But I can explain them to you by heart.

Q. Well, it explains the condition of your race, I suppose you mean to say, since the inauguration of President Hayes, and during the time of his administration?

A. Yes, sir.

Q. What has been the condition of your race in the South, so far as you know it, during the time of the present administration, and what is it at the present time?

A. It is just the same as it was before, only in regards of elections it is a little more bad than it was before in regards of the people casting their ballots.

By Mr. Vance:

Q. You say it is worse than it was before?

A. Yes, in regards to casting our ballots for whom we please.

By Mr. Blair:

Q. Won't you explain wherein?

A. In 1878, at an election we held in Caddo Parish, at a place that was called Caledonia, on Red River, they raised a riot there.

Q. Who raised a riot?

A. The white men did.

Q. Well, tell us about it.

A. The white men raised a riot and shot several colored men, which was reported.

Q. Did you see the riot or participate in it?

A. No, I never saw these things with these eyes; but I knowed about it, and I seen whilst they were going down there with guns, a hundred guns in one wagon and sixty in another, going down there with guns, and I seen some who came from down there. And whilst they was going on down there I would see colored men that would run up from down there. It was about thirty miles from Shreveport, below Shreveport, on Red River.

Q. What was the occasion of the riot?

A. It all broke out on that election, and I suppose that the colored men said that they would vote the Republican ticket as they chose, and they already had a majority in the box at the time when it first broke out, for they was voting the Republican ticket pretty fast. And when it first broke out they all squandered right away, and some of them attacked a colored man's house by the name of Madison Reams and caused him to leave his house, and they captured every gun they had in the house. They had guns, so they say, for the purpose of guarding the cotton-house, owned by Jere Bright, justice of the peace, and he had given Madison Reams, it is supposed, the privilege of having guns to protect his cotton-house, as some cotton-houses was fired before that time and they thought they might set his on fire. And I suppose he had nine or ten guns there, 'least so the man told me that run from there, that he had nine or ten guns there and they were there with him. He told me that the white men came and surrounded the house and took every gun that he had in the house. And after these colored men got shot by the white men about a hundred yards from the polls, near that distance, then when they shot these colored men, every one that they knowed had guns in his house they took them away from them, and then commenced shooting the colored men that had the guns, and commenced hunting for those that knowed anything about the guns being there. They went to running, and run into the fields, and they shot some men that didn't live in Caddo, but lived in Bossier Parish, and was over there picking cotton. They shot them down in the fields, in the cotton fields, and caused some of them to leave, and some went back. *

There is Jesse Williams, he ran from there and he went to New Orleans and was there a short time ago. And there was George Clark;

---

* A white deputy sheriff attempted to seize guns from the house of brothers Isaac and Madison Reams in the settlement of Caledonia on election day, November 5, 1878. Firing broke out, the deputy and a member of his posse were wounded, and two Black men were killed at the nearby polls. Dozens of armed white men then converged on the area and killed at least twenty Black residents who had fled to the swamps and woods. In December Lot Clark and William White, two Black witnesses to the killings, were taken by armed white men from a riverboat as they were traveling to New Orleans to testify. The two men were never seen again, and no one was convicted for the murders at Caledonia.

he ran from there, and he is at New Orleans now, or was a week or two ago. And Vernal Moore, he ran from there; and Monroe Brown, he ran from there; he is on Red River there. And there was Isaac Reams and Madison Reams, they both ran from there on account of that, and they are all scattered off somewhere now at other parts of the State. And there is Henry Glasgow; he is away from there on account of this very thing.

And there was several men that was witnesses before the United States court in some of these same events that happened down there, and they went down to testify as such, and they now are away from their homes. Henry Williams is one, he is away from there; and Fred Thaw, he didn't testify in that very case, but in another case that happened in Caddo; and Richard Pickett and Andrew Doty and Ben Williams—they two is in Kansas, they escaped and went home, and they could not stay, but left and went to Kansas. And several more are just in that fix, from the election of 1878; that being under President Hayes's administration.

Q. You don't find any increasing hope there for your race in that section of the country?

A. Not a bit.

Q. And the longer you wait the worse it seems to be for you?

A. Yes, sir.

Q. And you have concluded to get up and go out?

A. Yes, sir.

Q. You speak of outrages from your own observation and of those you had learned by inquiry from various sources?

A. Yes, sir; what I seen myself and what I heard from those that had seen 'em.

Q. Have you ever known any of these outrages you speak of to be committed by Republicans? If so, state the circumstances.

A. I will, if I can think of any. (Pondering.)

Q. Just state all about them?

A. Well, I have known some of the men who now pretend to be Republicans that have did some of these things in the past.

Q. I mean any who were Republicans at the time they committed the outrages?

A. (Reflecting.)

Q. I want to know if you have ever known of any Republicans who at the time these outrages were committed were engaged in them and approving them, and who were at the time Republicans and acting with the Republican party?

A. Well, I don't know of none myself; not one that was a Republican who was having anything to do with these outrages.

Q. Then the parties that have done these things have all been Democrats, have they?

A. Yes, sir.

Recross-examination of witness:

By Mr. Vance:

Q. Did you ever hear in all this time of any outrages committed by black people on whites?

A. O, I have heard some whites say that the colored people had raised arms and was raging against the white people, but when they came to investigate the matter they found it was false.

Q. When you heard the other side of the story, then, you did not think that the colored people really had committed any outrages at all upon the white people in that country?

A. Well, as a mass they have not, to my judgment.

Q. What do you mean by "as a mass"?

A. I mean that nine or ten or twenty colored men should get together and go to hunting and threatening and killing the white people—I don't believe they ever did.

Q. I am afraid you will have to take back some things you said a moment ago, as an honest man.

Mr. Blair. It is not exactly fair for the Senator to say that. I have never myself heard any such instance.

Mr. VANCE. The newspapers have been full of accounts of outrages on both sides.

Mr. BLAIR. It is very seldom such charges even are made. I do not recollect of seeing an instance in a Northern paper, Republican or Democratic, where a body of colored men, or "a mass," as witness calls it, were charged even with perpetrating political outrages; not one.

Mr. VANCE. There have been great numbers of them in the newspapers—the newspapers are full of them—if you will only read on the other side.

Mr. BLAIR. I have read very diligently the papers of both sides, and the Democratic press of the North has been tolerably ready to publish anything of that kind that comes to their knowledge, but I never saw in a Democratic paper that a body of negroes in the Southern country had committed political outrages anywhere—not one, to my knowledge. And I do not think the witness has exhibited any disposition to falsify or suppress the real truth, and he ought not to be indirectly charged with dishonesty.

Q. I will ask the witness whether any colored people, to his knowledge, have ever voted the Democratic ticket?

A. They have; some of them, in some places, but not freely. If they voted the Democratic ticket they have sometimes got whipped by the colored people, but not in my part, they didn't do that.

Q. Did you hear of its being done?

A. Yes; I have heard of them being whipped for voting the Democratic ticket, but when they came to investigate, it was more what that one that was whipped told on some Republican colored man, some false thing he had told about him, or something of that kind, and not for casting his vote—it was for something else besides that.

Q. Still some colored men have been whipped by their own people for being Democrats and voting the Democratic ticket?

A. Of course I have heard that was so in certain cases, but in most cases it was not for voting the Democratic ticket, but for something else.

Q. The man that did the whipping told you that it was not for that?

A. Yes; and when I got to questioning him pretty close he told me so, too.

By the Chairman:

Q. That is a new phase of the matter. Do the negroes whip each other down there?

A. Not often.

Q. Once in a while?

A. Yes, once in a while; when it is necessary.

By Mr. Vance:

Q. If they vote the Democratic ticket?

A. No; only so that they let others alone. Plenty of the penitentiary convicts vote the Democratic ticket.

Q. Do all the penitentiary men vote the Democratic ticket?

A. All of them don't, but a great many of them do. Many of them are in the penitentiary down there; they put them in every time they hold court, most; they send my race to the penitentiary.

Q. What for?

A. For 'most any little things they charge 'em with doing.

Q. What charges do they make?

A. Stealing a hog, or sheep, or such thing.

Q. You mean for stealing, and not for fighting?

A. Some for fighting and cutting.

Q. Well, it is all persecution, is it; they don't steal?

A. Some of them steal sometimes.

Q. Yes, they do! Well, the balance that don't steal are improperly convicted, are they?

A. We think they are sometimes; a great many of them are.

Q. Have they no colored men on the juries?

A. Yes; sometimes they have.

Q. And they convict men of their own race improperly and unjustly?

A. Well, it is a kind of fixing up the matter in such a way the men on the jury every time can't control the jury.

Q. Until quite recently the prosecuting officer in your place was a Republican, was he not?

A. Yes.

Q. And the judges were Republicans?

A. I didn't consider that——

Q. Well, I want you to consider it, then.

A. I didn't consider of their being Republicans in all cases.

Q. Well, were they Republicans or not?

A. I said in many cases they were said to be Republicans, but when they came to proving their Republicanism they was not there.

Q. They were not good Republicans, then?

A. If they had been thorough Republicans they would not have signed bills of indictment against Republican people as they do.

Q. But against all white bad men, and not against others?

A. Well, they could have told beforehand whether they were guilty or no, and would not have signed bills of indictment against colored men who were not guilty of the charges against them.

Q. Well, an honest man, whether Democrat or Republican, is not going to indict anybody without he knows it is right to do it, is he?

A. No; but he knows who is guilty beforehand—a right honest man does, before he hears the evidence.

Mr. VANCE. An honest man can judge after he hears the testimony. That is all.

Re-direct examination of witness:

By Mr. BLAIR:

Q. You have known, you say, of instances of hardship and improper convictions and sentences; I want you to explain about that, and state instances that you have known.

A. About men being convicted?

Q. Yes; men whom you have thought innocent, and were improperly convicted, and their sentences in some cases excessive even when they were guilty. Tell us about that.

A. Well, there have been some men really accused of things, and I judge from this: I have been on the grand jury there, and I have heard the testimony that came before the grand jury state that certain men did certain things—stealing hogs, horses, a cowhide, a bale of cotton or something of that sort, and when the man came before the grand jury to make his statement, and when it is proved up whether it is true or not, there ain't a word of truth in the statement he makes before the grand jury against the colored man, because we find in many instances cases come before us in the grand-jury room that on the very day this man was accused of doing this crime he was that day twenty or thirty miles away from there, and had been for two or three days. Therefore I believe a great many of these cases are false, and to get him to leave his crop so that his crop could be grasped by the man that made the charges against him. I have found cases of that kind before the courts.

Q. Such men have not been convicted and sent to the penitentiary, have they?

A. O, yes, sir; they have been convicted often and sent to the penitentiary in this way.

Q. And nothing done to remedy the wrong?

A. No; but we would investigate thoroughly and find the fact to be true, and besides those same men that were on the jury with me, knowing the fact, may be on other juries that would indict and convict.

Q. Have you known any instances where the punishment was very severe for the crime charged?

A. Against a prisoner who goes to prison you mean?

Q. Yes.

A. Well, when they put them in prison there they generally punishes them enough, by making them work hard and driving them.

Q. For how long a time have you known men to be sentenced there?

A. To the penitentiary?

Q. Yes.

A. From one year, I have known, up to as high as ten years—as long as that.

Q. For what offenses?

A. Well, some for stealing, some for cutting, and some for shooting and other things, but mostly for crimes like that.

Q. Stealing what?

A. Horses, cows, hogs, cotton, corn, and other things they steal.

Q. Were these persons kept in close confinement, or within the prison, or were they allowed to come out?

A. They allow them to come out to work when they want them to work, because they works them down in our State.

Q. They are not kept in the penitentiary necessarily, then, but may be worked out?

A. Yes, sir.

Q. What do they work at?

A. They work on the railroads and on the farms too, down in Baton Rouge Parish; I have a place in Baton Rouge Parish.

Q. How are these convicts treated when they are taken out to work?

A. Very rough.

Q. In what way?

A. I have seen them whipped, and one day I seen one of them shot down by the man in charge of them; he said that the man tried to get away from him.

Q. Do they work for the railroads, or for corporations on the railroads?

A. I don't know, because I don't know if there is any corporation railroads in Baton Rouge.

Mr. BLAIR. That will do.

Recross-examination of witness:

BY THE CHAIRMAN:

Q. You say you never heard of negroes killing the white men down there?

A. I have heard of colored men killing white men down there.

Q. Do you remember hearing of Billy Brownlee and Beverly Ogden being taken out and shot to death by a gang of fifty colored men?*

A. In Bossier Parish?

Q. Yes, you have got it right; that is the parish.

A. I have heard of that.

Q. Well, what have you to say about that?

A. I have only heard of that; I was in the Army when they said that was done; it was in 1868.

Q. Have you heard of this gang of forty or fifty men taking them out and shooting them at a hitching-post?

A. I heard of that—yes, sir.

Q. Did you believe it?

A. Well, I did believe it when I first heard it.

Q. Well, do you believe it now?

A. No, sir, not exactly; I don't since then.

Q. What is the reason you do not?

---

* In late September 1868 a drunken white trader from Arkansas shot at and missed an elderly Black man on a plantation in Bossier Parish. The trader was seized by freedmen from the plantation and chained to a tree while his wagon was pillaged, then released. After a white posse began killing people in Bossier Parish on September 30, a group of armed Black men shot James Brownlee and Beverly Ogden, two white men they believed were involved in the killings. Agents of the Freedmen's Bureau reported that white mobs then killed at least one hundred Black persons in the area over the next several days.

A. Because I heard the colored people state something in regard to that that makes me doubt it since.

Q. They said these men were not killed by the negroes, did they?

A. Yes, sir; they said they was not.

Q. They said that these men were not killed by negroes?

A. Yes; that is what they say.

Q. Whom do they say they were killed by?

A. Some of them says they was, some says not.

Q. Did you hear any deny it?

A. Yes; two said they were not, and I heard two say they were.

The CHAIRMAN. Well, that is all.

PART II

Statement of Outrages Committed in Louisiana during the Years 1865 to 1866

Statement of Affairs and Outrages in the South, 1866

Statement of Specific Cases of Outrages from 1866 to 1876

Affidavits of Colored Men

The White League in Louisiana

STATEMENT OF OUTRAGES COMMITTED IN LOUISIANA DURING THE YEARS 1865 TO 1866

[Compiled by HENRY ADAMS.]

In the parish of De Soto, La., near Logansport, on a plantation owned by a man named Ferguson, the white men read a paper to all of us colored people, telling us that we were all free, and that we colored people could go where we pleased and manage our own affairs, and could work for who we pleased. The man I belonged to, or who had me in charge, told me I could work there, or work wherever I wanted to; but it was best to stay there with him and his family on his plantation, because the poor white people did not like a rich negro no how. I had at that time three horses and a fine buggy, and a good deal of money, both gold and silver, and the most of them knew I had plenty of money, both blacks and whites; and they said to me it would be best for me not to go about then as I did before, for some poor white man robber or Klu-Klux might kill me.

I told them I feared God but not man, for He knew what was good. He said the bad white men was mad with all the negroes, because they were free, and they would kill you all for fun; for, said he, I do not want them to meddle with you; if they do they will have me to kill. I told him if I was free, I have to be free, but if I was not, then I would be a slave as I had been ever since the 16th of March, 1843, the day I was born, and that if I could not be free here where the slaveholders are and with them, we had all better leave the slave-holding States and join some of the foreign States and nations. He said it was no use of that, but stay where we were living, and we could get protection from our old masters. I told him I thought that every man when he was free could have his rights and protections and protect himself. He said that was true, but the colored people could never protect themselves among the white people. There was too many bad white men that would all the time be killing colored people, for no other reason than because they were free and may get well off, and some white girl might make much of you and such colored men and boys like you, smart and always with a plenty of money, horses, and other things, might want to marry you, and then they (the mean white men) would kill you; and that if one of you attempt to take up for one another, they would come fifty or more white men to help kill you, against one that you would find who would help fight for you and your colored race. So you all had better stay with the white people who raised you, and not leave them, but make contracts to work for them by the year for one-fifth you all make, and next year you can get one-third, and the next you may work for one-half you make, and by that we may be able to protect you from the bad white men, and keep them from killing you all so much. We have contracts for you all to sign, and to work on for (10) ½0 you make from now until the crop is ended, and then next year you all can make another crop and get more of it.

I told him that I would not sign anything, for I am a slave, and belong to a white girl about fourteen years of age; her name is Nancy Emily Adams, and I expect to work for her until God frees me, and then I will go where I pleases, and will go to some free State where I can be free. The boss man was named W. M. C. Carrods. He then said to me, you are all as free as I am. Sign this paper and get yourselves another home if you want to, or keep the same. I said if I cannot do like a white man I am not free. I see how the poor white people do. I ought to do so too, or else I am a slave. You says we must carry a pass to keep the white men from killing us, or whipping us, so I think still we are all slaves, and I will sign no paper. I might sign to be killed, and I believe that the white people is trying to fool us to see if we are fools enough to go off to work for ourselves, and then everywhere they see one of us they will kill us and take all of our money away what we work for, and everything that we may have. But he said again, "You all are as free as I am, and as any white man, and sign this contract so I can take it to Mansfield to the Yankees and have it recorded." So all of our colored people signed it but myself and a boy named Samuel Jefferson, and Manuel Adams, and John Jefferson; all who lived on the place was about sixty, young and old. My mother lived at one of my young master's place, and belonged to him. My father lived on the same place with me. Both of them were old people. They was not allowed to quit the places and live together during the entire year of 1865, and not until the next year.

On the same day or the next after all had signed the papers or contracts, we went to cutting oats. I asked the boss could we get any of the oats? He said no; the oats were made before you were free. I said it is some of the crop we made, but we did not get any of it. We made about eight hundred bushels. After that he told us to get timber to build a sugar-mill to make molasses; we did so. On the 13th day of July, 1865, we started to pull fodder. I asked the boss would he make a bargain with me to give us half of all the fodder we would pull and save. He said we may pull two or three stacks and then we could have all the other. I told him we wanted to make a bargain for half, so if we only pulled two or three stacks we would get half of that. He said, "All right." We got that and part of the corn we made. We made five bales of cotton, but we did not get a pound of that. We made two or three hundred gallons of molasses and we only got what we could eat. We made about fifty or seventy-five bushels of pindar;* we got none of them. We made about seven or eight hundred bushel of potatoes; we got a few to eat. We split rails three or four weeks, and got not a cent for that; so in September

---

* Peanuts.

of same year I asked the boss to let me go to Shreveport. He said, "All right; when will you come back?" I told him "next week." He said "You had better carry a pass." I said, "I will see whether I am free by going without a pass."

So the next day I left, and got about six or seven miles from home. I met four colored men, and they asked me where I was going. I told them to Shreveport. They told me that they had seen four or five large crowds of white men armed on the road, and they had taken everything they had away from them—a horse and other things, and beat them badly. I then thanked them, and went on my way and got to a white man's house, and asked him if he would keep my horse until I came back from Shreveport? and he said yes, and take good care of him. My horse was worth two hundred dollars in gold. I then went on towards Shreveport, and met four white men about six miles south of Keachie, De Soto Parish. One of them asked me who I belonged to. I told him no one; so him and two others struck me with a stick, and told me they was a going to kill me and every other negro who told them that they did not belong to any one; but one of them who knew me told the others to "Let Henry alone, for he is a hard-working nigger, and a good nigger, and I will fight for him." They left me, and I then went on to Shreveport. I seen over twelve colored men and women beat, shot, and hung between there and Shreveport. Every day while I was in Shreveport there were about fifty or sixty colored people running away from the slaveholders, and coming in the city daily; and staid there three days.

So, late on Saturday evening I left the city and rambled about fifteen or sixteen miles south, and stopped for the night. During the night several white men came up to us and robbed us of thirty-eight dollars; me and my companion was on foot. Sunday I went back home in De Soto Parish, got my horse from Mr. Franks, and he was all right. When I got home, the boss was not at home. I asked the madame where was the boss? She says, "Now, the boss; now,

the boss; now, the boss! You should say master, and say mistress—
and shall, or leave this place; we will not have no nigger here on
our place who cannot say mistress and master; and you shall, for
you all are not free yet, and will not be until Congress sits, for
General Butler* cannot free any one, and you shall call every white
lady misses, and every white man boss, master." During the same
week the madame, Mrs. Frances Carrods, taken a stick and beat
one of the young colored girls, who was about fifteen years of age,
and who is my sister, and split her back. The boss came next day,
and take this same girl (my sister), whose name is Katie Carter, and
whipped her nearly to death; but in the contracts he was to hit no
one any more. So, after the whipping, a large number of the young
colored people, all kin to her, taken a notion to leave, and the next
day she left. Her father was then living there too, and also three
brothers and a sister.

On the 18th of September, I and eleven men and boys left that
place and other places in the same settlement and started for
Shreveport. We all got to Keachie, a little town. I had my two
hundred dollar horse along; my brother was riding him, and all of
our things was packed on him. Out come about forty or fifty armed
men (white) into the public road and shot at us all, and taken my
horse; said they were going to kill every nigger they found leaving
their masters, and taking all of our clothes and bed-clothing and
our money. I had my pocket-book in my saddle-bags on my horse
with one hundred and fifty dollars in gold, and they got it all; so I
had to work away to get a white man to my boss to get my horse.
Then I took my horse and another horse and got a wagon and went
to peddling, and had to get a pass, according to the laws of the
parishes, to do so.

---

* Union Major-General Benjamin F. Butler (1818–1893) had commanded the
Department of the Gulf in 1862. Edward R. S. Canby was the military com-
mander in Louisiana in September 1865, serving under Philip H. Sheridan, com-
mander of the Division of the Gulf.

In October and November and December I was searched for pistols and was robbed of $250 in goods and money by a large crowd of white men with Henry Smith and George at their head, and the law would do nothing about it. This was at or near Thomas' place, near the line of Texas and De Soto Parish, and they shot at me twenty times during the same day. The same crowd of white men broke up five churches (colored) and from time to time broke up churches everywhere the colored people held them; and when any of us colored people would leave the white people, they would take everything we had, during the year of 1865; and when any of us left we had to run away. I ran away, as also did most of the rest, and the white people did not sympathize with us; they would take all the money that we made on their places when we went to leave; and they killed many hundreds of my race when they were running away to get freedom. After they told us we were free—even then they would not let us live as man and wife together. And when we would run away to be free from slavery, the white people would not let us come on their places to see our mothers, wives, sisters, or fathers. We was made to leave the place, or made to go back and live as slaves.

To my own knowledge there was over two thousand colored people killed trying to get away, after the white people told us we were free, which was in 1865. Many of the colored people were killed, but the white people pretended to know little about it. I seen some shot dead because they left with a white woman. This was after they told us we were free, in the year 1865; this was between Shreveport and Logansport.

STATEMENT OF AFFAIRS AND OUTRAGES IN THE SOUTH, 1866

[Compiled by HENRY ADAMS.]

In the year 1866, in the parish of Caddo, State of Louisiana, I seen hanging to a limb of an oak tree about six miles south from Shreveport, the body of a colored man—he was dead when I seen him. About six miles north from Keachie I saw a wagon belonging to a colored man burning with all his things; even his mules were burned to death. While on my way to Sunny Grove, I seen the head of a colored man lying side the road. Whilst traveling on my way to De Soto Parish a large body of armed white men met me and asked me who I belonged to. I answered them and told them that I belonged to God, but not to any man. They then asked me where was my master? I told them the one I used to have was dead, and I have not had none since 1858; worked for those who would hire me and pay the largest price, as I was still a slave, and during the time I was passing through this parish a black man was not allowed to preach the Gospel anywheres, any more than he was before, in 1865. As he was, he daren't to preach such doctrines as was suitable to the congregation, and a truth from the Holy Bible, but he had to preach just what they (the white men) wanted, and what they told him to preach. My father was a preacher, and he is even until this day, and they all, or least the most of them says they cannot preach the gospel as they wish, for the white people did not nor do not allow them to do it. For the white men says the preachers make meaner niggers, and that they cannot rule the nigger. I have heard them tell the colored men to not preach such doctrines as that to the nigger, because the nigger will get above himself and above their business; and if you do, you are in danger of losing your own life.

Such is the language they used to the colored preacher, for they said they will not stand such to be preached. They told me that I must give up all that I got to them, because they had the law in their hands to take all of what a nigger had. So they said to me give us your money and your whisky, your horse, and then you can live; but if you don't, you have got to die right here; so I had to give it up to them to save my life, and I then reported to the courts, but the law would not do anything about it.

So the next incident what I saw was when I was passing a place—I saw white men whipping colored men just the same as they did before the war, or before freedom in this State. I saw white men take a colored man because he had been a United States soldier; they beat him all but to death; that was between Shreveport and Logansport, in the parish of De Soto. I did not know his name, but I heard him cry, saying that I will not ever soldier again no more if you will not kill me, and they made him swear and curse all of the soldiers in the United States Army, and the officers of the Army also.

Manuel Adams, my cousin, and myself was on our way to Logansport, De Soto Parish, and about one mile from that place we were surrounded by six armed white men, who taken us and then demanded us to give up our watches. Manuel having his watch in sight, they took the watch from him, but they did not see any watch on me. They turned our pockets and searched us for money, but we did not have any, so they told us if we ever told any one about it that they would kill us on the first sight, and asked us if we had rather die than to keep that to ourselves? We told them that we had rather give them all we had in the world than to die and go to hell. They said that we were right to keep it to ourselves.

The next incident of importance that came beneath my observation was the finding of ten or fifteen colored men floating in Red River; this was in the year 1866; some of them was tied by the sides of logs, some with ropes round their necks; some of them was shot, and some had their throat cut; this was between a plantation called

Gold Point and Shreveport, on the parish line of Caddo and
Bossier.

On the steamboats plying in Red River I have seen colored men
knocked off the stage planks and guards of the boat by the mates
and other white men; and they were whipped and knocked and beat
by them at all times; this I saw with my own eyes, and heard white
men say to colored preachers in that part of the State that
there was certain parts of the Scriptures that they must not preach
to the colored people; so I asked the preachers what parts of the
Scriptures was it they did not want preached. They said the colored preachers must not preach about Joshua and the children of
Israel, nor about Jeremiah and the children of Benjamin, and told
them that if they preached such doctrines as that, they would be
killed, for they, the white people, would not stand it; also the colored
ministers in the State say they never have preached the gospel as
they wished; they say they are afraid to do so.

Again, in the year 1866, I was traveling between Shreveport and
Alexandria; I saw white men riding in their field with their bull whip
in their hand over colored people just the same as they did in 1858.
On some plantations, in the year 1867, I seen white men knock and
beat colored men; also, I seen them knock colored people off stage-
planks on steamboats on the river, and I have seen them compel
colored men jump out into the river waist deep in water with a rope
in their hand, and sometimes the water was over their head, and
they would bank them anywhere on the river without a cent of
money in their pocket, and not pay them a cent for their work, and
would threaten to kill them if they reported them or had them
arrested. Colored passengers on the steamboats would pay second-
class fare, and the officers of the boats would compel them to take
third-class fare; and some would pay first-class fare and they would
have to eat at the third-class table, and would not even give them
a place to sleep. I saw all this occur between New Orleans and Fort
Jackson, La. And in parish prisons in this State any colored persons

found in such places who having been a United States soldier or is a soldier, is starved half to death while in prison, and is treated worse than a dog.

And in 1868 the same thing was still going on between New Orleans and Fort Jackson. I landed at a plantation below New Orleans called the Magnolia plantation; the boat laid up there all night; I heard a gun fire twice and then saw two colored men running. I hailed them and asked them what was the matter. They said they had been working there two or three months, and they had not been paid in full since they had been there and they had asked the boss for their pay as he had threatened to whip them that day; so again that night they asked him to pay them what he owed them, and he told them all right, then he took his gun and shot at them, and did not pay them a cent. I saw on two other plantations white men whipping colored men; this was going on between Fort Jackson and New Orleans. In 1868, at that time I was traveling and paying first class fare on board of steamboats and receiving third-class fare; these boats were the D. G. Brown, Alice, and the St. Nicholas; the colored passengers was treated outrageous, and in the plantation quarters I was told to leave by a white man, who asked me what I wanted and what I was doing there. I told him that I came up there to see some of my race that I knew; he told me that he did not want any negro soldiers around him and he did not want them on his place. I told him to not call me a negro, that my principle was just as good as his'n, and if anything better; he submitted to that, but still told me to leave, and I left and did not get to see any person that I wanted to see, and any one that wanted to see me had to leave the place to do so.

In March, 1869, I saw three colored men knocked off the stage-plank with a billet of wood by the mate on the steamboat and then made get ashore, and never paid them a cent of money. And colored passengers who had paid first-class fare was made to eat at the third-class table, and nowhere to sleep. In April five colored ladies paid first-class fare on the steamboat Ella May, and they would not give them any place to sleep and nothing to eat. I saw again on a steamboat two colored men pay first-class fare from Baton Rouge to New Orleans and they had to eat at the third-class table, and sleep on boiler deck. I saw two colored men (boat-hands) put ashore and left them on the river side, and did not pay them a cent, and their homes was in New Orleans. On four or five different plantations white men whipped colored people, and I heard the colored people hollering O, pray master; this was at night. I then had a prisoner, carrying him from Fort Jackson to Baton Rouge penitentiary on the Lotus No. 3. I walked about on the boiler deck, and stopped and stood awhile, when I was ordered down stairs by the captain of the boat; he told me that no d—m negro soldier could stand on the boiler deck of his boat. I told him I meant no harm, that I just walked up there to look about; but he told me to get down stairs, and if I did not go he would have me put down, and if that did not do he would land the boat and put me ashore. I had charge of a prisoner and one guard, and I was quartermaster-sergeant at the time of Company B, Twenty-fifth United States Infantry, stationed at Fort Jackson, La., in June, 1869.

So I went down stairs, and when we landed at Baton Rouge I reported to the commanding officer there, and then went on to the penitentiary, and there I saw a white man knock down and stamp on a colored man; it was some of the officers of the penitentiary; they told me there they were whipping them constantly every day. When I started back from Baton Rouge to Fort Jackson I went on board the steamboat Governor Allen and asked the clerk to take us down to the city, and he told me he could not take no d—m negro soldiers on government transportation, but if we paid our fare they would take us down. So I reported back to the commanding officer, and he told me to wait for another boat, and I did so in about two days afterwards. On that boat I saw two colored men struck and kicked about by a white man called the mate.

On or about the latter part of September, 1869, I left New Orleans
for Shreveport on the steamboat Jefferson. I was then just discharged
from the United States Army; so I paid first-class cabin fare. There
were about sixteen colored passengers on board the boat, all being
discharged Union soldiers, and six others—citizens. Yet they said
they only charged us second-class fare, though we paid $20.00
each—same as they charged the whites—and yet we eat every meal
at the fourth table. They promised to give us beds in the hall, and
promised to feed us at the second table; but they made part of us
sleep on the boiler deck, and part of us on the lower deck, and told
us when we complained that we either had to abide with that or
take worse. I sat up all night for four nights to keep from sleeping
on such places as was given us. I also had some freight on board,
and they charged me the sum of ten dollars and some cents for my
freight; yet a white man who had the same amount of freight was
only charged seven dollars. I landed in Shreveport, Caddo Parish,
La., September the 25th, 1869, and went about trying to rent a house,
but it was rumored all over town that a boat load of discharged Union
soldiers had come, and the whites would not rent us their houses.
Finally we came up with a Baptist preacher, and he let us have his
house.

   After we had been there a few months the white people began
saying they were going to kill us; to kill all the discharged negro
soldiers; that these discharged men were going to spoil all the other
negroes, so that the whites could do nothing with them; for the
colored people would get these discharged soldiers to look over their
contracts and agreements they had made with the white people who
they were working for. I would tell them to go and have a settlement of accounts, and get what was due them, and pay what they
owed. I figured up accounts for them, and often seen where the
whites had cheated the colored people who had made contracts with
them out of more than two-thirds of their just rights, according to
their contracts. I told a great many of them to take their contracts

to lawyers and get them to force the parties to a settlement; but they told me they were afraid they would be killed. Some few reported to the court, but told me afterwards that it did not do. Some even were whipped when they went home. These white men told them if they would take a whipping they might go, but if they did not take the whipping they would have them put in jail, as it was a general rule they had of going to the colored people and telling them they had a warrant for their arrest, or, an order to seize what they had, and they would seize all the colored people had.

I went to many of the colored churches throughout the country, and conversed with the preachers, and they told me they were afraid to preach their opinion. One day I was riding with a young colored lady along the public road between Shreveport and Greenwood, and a crowd of white men rode between me and her and ordered me to leave, and for her to stand still, and told her she was too pretty a girl for such damn black negro as me to be riding alongside of her. I told them if they wanted to kill me they could do so, for I was not going to leave her. They asked me then who I was; I told them I was a Texian; I did it to save my life. They said, "So long as you are a Texian we won't kill you; but if you was a Louisianian we would kill you right here." I seen the same crowd of men get after a colored man, and made him run off and leave the girl he was with, and they then done to the girl what they wanted, and then put her upon her horse and told her to go.

In Shreveport, in a merchant's store, I had taken a colored man's cotton receipt to see what it brought, but the merchant ordered me out and talked about putting me in jail, and I had to get out of there. I seen colored men put in jail many a time in this State because he could not count his money; the white men would pay colored men their money in large bills, and when they would ask them to change them a five or twenty dollar bill, whichever it might be, they would not give them back in change half of their amount. I have seen at auction sales colored men bidding on things to the amount of the money they knew they had to pay for them, and when they would give it to the white man to count they would not find enough to pay for them, as they had knocked them off to these colored men. They would then put them in jail, and some white man would bail him out and make him work for him three or four months; yet his fine was not more than seven or eight dollars.

From December, 1869, up till July, 1875, my mother and father lived in De Soto Parish, and I was informed by some of my best-friends, both white and colored, that I had better not go down there to see them; if I did I would never get back to Shreveport alive. My life was threatened; the white people of that parish said no d—n negro that soldiered against his master should come in that parish. They said if I came down there I would ruin the other negroes, and put devilment in their head, so they (the white men) could not rule them at that time. Half of what I was worth was in De Soto Parish. In 1870, I seen a white man buy a bale of cotton from a colored man, weighing five hundred pounds, and paid him only twenty-five dollars for it, and cotton was then worth 25 cents per pound. I saw two colored men come out of the woods, and they told me that they had not been out of the woods for seven years. They came out in 1869; one was named John Dunlow and the other Billy Scrapp. They said they had seen crowds of white men kill more than two hundred colored men while they were in the woods. That is why they thought they were not free.

From the latter part of 1867 till 1869 I done much traveling along the roads west of Shreveport—on the road called Jefferson Road. I saw stuck on an old stump the head of a colored man; I inquired of some colored people why and who put it there? They said that some white men brought from Shreveport a colored man who they killed and put his head on the stump. Thousands of colored persons told me they were driven from home and their crops and all they possessed taken away from them, and that exists even now. I was at an election in 1870, in November, in the city of Shreveport, and I heard white men tell colored men that if they voted the Republican tickets that they would not let them have any more credit, nor would they bond them out of the jail; that they would have to go to the d—n Yankees or carpet-baggers to take them out, and the colored men told them that they were afraid to vote the Democratic ticket because they might make them slaves again. Many of them asked me what did I think was best? I told them I was nothing but a rail-splitter and wood-chopper, and did not know anything about politics; had never seen a poll for an election before, but thought if we voted the Democratic ticket we would have to carry passes from one parish to another and from one State to the other. I told them as to our freedom, our rights, and our votes that no Southern man was our friend; only the Northern men, Army officers, and United States troops were our friends; that the Southern people would always be arrayed against us as long as we lived because we were free.

In Shreveport large bodies of armed white men would go to break up our churches, during the same year, and on Sunday night before the election, and Monday also, a large body of armed men (white) went out and about to scare colored men from coming to the polls to vote the next day. So the colored people met them and told them to go back, for if they interfered with the churches that we, the colored men, would burn the city; but they did not go back, and it frustrated the colored people so they got scared and the churches were broken up. Tuesday, the day of the election, one colored man named Squire Norman, was killed by a Jew for distributing tickets (Republican) to the colored people. I was told by several white persons on that day that they had me spotted; said I was spoiling the other negroes so they could not do anything with them, just because I told them to let my race vote the Republican ticket; let us Republicans advise Republicans, and the Democrats advise Democrats. They told me all such negroes as me had to be killed; I told them if they did kill me only give me my rights while I am living.

About three miles from Shreveport I saw four white men
(wagoners) throw a colored man flat on his belly and whip him until
he digested all over himself and had him as bloody as a hog. I asked
them what made them whip him; they told me he had told them a
lot of damn lies, and they wanted to learn him to tell the truth; they
said that is the way they do negroes in Texas; we make them do
what we want them to do. During the year about twenty-five colored persons showed me their contracts and their account sales of
their cotton; and their accounts due their employés and merchants,
after balancing all, I found they had been swindled out of about
seventeen hundred and ninety dollars. Some went to law to recover
it, but it did no good; the courts were against the colored man; those
that did not go to law were better off, for those that went to law
some of them were killed, some whipped, and some ran away. Many
that did not even go to law were whipped also; I seen three white
men go into a colored man's grocery in Shreveport and run him out,
his mother, wife, and all his family, and took charge of the grocery
themselves, and invited other white men to come in and drink. The
colored man who owned the grocery was named A. Leroy. While
the white men were in possession of the store a colored man went
in there to buy something; so they captured him, took a five shooter
from him, a pocket knife, and all the money he had. His name was
Hyam Coleman. They told him, after they had robbed him, to march
on before them; that they were going to kill him. Seven or eight
colored men and myself made them turn him loose, and made them
leave the grocery; so the colored man got his store back again.

In February, 1871, a crowd of white men approached the house
where I lived and sent me word by one of their number to leave
home; they had made threats the day before that they intended to
kill me and also all the discharged colored soldiers in and around
Shreveport, Louisiana. But I did not leave my house; I staid there;
I had made up my mind to face the battle. They told me their
reason for wanting to kill me and all discharged colored soldiers

was because they were ruining the other negroes. They had already jumped on several of the discharged colored soldiers, but they got as good as they sent. These colored men were then arrested and put in jail, and charges made against them; but the case was so plain they came out clear. While those men were in jail, then they approached my house; they were about fifty strong, yet they did not attack us. Then crossing Red River on my way to Homer I saw a white man on the ferry beat a colored man badly, giving him about twenty lashes as hard as he could put them on, and the man was afraid to raise up his head. Whilst in Claiborne Parish I saw two white men with double-barrel guns after a colored man. I asked him what he done; he said he had asked a white lady to let him enjoy himself with her; they said if they caught him they would kill him. I saw one of the same white men go to bed with a colored woman two or three successive nights. During the time I was in Claiborne Parish in that same year I saw more than twenty-five colored persons who told me they had been whipped, their crops taken from them, and then they were run away whenever they would ask for a fair settlement. There was several white men in that parish to my knowing who had colored women as sweethearts, nor would allow a colored man to talk with them. In every part of the State where I have been I have seen the colored children barefooted, half naked, and bareheaded, and even half starved on their way to school, and in parishes there was no public schools. The colored people in these parishes works for shares of the crops, one-third they makes, and their employers find them something to eat and farming utensils, giving them rations for man and wife per month the following: Two bushels of meal and twenty pounds of pork, nothing else. I have seen white men go in colored men's houses and drive their wives out to work, and call them dam bitches, and tell them if they don't go to work they must leave their places or pay rent for the houses they live in, and their husband's crops will be taken to pay the rent.

In 1872 I was on my way from Shreveport to New Orleans, and I seen four colored men badly whipped by white men on two plantations on Red River. Two of them lives on a plantation on Mississippi River and in the State of Mississippi, and I heard white men curse and abuse colored ladies on the plantations at different landings on the river where the boat would land. I heard two white men ask a colored man to let them see his revolver, and he did so, and they kept it and did not let him have it any more; he asked for it; they told him he had no right to one; none but white men should have them. In New Orleans on the levee I saw six white men club a colored man near to death, and then threw him on his dray and carried to jail, because he called one a d—m s—n of a b—tch, made a charge against him and made him pay fifteen dollars. Between New Orleans and Baton Rouge two colored men was knocked overboard, and one put ashore without giving them a cent for their work. At Baton Rouge one of the penitentiary men knocked down a colored prisoner with the butt of his gun, and beat another with a billet of wood. The prisoners told me that not a day passed but that half of them was beaten in this manner; they were treated outrageous. Between Live Oak Grove and Fort Vincent I saw three white men whip a colored man, his wife, and three children. I asked the man why they had whipped him, and he told me that was a common thing in this country. They did not have clothes enough to hide their nakedness. In Saint Helena Parish I saw a colored man buy a horse from a white man for $150; he paid him $25 cash, and was to pay the balance when he gathered and sold his crop; so the colored man was not able to pay at the time, and the white man took the horse back and did not give him a cent of his money back. And there thousands of such cases in this State like that, but I cannot at present mention any more of them.

In 1872 me and my cousin owned a house and two lots in Shreveport, and had a good well on it. It was worth $1,000 and about one thousand dollars' worth of improvements. The lot measured 80 by

121½ feet. The white people in Shreveport took a notion to run a street through my place, and done so during my absence. They took all of my improvements off, filled up my well, and had taken the best part of my furniture, and I have never seen it since; and only gave me $1,200 for it. I did not agree for the place to be taken in no such way, unless they paid me $3,000, as I had been offered that for it. And they took $130 out of the $1,200 for a lawsuit, and they put it in law themselves. So I just considers that they robbed me out of $1,930; and they would not allow either one of us to have a word to say in court, nor allow us to pick a jury, nor let a colored man serve on our case. They said their reason for doing us as they did was because they did not want no discharged colored soldier to live there. So when I arrived home I went to the court for redress, but soon found there was no justice for a colored man against a southern white in the courts.

About twelve miles from Shreveport, in the parish of Caddo, on the plantation of a man named Douglass, I saw six colored men's entire crops taken away from them by a white man and he still swore they were still in his debt. In November, 1872, at an election held in Shreveport, La., I saw colored men shoved back from the ballot-box. At Sumner Grove—I went there to try and vote and was prevented from voting by a white man by the name of Andrew Pickens—about fifteen or twenty of them surrounded me and swore I had voted, and was going to put me in jail; and so they would not let me vote there. So I did not vote at all for President nor anybody else. And the colored people was generally kept back from the ballot-box by the whites of the parish of Caddo. The city of Shreveport was so crowded that nearly all the colored men could not vote; yet there was many who had a chance to vote but was afraid to vote for fear of losing his life or his crop; they told me themselves they were afraid. I counted six hundred and twenty that did not vote but tried hard to get a chance to do so. I saw a colored man who was killed at Shady Grove by another colored man that voted a

Democratic ticket. The man he killed was a true Republican. But the Democratic colored man was cleared by the Democratic court.

In the year 1873 I served on the grand jury in Shreveport in the parish of Caddo; and there were ten colored men on the jury and six white. The colored prisoners told me that they did not get half enough to eat; some of them told me they were beat and whipped in jail by the jailer, a white man; and the white men on the grand jury tried to find a true bill against every colored man that was indicted by a white man. I saw little colored boys in there for stealing one can of oysters. I seen little girls in there for stealing such things as thimbles, scissors, &c.; and was several colored men in prison, and only two white men were put in jail for crimes they had committed; and most all the colored people whose cases came before us were indicted by white men. There was several colored ladies. There was no affidavit made against any white lady. The judge, lawyers, district attorney, and foreman of the grand jury and clerk all favored the rich man (white). That is my opinion, however preposterous it may seem. All the cases that were fixed and came up during that sitting of the court there was but one white man tried, and it was for killing a colored man in cold blood, and he was cleared; but his trial was, and had been, standing for more than a year. The prisoners had not near enough blankets to keep them from catching severe cold and suffering untold misery.

During the year 1873 I saw many colored people swindled out of their crops. I led them into the light how it was done, but they were afraid to make affidavits against them. It is generally in this way that the white people rob the colored people out of two-thirds of what they make; for instance, the contract for one-third or one-quarter of the crop that is made as the case may be. They take it in every bale, and will not divide it at the gins, but ship it to the city; then when the cotton is sold they figure and figure until there is but little left to the colored man; then they do not settle, but wait until the next crop is pitched, say in February, and sometimes even in June, before they will say the cotton is sold. Generally about March they commence settling with the colored people. Some divides the cotton at the gin, but very few of them does, and it is in this way in which they plunder the poor colored men in this State. In the year 1874 in the month of January, I was in the parish of East Baton Rouge and St. Helena; also during the month of February and also in the parish of Lexington I seen colored men cheated out of their crops. I saw a white man from the town of Baton Rouge go to Strong Point, or North of Strong Point, La., and take a poor colored woman's bale of cotton and had it taken to Baton Rouge and sold it for a debt that a colored man owed him. A woman named Rachel Hopkins and her children made the cotton; I seen a colored man that lived in the same parish shot. His name was Shoemaker. He said that the white man shot him because he could not make him stop hunting with his own gun in the woods.

I also saw many colored people in that part of the State who told me that the white people would not pay them for their work, and would take all their crops every year, and had been doing so ever since the surrender. They, the colored people, told me they had tried to live upon government land but it all had been taken away from them, and they could not live on any land but what they would buy from white people. They told me all the colored people that were or are living on government lands was every two or three months put in jail, and the land taken away from them and the whites claimed the land themselves. Those colored people who still lived on government land had no stock, and had to hire horses or mules at five and ten dollars per month; yet the whites would pay them only fifty or seventy-five cents per day for their work and they had to feed themselves and seventy-five cents per hundred for splitting rails.

In Baton Rouge on the 17th of February, I seen white men ride on horseback into colored people's groceries and houses. On the 3d of March I saw the mate on a steamboat at New Orleans knock a colored man off the boat in the river and nearly break his head.

In going from Shreveport to New Orleans I seen along the banks of Red River colored people who were afraid to talk with me at landings; some would ask me if the times would never get any better. I asked several of them, do you not live well? do you not get all you make? They told me no, that the whites take all we make along on the river, and if we say anything to them about our rights they beat us, shoot us, and shoot at us to scare us; so we are afraid to tell everybody how they do us, for we are afraid they will shoot us; we wish to God that Gen. Grant would do something for us. I told them if the men you all live with this year do not give you all what belongs to you just like he has promised, you all must leave that place and go to another, and if he does not fulfill his part of the contract leave that place also. They told me if we do that we will have to be all the time going from plantation to plantation, for all the white men here are alike on this Red River, for what one of them says to us they all say, and what one of them do to us they all do; so none of them is any better than the other. We have been working hard ever since the surrender, and have not got anything that we can carry off the places if we attempt to go. Such is the case all along the Red River. A few of us can run away at night, but a very few. In some instances old missus tells old massa we have or he has been a good nigger and worked so hard, let him have that old horse and wagon, that cow and hog, and some of that corn, and one bale of cotton. Only a very few even gets this much, although they have worked on that place for three or four years since the surrender. He says to me, look at aunt Nancy, she has to wait on old missus for four or five years for nothing; that is the way nearly all the whites do us on Red River, and when we go to vote they ask us what sort of a ticket we are going to vote. We tell them a Radical ticket; they tell us to vote their ticket (Democratic). We tell him we cannot vote that ticket; then he tell us if we do not vote their (Democratic) ticket we have to get off that place and leave just as you came, and carry nothing away; you all brought nothing, and you shall carry nothing off; and that is the way the whites do us about voting; and if we don't do like they say they will kill some of us; run some of us off, and make us leave our crops; beat some of us nearly to death.

In Shreveport, Caddo Parish, La., in April and May, I could see every day colored people (women & men) and they told me they were coming from the country because the whites were running them away from their place, shooting some, killing some, and beating others, on account of their crops and the contracts; when they would ask them to pay to them their part of the crop according to the contracts the whites would then bring in old bills and say to the colored people, you owe me this, and I want it paid; the whites would then take all the colored people had, horses, mules, hogs, cows, chickens, beds and bedding, and then run them off the place or kill or shoot them. The white men killed during them two months eight men and boys (colored). The bad men (white) in this part of the State have organized themselves into bands, called White League, and white man's party, and they ride through all the parishes of the State, and threaten any white man or black man that gets the nomination on the Republican ticket shall be killed. The parish of Caddo was infested with such men and talk, and even the Democratic newspapers spoke it plainly. And if any colored man voted the Republican ticket he should not have any work. All this was done and said before the election came off.

In the parishes of Caddo, De Soto, Webster, Claiborne, and Bossier, the Democrats broke up all the Republican clubs but the one in the city of Shreveport, called the Mother Club; but they sent a large crowd of armed men to break it up; but a white man named J. M. Wilson had rented this house to a colored man named J. J. Williams, for a business house, and promised him to protect his house as he did his own; and he did so at the peril of his life, and was arrested and carried before the mayor's court, and a large number of colored men appeared before the mayor's court in defense of Mr. Wilson, which saved him. Then the club was arraigned before the mayor's court, and the right to hold club meetings was discussed. The chief of police, who was white, George J. J. Horem and J. C. Moncure of the city forces, asked who was the president of that club? So I says to them, I am the president; my name is Henry Adams; why do you ask me that question. Because says he, "if anything is done in that club, we will hold you responsible for it." I says to him, you can do any thing to me or my race because we are all black and were born slaves; but if we cannot hold our club-meeting, we will petition President Grant the right to hold our club-meetings. They said you can go on and hold your club-meetings, but do not make any fuss, and if any body of armed men interfere with you all we will stop them.

The next week after that they issued an order to all the ministers of the colored churches in the county and city that they must hold no meetings of religious character in their churches after half-past nine o'clock at night. I was at a friend's house, where there was a corpse, and about twenty armed white men came to the door and told us colored people not to sing or pray over the dead; if we did they would put us all in jail. About this several colored churches, schoolhouses, and arbors was burned. During the campaign in the parish of Caddo I seen armed white men go to the places where Republicans held their meetings, and would try to make them take back what they would say against the Democrat party. At a place called Spring Ridge the Republicans were not allowed to speak what they wished. At Carry Stay, Greenwood, and Camp Blow on Red River, the same thing was done; a large crowd of white men went to all the places and threatened to shoot and kill any Republican that spoke what he wished. At Mourning Port the whites sent word that if any Republican went there to hold a meeting, he would and must be killed. Judge Levisee* and Col. C. W. Keeting both

---

* A Confederate veteran, Aaron B. Levisee (1821–1907) served as an elected district judge, 1868–74, and as a Republican in the state house of representatives,

were nominees on the Republican ticket for the House of Representatives, and they could not make a speech for fear of being killed
by the armed white men who were at every place where a meeting
was held, or to be held.

And on the day of the election, in November 1874, I was United
States supervisor at the box-poll there, at Tom Bayou, in the parish
of Caddo, about fifteen miles southeast of Shreveport; there were
ninety-nine votes cast—fifty-nine were colored men. The whites told
all the colored men that voted at that box, if they did not vote the
white man's ticket, or people's ticket, and voted the Republican
ticket, they would kill them before they could get home; and that
their wives and children should not have anything on their places.
Some told them if you do not vote at all you are damn rascals, and
you have forty B. C.* at the gin; twenty B. C. are yours, and you
will owe me nothing if you will vote the white man's ticket. But the
colored men told them they would vote nothing, neither for one
party or the other. The Democrats told them they knew the reason.
You want to vote the damn radical ticket, says the white man; and
if you don't vote our way you had not better start, or go home, for
we are going to kill every damn nigger that votes the radical ticket
to-day. This is a Democratic hole, and it shall go Democratic or we
will kill every nigger that we see; so a great many colored men left
the polls. J. J. Ward, Joe Carrows, James Bointon, Charley Jones,
Wm. Robinson, and several others (white men) had large revolvers
all around the polls, and told the colored men that they had to vote
their way or die. So all that voted at that poll, voted the Democratic
ticket; but seventeen colored men, who voted the straight Republican ticket. But of them who had any crops it was taken away from
them; so they told me. The colored people all over Caddo Parish

---

1875–76. A Hayes elector in the 1876 presidential contest, Levisee testified that
he had been offered a $100,000 bribe to switch his vote to Samuel J. Tilden.
* Bales of cotton.

told me that they who had voted the radical ticket, and had any crop, it was taken away from them, and a great many of them was run away from the places. I made a protest before the United States commissioner against the box at poll 3, and made a statement as to what I knew and had seen; so I afterward saw my name published in the Shreveport Times, saying I should be killed for making that protest; also several other colored men who had made a similar protest. They all ran away but myself.

So in 1875 large crowds of colored people were moving every day from Caddo, Sabine, De Soto, Red River, and other parishes trying to get homes, as the white men had taken everything they had away from them, and had then run them off; and they had to call on the United States military officers to help them to move away from the South and slaveholders, for they will not let them have anything, not even their wearing clothes, corn, cotton, nor anything. I travelled through Grant, Bossier, Claiborne, Webster, Natchitoches, De Soto, Caddo, Red River, and Jackson Parishes, also through some counties in Arkansas and Texas, and saw many colored people destitute. I seen on some plantations on Red River where the white men would drive colored women out in the fields to work, when the husbands would be absent from their home, and would tell colored men that their wives and children could not live on their places unless they work in the fields. The colored men would tell them they wanted their children to attend school; and whenever they wanted their wives to work they would tell them themselves; and if he could not rule his own domestic affairs on that place he would leave it and go somewhere else. So the white people would tell them if he expected for his wife and children to live on their places without working in the field they would have to pay house rents or leave it; and if the colored people would go to leave, they would take everything they had, chickens, hogs, horses, cows, mules, crops, and everything, and tell them it was for what his damn family had eat, doing nothing but sitting up acting the grand lady and their daughters acting the same, for I will be damn if niggers ain't got to work on my place or leave it.

I seen in my travels through many of the above named parishes, whilst I was acting United States scout, a large number of colored people killed at different times and places by bad white men or slaveholders; also some white northerners who would attempt in showing the colored men their rights, and protecting them in the same; many of such men have been killed. Even some white men has killed other white men for killing colored men on their places. I received several written statements from colored people, which I will embody in this statement at the proper time and place. I seen several whipped, shot, and badly beaten by white men. I seen white men riding with the bullwhip on their shoulders in the field and driving the colored people just as they did in 1849 and 1855. I passed places where the bones of the colored men were laying where these poor men were burnt, hung, shot, and most unjustly murdered; and hundreds driven away from their places and families, and their crops taken away, and even ordered to leave the State or they would be killed by the slaveholders of the South. I have seen several colored men who were shot and wounded, and they told me that they were shot by white men because they protested against them taking their crops, stock, &c.; they even went so far as to take the colored men's daughters and make them sleep with them, taking many of their children to wait on them, and would pay them nothing. Many colored men who lived upon government land was killed, some shot, some hung, but not dead, and made to leave the land they were homesteading upon. They would sometimes be shot for refusing to lend a white man their horse or wagon.

On Black Bayou, in Caddo Parish, I found about forty colored children who were taken away without their father or mother's consent, and without even any pay. I might say made them slaves to wait on them. In De Soto Parish I found five in a similar condition. In Sabine Parish I found three. In Bossier I found six; in Webster four; and several other parishes in this State the same thing is practiced. In several counties in Arkansas and Texas the same thing is practiced to my own knowledge. In fact in Louisiana it is almost universal. Some are even taken away from their parents for debt. I seen a colored man who was appointed to take the census refused the names of white persons. I have a knowledge of white men who would sell cotton for colored persons in the city of Shreveport, and the bale of cotton bringing $65, and they would pay them $49 and tell them that was money enough for a nigger to have. That was in the year 1875. They would buy cotton from colored people when the cotton was selling at 12 and 12½ cents and pay them from six to seven cents. And a bale of cotton weighing from 450 to 500 pounds would pay them from 35 to 40 dollars per bale. I was present some time myself, and saw with mine own eyes. Sometimes I would sell some of the same cotton and show them the difference. They tell the colored people they sell them meat at 7 cents per pound, or 10 or 12½ cents, and when the white men make out the accounts he makes 75 pounds 100, if 150 he makes it 200, and charges five cents more on every pound. I picked cotton of Forster plantation, and I seen the white men that weighed the cotton when the draught would weigh 75 pounds they would check 50 pounds; or if it weighed 100 or 150 pounds, they would check it 150 or 200, and so on; yet they were charging colored people 15 and 21 cents per pound for meat, and beef from five to 10 cents per pound; ten or fourteen pounds of flour for $1; tobacco 25 and 60 cents per plug; meal 25 to 45 cents per peck; sugar 15 to 20 cents per pound, and coffee in proportion.

Many of the hands on the place bought much of such articles from the boats or the managers of the places; yet a very few of the colored people on the places were allowed to dispose of any of his cotton that he makes or has made on the place without the permission of the white managers of the places. I worked on James Hollingsworth's plantation, and the same thing was practiced on that place. Those places are called the Gold Point place, Cash Point place, and the Douglas plantation, all on the Red River in Caddo, Bossier, and Red River Parishes. The same work and treatment was extended to all the colored people throughout North Louisiana in general. On Dr. Vance's plantation, where I have often worked, I have seen the same; even from the mouth of Red River to Jefferson, Texas, no difference can be seen; even in the bordering counties of Arkansas and Texas where I have traveled I see the same, as it was my business to look around and ascertain as far as possible into the treatment of colored people by the whites.

In December, 1875, I went with a large delegation of colored ministers to attend their annual conference in the city of New Orleans. We came down on board of the steamboat Texas, and in conversation with them regarding the treatment of colored people by the whites in their respective districts, they told me that the colored people seen hard times, and underwent the same treatment as I had told them the colored people suffered in the various parishes I had been traveling through; and in some parts even worse. One of them told me the white people made him get off his horse and get on his knees and pray for them, and then afterward threatened his life, and when he got up he had to get up running. Elder Albert, from his district which includes Bossier, Caddo, De Soto, and Red River Parishes, told me that he had taken passage on the steamboat Kouns for Coushatta, in Red River Parish, but she brought me to Grandscore, 100 miles below my destination, and put me off under a bluff bank about a hundred or more feet high; and I had to remain there until I could get passage on some other boat. I landed at East Baton Rouge on the 2d day of January, and found great excitement prevailing throughout the parish, as well as in the city, caused by a colored woman being killed the day before. She was taken away from the officers of the law by an armed body of white men, about sixty or sixty-five, and brutally murdered, having a suckling child at the time. On the 5th day of January, about 8 or 10 miles from the city, I met a colored man coming to Baton Rouge; I asked him where he was going; he told me he was running away from where he was living to save his life; that the Regulator Coal Oil men (all white) had just killed his son and burnt him up with coal oil, and he feared the same fate would befall himself. And whilst I traveled through the parishes of East Baton Rouge, Saint Helena, and Livingston, and East Feliciana, I found colored people running helter-skelter throughout their parishes seeking refuge and safety. I met a colored man named Jake Kintning, and he showed me an order given him by the whites, which read as follows:

> East Baton Rouge Parish,
>   *State of Louisiana, January,* 1876.
> Jake Kintry, we give you five days to leave your place, and move all you possess away. Unless you do, your things, your wife, children, house, and all will be burnt; your horses, corn, and all.
>
> COAL OIL COMPANY.

I also seen three colored men together going to the town of East Baton Rouge, and they told me that they came from Saint Tammany Parish, and that they were going over on the other side of the Mississippi River, for the time was very hot where they came from; so I asked them how, and they told me that about three or four colored men had been killed in that parish in less time than three weeks; and told me that if I go far in that parish, I would believe what they told me. I had a gun, also another colored man with me, named Major Edwards, had a gun. So, when we had gone about three miles, after leaving those three colored men, we met five white men, who asked us where we were going. We told them we were traveling. They said "we thought you all were going hunting; and if you were, we were going to take you both up and turn you all over to the captain of our company." I asked them for what. They then said, "we have orders that all colored men caught hunting in the woods with guns, to take them up and turn them over to Captain Montgomery, and if they cannot give a good account of themselves, to hang them to a limb or burn them up, and we will do both of you in that manner. We are called 'Regulators' and 'Coal Oil Company,' and we will have you niggers to know that you shall not hunt in this country."

They then left us; and we went on about eight miles further east, when we met about fifteen or twenty, all armed with revolvers. They asked us where we were going. We told them that we were going to see our people. They said "all right; we thought you were negroes from some other part of the country, and coming here to put the devil in our negroes' heads, and we was just going to kill you both, as we did when we burnt that negro, Joe Johnson's, houses down, and him in it, about a month ago. We thought you two was like him, could not be taken; but we took the black scoundrel and killed him. We will not allow any more negroes to hold office in this parish, nor anywhere in this section of the country, for this is a white man's country, and we whites will rule it over you negroes." They told us we could go on, but better not let them hear a word from us; if they did, they would kill us in time to come.

Next day I was traveling through East Feliciana, and met several colored men going out of that parish. I asked them what they meant by running out of their parish and going to other parishes. They told me the Regulators and Coal Oil men would kill them, for the white men said they were going to kill every colored man who had voted the Republican ticket, or make all of them vote Democratic, as they had killed John Gair,* and had got him out of the way, and intended to get every leading colored man out of the way, and they (the whites) would have everything their way, and that we all had better leave

---

* John Gair (1841–1875) was a delegate from East Feliciana Parish to the state constitutional convention of 1867–68 and served as a Republican in the state house of representatives, 1868–70 and 1872–74. Gair was shot to death by a mob in October 1875 that also hanged Elizabeth Mathews, his sister-in-law, after they were accused of attempting to poison her white employer.

the parish. East of Clinton I seen a large crowd of white men and four colored men coming towards me; so, when I met them, I asked them what those armed white men was going to do. They were hunting some colored men they wanted to kill, but the colored men had done run off, and they would not catch him. So the next day I had got out of that parish and went in other parishes, where I found the same terror reigning; in fact that part of Louisiana is in a horrible state.

I went to a house where a colored man who I was acquainted with lived named Joe Johnson, but I found his home was burnt down, and as his house was near mine, I went on to see what had been done to it. When I came to Madison Jurille's house I met Joe Johnson's wife, and she related to me the following sad story, alas but too true: She said to me that she had lost her husband; that he was burned to death in his own house; that him and I had worked together, but he was gone now to return no more forever; but, thank God, he is gone to rest. He asked me not to grieve for him. They made me and my children wrap our heads up in bed-quilts and come out of the house, and they then set it on fire, burning it up, and my husband in it, and all we had. They then took all my husband's papers from me. There were about fifty or sixty of them. They killed him because he refused to resign his office as constable, to which he was elected on the Republican ticket. They sent him several notices, warning him to leave his place and resign his office, but he said he would not until his time was out. So they warned him the last time, but he did not leave, so they burnt him near to death; at least they thought he was dead, but he was not quite dead; he got out and fell into a hole of water and lay there; but all the skin was burnt off of him. So the white men saw him and shot him, and he lived four days and died, and leaves me, a poor widow with a housefull of children, and no one to help me. She then asked me if I thought those white men would be punished for it. I told her I did not know, perhaps some day, but not soon, as I knew that white men had been killing our race so long, and they had not been stopped yet; as all whites who had owned slaves believed they could kill as many as they wanted in the States that existed before the war, and the poor woman shed tears and cried aloud, "O, Lord God of Host, help us to get out of this country and get somewhere where we can live."

I then left and went on the east side of the Amite River, and went through that country, and I was told that several colored persons had been badly whipped and murdered by white men; and also a large crowd of whites rushed upon a colored church masked and frightened the colored people very much, and caused them to run off from their church and nearly killed themselves, and many of them was afraid to go back to the church; and in various parts of Livingstone and Saint Helena Parish I seen colored people badly abused by white armed men. I saw an old colored man named Stephen Morgan, living in the parish of Saint Helena, and he told me that he stored cotton with a white man named Mr. Greagers, a merchant at Baton Rouge City, and said merchant sold his cotton. Two or three years after the sale of his cotton, he came to the said merchant for a settlement, as he owed the merchant one hundred dollars, but had given him two bales of cotton extra to settle that account. The merchant then entered suit against him, and got judgment, and he, Morgan, had to pay the debt the second time. He also said to me that the most of the white men throughout the country, that is, in these lower parishes, act that way whenever they can get the least hold upon the black man. Morgan has a good place of his own, yet he told me if he could get away he would leave the white people of the South, and go where he would be in peace.

I went over then to East Baton Rouge Parish and I seen four or five colored men crossed the road ahead of me, and I went up to them and I asked them where they came from, and where they were going, and they were leaving Mr. Alexander's plantation, because the armed white men went on that place last night and killed a colored man about killing his own hogs, and they knew if our race had to be killed about anything that was their own, that it was best for them to leave. I then asked them where they intended going, and they said they were going out of the State, or at least out of this part of it, until General Grant would send soldiers over to this country. I also seen several colored men on the same day going toward Baton Rouge, carrying bundles, carpet-sacks, and saddle-bags upon their backs, and they also told me they were going to leave this part of the State, as it was no place for colored people to live in; I told them I agreed with them, for I just had left my place back of Stony Point, where I found my place destroyed—houses and fences—and in fact all improvements thereon burned, and those who lived near around told me it was burned by the coal-oil men and regulators, and other styled white men; so then I told them they were right to leave; I myself was going to leave in a few days; and then one of the colored men said, "Yes, I have been justice of peace here in this parish, and a crowd of white men came to my house and took me out and whipped me nearly to death to make me resign my office; so now they may have it." So then Wesley Williams, colored, said he had been a justice of peace in Stony Point, but I give it up because Bige Fairchild, a white man, and a large crowd of other white men came to my house and told me that I had to resign my office or be killed; so I told them to take the office and let me live, and I would leave the country; so I am leaving that part of the country now.

In the city of Baton Rouge I seen a number of penitentiary convicts was working on the side of the road, and near them was a white woman and some colored men, and they told me that the guards do not mind shooting the prisoners no more than they would of shooting hogs, for, said they, we have seen them shoot and kill a good many of the convicts while they were working outside of the prison yards; that they keep dogs to run them, in other words to train them; for should the convicts run a little too fast they will put chains on him, and often they would say he attempted to run away, and then they would shoot him and place his name on the dead roll. I seen the convicts that had just been leased, and I asked them was this facts; some of them had been in there six and some of them ten years, and they told me it was true, and even much worse, so much so that they did not want it known outside the penitentiary. A colored man told me that about two or three weeks ago, that the white men had taken a young girl, colored, and tied her to a horse's tail, and run with her three miles as fast as the horse could go, and killed her; and they nor has any of the white men been punished yet for any of the crimes done in East Baton Rouge. They also told me that at the election in 1874 the whites beat, shot, and killed a great many colored people in that parish. A colored man named Job Harris told me that he had to run away from Stony Point to save his life. He had been helping Joe Johnson, the man the white men had killed by burning and shooting him; they got after him, and he had to leave his home to save his life, and of all his labor he got nothing. Bige Fairchild was with that crowd that run me away.

The same crowd of white men shot at Mr. Stillman, the postmaster there in 1874, but, by his bravery, he backed them out. He was a Republican, and the white men says no Republican shall live there, much less run for or hold office, or aid the damn radicals to elect any one. One night, whilst I was in the city of Baton Rouge, I seen about fifty or a hundred men, all white, and armed, come in that city and went to the jail, and took a colored man out and carry him off; and he never been seen or heard of since. Two days later I left for other parts of the State. On the 2d day of January, I was in New Orleans, and conversed with colored men from several parishes in this State. So I asked them concerning affairs in their respective parishes, and they told me that in their parishes murder, whipping, and other crimes were predominant. Also the colored people were robbed and plundered of their crops and other possessions, and in many instances run away because they had voted the Republican ticket. Some colored men were afraid to tell me the

exact state of affairs in the parishes from whence they came, and
where they had lived; that many of them worked on sugar and cotton plantations, and made large crops, often varying from fifteen to
forty bales of cotton per family. Yet they had not had as much as
twenty-five to fifty dollars cash money at the end of any one year.
That they always, at the owner's mode of settling, was in his debt.
Yet they did not even have half enough to eat or scarcely anything
to wear, and their indebtedness never exceeded one hundred and
fifty dollars per year on an average per family.

Along the Mississippi and Red River valley or basin the colored
people have to pay from five to twenty dollars per acre for land, and
they could not make anything at such prices, and the few that makes
anything at all has to aid the white people in cheating the others
of his own race and color out of his money and crops. That is when
the colored man gets what he makes; they have to do that or not
make anything. No year since the war but this has been and is still
the case. The white people do not allow us to sell our own crops;
and when we do, we do it at the risk of our lives, getting whipped,
shot at, and often some get killed. I have conversed with colored
men here from Mississippi, Alabama, Arkansas, and Georgia, and
after telling them of the cruelties, abuses, murderings, and other
treatments too heinous to mention, they have told me that in the
States where they live it is just the same; and you may say we have
told you so, for we live in there and must know, and we wish to God
we could get out of the ex-slave States and ex-slaveholders and go
to where we can live in peace and quietness, without continual fear
of our lives. Says one of them who was from one of these States,
"Do you think we will do better if we were to ourselves and out of
the South?" One colored man from Georgia spoke and said, "Yes;
for we will get our rights at law, our lives will be protected; we will
get what we make, our crops or their value; if we get in jail, we will
have a chance to get bond and a chance to prove our innocence,
and not be taken out by a mob and hung or shot before they know

whether we are guilty or not; and may not have to work on the railroad or levees in chain-gangs when we are not guilty of any crime, and not to be whipped as if we were dumb brutes; nor hated because we are black."

So one colored man from Mississippi asked me what I thought we the colored people should best do. I told him we had better petition Congress and the President of the United States to set apart a territory for the colored people (our race) in the western part of the United States or appropriate money and send us to Liberia, where our forefathers came from; for then we will be living with our own race and people, and under a government with our race as presiding officers. A man (colored) from Texas asked me did I think we all could live in Liberia. I told him yes, for there were thousands of our race there already who had left this country; and another colored man said yes, for I am going to Liberia some time this year myself, and you all had better go too, and take heed to what Mr. Adams tells you, for he is a man that loves your race. So one of them asked me where I lived when I am at home; I told him Shreveport, La., but was working for my race to get them to leave the Southern States; and I want to know if you intend still to live with these ex-slaveholders; and that I hope that all of my race will leave the South; for, said I, the God of high heaven will put a curse should we continue to live with our former masters and ex-slaveholders, who are not enjoying the same rights as he has ordained that we shall enjoy in our own native soil; for God says in His Holy Word that he has a place and land for all his people, and our race had better go to it; and I hope that all of you who are here, when you go home to your States, will tell our race that myself and all others who loves our race has petitioned the President and Congress of the United States for a territory for ourselves, or to appropriate money to carry us to Liberia.

We went back to Caddo in September, 1874, and organized an organization called the Colonization Council, for the purpose of

bringing our race together to aid by unity the moving of our race
from the Southern States; as we all could testify to the same brutal
treatment done us by the whites in the South. I said to all, let us
go home and prepare to vote and try to carry this election, and then,
if we find the country no better for us, we must then go to work
and try and get our race to leave the Southern States where we have
been slaves, working the land for our masters. So a unanimous voice
was the answer, and yes was echoed by all; and we agreed to it, both
women and men that were assembled at that conference.

I then left the city of New Orleans for Shreveport, and on my
way up the river at different landings where we touched I got several statements from the colored people; how they were treated,
and how their crops were taken from them, and their wives also,
and run them off the place. Eight colored men stated to me what
I now reiterate; they also told me the whites had taken their horses,
mules, wagons, and all they had pertaining to them; that they were
in their debt; even corn, hogs, and all their cotton, yet they owed
them nothing. Sold all they had for taxes when they owned neither
real or personal estate; even took bed and bedding for taxes. The
same is done in Harrison County, Texas. The parties who made
the statement were men living in different counties in Texas and
different parishes in Louisiana; and thus it has been ever since the
war. Even the elected officers of the Republican party undergo the
same treatment.

During this campaign I was often attracted by crowds of armed
white men, who told me if I was canvassing for the damn Radical,
I had better not come in their place. If I did, I would not get off. I
was then canvassing for the Radicals, as they called us, organizing
clubs of my race for the canvass, and on some plantations I was
not allowed to organize clubs either on or about their plantations.
On the river plantations, where the boss did not want office, or the
colored vote to support him, he would not let me canvass on that
plantation, as he would say he did not want no negro politician on

or about his place. But if he wanted office and wanted the colored vote then he would let me organize a club on that place so long as I was fighting some Republican candidates, and favoring some of the white men of the place. I often had to leave my race ignorant of what politician to vote for.

In June, about the 21st, a delegation left Shreveport, including myself, to attend the State convention to be held at New Orleans on the 28th of the same month in 1876. So then when we took passage the chief officer of the boat told us if we would vote for a white man for governor of the State in the convention he would carry us in the cabin (cabin fare) for ten dollars. We asked him who he wanted us to vote for. He said any white man, who was born in Louisiana. We said we would vote for Col. George Williamson.* He said, all right, we could go the round trip for twenty dollars. On our way down I seen the mate knock the blood out of one colored man, who was working on the boat, and knocked him off the stage-plank; and at a wood-yard, he struck another colored man with a stick of wood, and hurt him very bad. The colored man who worked on that boat told me it was a common thing, for often the mate nearly killed some of them, and never anything done to them about it. And on our way back to Shreveport, we took passage on the steamer C. H. Durfee, and at or near Alexandria, on Red River, the boat got hung on a snag, and the mate struck a colored man on the boat, and made him jump into the river waist deep; and did the same several times between there and Shreveport. This was about the 30th of July.

I went to Claiborne Parish and tried to organize clubs; I had together about ten or twelve colored men, when along came three white men, and said to us, "What are you damn niggers doing here?

---

* George Williamson (1829–1882), a lawyer from Shreveport, was nominated for governor in 1872 by a Reform convention, but withdrew from the race after the Reformers decided to support the Democratic candidate. He later served as the U.S. minister to the Central American States, 1873–79.

If we catch you damn niggers trying to organize here we will kill half of you; as that is our business." So we left there and went down to a little place called Argenars; and to another place called Forrester Grove, to a church, and was talking to some colored men about organizing a club there. The colored men told us we might organize it, but when the whites found it out they would break it up unless we vote, or say we vote, for some white man on the Democratic ticket. I then asked them, did the white men interfere with them about voting, or take their crops from them whenever they voted the Republican ticket? They told me, "Yes; unless we voted for some white man they told us to vote for, and some of us owns our own land and homes, and so we cannot vote at all; but when we can vote we vote Republican, out and out, or not vote at all; yet some of us only votes for members of Congress; sometimes district judges; but if we get a fair chance to vote, we vote the whole Republican ticket." I then asked them, did they believe we would be any better off to vote, or hold office; and all of them answered (but one) "No, and we think it useless to try any longer; for the white men of Claiborne Parish has killed every good black man in our parish that tried to lead us right."

We know that a great many colored men has been killed in this parish, also in the parishes of Jackson, Union, Webster, Claiborne, Lincoln, and Bienville; also there has been some killed in Bossier; for I was there myself and another colored man went with me through these parishes, and heard these statements in conversation with them. Two men said to us, "Look how the white men killed Bill Undrees,* because he was a member of the legislature, and held an office, and we all could go to him for instructions. Look how they burnt to death those three colored men, because some

---

* Possibly a reference to William Meadows, a freedman from Claiborne Parish who served as a delegate to the state constitutional convention of 1867–68. Meadows was shot to death in front of his family on his farm in May 1868.

white woman lied on them." Yet, said they, we could live here and get our rights in the Southern states, if the man we elected to office would do what General Grant tell them to; but these men, when we elect them, do what the ex-slaveholders ask them to do, or pay them to do. So it is best for us to stop voting until things are fixed and carried out better.

But many of the 27th said, No; not stop voting; let us vote for President and Congressmen, for, as Mr. Adams says, if then things are not better, we will all leave the ex-slaveholding States." But, said they, Look how the white men shot Peter Williams, in Homer, in the year 1874, when we all was marching through that town. They shot him because he had charge of us. So, after they shot him, Joe Calvin took charge of us, and we went on to Homer, and these agreed to vote the straight Republican ticket in full. After voting we went southeast of Homer to a church called Saint John the Baptist. There was a large gathering of colored people and a few whites. I got together about twenty or twenty-five colored men, and we went out on the right side of the road and asked them would they go to Homer to-morrow to the meeting and hear the Republican governor and lieutenant-governor speak. Several of them asked me who was the republican governor and lieutenant-governor. I told them it was S. B. Packard and C. C. Antoine* was our candidate for governor and lieutenant-governor; so they told me that the white people around there had told them that every one of them that went to hear the Republicans speak, they, the white men, would take every bit of corn from them; and if they voted a Republican ticket and did not vote for Tilden and Nicholls,† they would take all of their

---

* Stephen B. Packard (1839–1922) was inaugurated as governor on January 8, 1877, but was forced to surrender his office on April 24 after President Hayes withdrew the troops guarding the state house. Caesar Carpentier Antoine (1836–1921) was born a free person of color and served in the Union army. He was lieutenant governor of Louisiana from 1873 to 1877.

† See footnote on page 99.

cotton too, and would not let them have no supplies nor anything to live on for the next year.

They also told me that all the white people that had colored people on their place working their crops was Democrats, and they had already said that any colored man living on their places that voted a Republican ticket should receive nothing for their work for this year; and also any negro that was caught trying to get the negroes to vote the damn Radical ticket, he would be killed or run out of the country. I then asked them would they all join a club. They told me, no, sir; we would like to join a club, but if we did so, we would all, or nearly all, of us have to vote the Democratic ticket, or we would have nothing; for we would have our crops taken away from us by the whites if we did not vote for their nominees; and while we were talking two or three white men passing by us said to us, "What are you damn negroes doing there? You all are trying to do something against we white people, and we believe we will shoot every one of you."

So all the colored men left; some went home, and some went to the church of Saint John, the Baptist. I also went in the church; and some who knew me by name, asked me to ask an educational speech; so I consented, and began to say something respecting us freedmen, and how long we had been free; how fast we had improved in citizenship, and that we would soon overtake some of the white people if we continued as we had started; and I further said we ought to elect men to office that would always give us free schools. At that part of my speech three white men came in and leaned upon the benches in the church, and some of the colored men who had been run by white men that night, jumped over the benches and ran out of church, and then a good many more followed them and left only eight or nine who remained with me while I was speaking; so the meeting was broke up, and I left there on the 30th of September.

Many colored people told me they had an idea of going to the meeting and hear S. B. Packard speak at Homer, and a great many

did go; but those who were working on shares of the crop raised
did not, as they feared the white people would take away all they
had and would make, as they had already threatened to do so. In
my travels through Jackson Parish, in many parts of it, I found colored people who were afraid to even take a newspaper from me,
especially if it was Republican. But if it was a Democratic organ,
they could take it without fear; as they said the white men of the
place did not allow them to read Republican newspapers; for the
whites said it was for the purpose of making up Radical clubs, and
they told me I had better get out of that parish, for all of Mr. Kidd's
men would get after me. I then asked them who Mr. Kidd was, and
they told me a white man, and all of his followers were white men.
I asked them what Mr. Kidd had to do with me—talking to men of
my own race—that I was not going to say anything to the white
people; I came here to talk to you all, and I hope you all will hear
me. They agreed to hear what I said, but, said they, this white man
on this place will not allow us to vote or act as we wish.

I then said to them, why don't you all leave him and go some-
wheres else; because, said they, these white people will not let us;
and if we run away, they will take everything we possess; so you
see we cannot leave all we have got. Then, say I, why do you not
go to law and have the white men arrested for the manner in which
you are treated by them? We have, says they. We have resorted to
the courts, reported to the Federal officers when they were here,
but it is no use to try and get anything done to those white people
who treat us so, as the ex-slaveholders has the money, and with it
they can buy the courts and officers of the law; for I believe if they
were to kill ten thousand of us colored people and were arrested
they could get clear. Whilst we were talking two white men came
along and asked us what we called that, was it a council or a political
meeting. The colored men said neither one. They then said to us,
if you want to live happy you must have nothing to do with the damn
Radical party this year, for we are going to elect Tilden and Nicholls,

and we will have the damn Radicals afraid to hold up their heads in this State. So you negroes who do not want to die hard by our shot-guns had better not have anything to do with this damn Radical ticket. Now, says they, "Don't you understand?" and the colored men say yes, sir.

Then I left and went through two other parishes and into the par-ish of Webster, but found a little better feeling existing there among the whites and blacks, yet many of them told me that the whites had taken away a great many of their crops, and some of the colored men had been badly beat, and whipped, because they sold their crops without the owner of the place's permit, and some were warned if they voted a Republican ticket they (the whites) would close their debts on them, and give them no more credit, or furnish them the next year. I left, and went over to Bossier Parish, where I found a very large crowd of colored men assembled at Belleview, and had a talk with the colored men from all parts of that parish. And nearly all of them told me the same story I heard in and through the other parish. They told me they intended to vote the Republi-can ticket, even though they thought they would be killed by the Democrats. As the Democrats did not free us, and now they do not want us to vote the Republican ticket; but we intend to do every-thing the Democrats don't want us to do; because they had us slaves once, and they want us slaves again; and now we intend to vote the Republican ticket at the risk of our lives. Of course we know that the white people own all the plantations in this parish, and will take everything we have from us, and kill some of us, and beat some of us, and put some of us in jail, and make false charges against us, just as soon as we vote the Republican ticket. But let come what may we will vote the Republican ticket throughout, and for every man on it.

And whilst I was talking to my race five or six white men came near, and says to me, "Old man, what office is you running for; and why are you trying to get these colored men to vote the Radical ticket?" I said to him, "to help elect our nominees." They asked me, "Who are your men?" Says I, "every man on our ticket, from Hayes and Wheeler* down to the last man." They then asked me where I lived, whether in this parish or State, and where I was raised at. I told them I was born in the State of Georgia, and lived there awhile, and was then brought here to this State, on the line of Louisiana and Texas when a boy, and was first in Louisiana and then in Texas until the war in 1861. They then asked me if I had been in the Army; I told them yes, I had been in the army three years since the war. So they said, "That is the reason why you tell your race to vote the Radical ticket; but we will carry this election for our State, or we will kill every negro and damn radical in the State; mark our words for that. Go ahead; you will see it if we will have to fight for it." I said, "All right; all I want is my race to vote the Republican ticket."

I went then through the parish of Caddo, and at or near Mowning Port I met a large crowd of white men, and they said to me, "Is you a Radical politician?" I told them "No," I was a laboring man. They then asked me if I was not trying to get negroes to vote the Republican ticket? I told them "Yes"; so they said to me, "You had better leave this part of the country, as you might get your head shot off." And then they asked me how me and Bill Harper stood? I then told them how it was. They asked me what was my name; I told them Adams. They said to me, "Is your name Henry Adams?" I told them "Yes." "Then you are fighting Bill Harper and George L. Smith?" I told them "Yes." Then says they to me, "Go ahead; just so we defeat them two damn rascals, we don't care if all the other men are elected on the Republican ticket in this parish."†

Two days afterwards I went to Bossier Parish, down to Bossier Point, and a white man halted me and asked me where I was going,

* William A. Wheeler (1819–1887) was a Republican congressman from New York, 1861–63 and 1869–77, and vice president of the United States, 1877–81.
† Harper was reelected to the state senate, while Smith was defeated in the congressional election. (See also footnotes on pages 75 and 126.)

and if I was canvassing for the Republicans. I told him "Yes; but I am canvassing among my race, and not the white race." He says, "We white men have sworn to kill every negro we catch teaching other negroes to vote the damn Radical ticket; so I had better kill you." I told him I thought it very hard that we colored people lived with the white people, and made you all rich, and now must not tell our own race how to vote; and yet you white men go everywhere and tell your race how to vote, and who to vote for, and we colored people says nothing to you at all. We do not tell you all to vote our ticket; so for God sake let me alone, for I will teach my race until I die. So he says to me, "Give me your hand, for you are an honest and good man; go anywhere you please." So I passed on through that parish, and when I got to Doctor Vance's plantation, on Red River, about ten miles north of Shreveport, I stopped, and was telling the colored people about voting, and who was the best to vote for; and Dr. Wyatte Vance said to me that he did not allow any colored man to say anything about voting to any colored man on his plantation; "for," said he, "they all shall vote as I say vote; and if I catch any negro on my place trying to get negroes to vote the Radical ticket, I will shoot the top of his head off." I told him I would not go on any man's plantation that told me not; but I could call a meeting in the public road, and would then tell them all about how to vote and who to vote for. So he said to me if he caught any negro holding club meetings anywhere about his place, he would kill the last one of them, "and we intend to kill every negro in the State that votes a Republican ticket, but what we will carry this State and elect our governor and State ticket; so I want you to keep away from my place, unless you come on my place to work, as you did on Hamilton & Co.'s plantation; as I happen to know you, and that you are a good negro to work and carry on business, I will let you go." And all the colored people I had a talk with told me Dr. Vance had taken nearly all their crops every year that he would make contracts.

Passing along the line of Arkansas and Louisiana, I seen many colored people on the roadsides, in the fields, and at their houses, and they told me that they could not vote anywhere, for the white people all through this country wants us to vote for them and their ticket; but we are all going to vote the Republican ticket this election, and if the Democrats kill us, beat us, or take our crops, as they have been doing here all the time, we will leave here and go and hunt us another land. I told them that was right. I met some white men on the road, who asked me where I was going. I told them I was going to see some of my people; and they asked me if I was going to tell them to vote the Republican ticket. I told them I could not do otherwise. Says they to me you had better leave this part of the State; if I did not I would get killed. Says I, "All right, gentlemen, I will leave; but I will see my race at another time, and they will all vote as I vote." And they told me if we voted the Radical ticket they were going to carry the election, and elect their President and State ticket, or kill every negro in the State. I said nothing more, but left; and on my way to Cotton Galley, near the line of Bossier and Webster Parish, I seen many colored people, and they told me that the white people had told them that if they voted the Radical ticket they would not furnish them anything, but would not let them have a thing off of their plantations, and they should not have any club meeting about or in that part of the State. So I am advised by the colored people to not attempt to organize any clubs there.

I left, and met white men all along the road I was traveling, asking me where I was going and what my business was, but I never would tell them nothing. At some places the colored people talked as though they did not care to vote, for fear of the white people taking away all they possessed and run them off the plantation. After the large meeting at Longview, in Bossier Parish, I left and went above Benton, at or near Gum Springs; and I staid there all night, with a large crowd of men and women, colored. Some of them told me they had been working on the Widow Dickson plantation since 1866, and some since 1868, and some ever since the war, and before the war; and they told me that they never could get a settlement with the owners of the places, and that they had made from five to thirty-five bales of cotton per family, and they had never drawn as much as one hundred dollars during the entire year; and that Mrs. Dickson do not permit them to ever take off the plantation in one year two bales of cotton, charging them from ten to fifteen dollars per acre, and sometimes one hundred pounds lint cotton per acre, and allow them no credit, only what they got from her, and give to her her own price. I seen some of their bills, and found them charged from 35 cents per pound for meat, and even 40 cents per pound, when the same meat was selling for 12½ cents per pound. Meal $3 per bushel, when it was selling for $1 per bushel. I seen their accounts from 1866 to 1874 kept by them on their memorandum books. I also seen where they had receipts for horses, and mules, and made to pay for them again. Many were there from all parts of the parish that night, and the most of them told the same story about the treatment they received from the whites in that parish.

The next day all up and down Red River on the plantations, I seen colored men and women, and talked with them about how they were getting along; and they would say to me, if we cannot do any better than we have been doing here since freedom, we had better leave the country and migrate to Africa. So I told them that if we cannot vote this election and elect our men, Republicans, without the whites taking it away from them and us, as they have done for some time, we will and can go to Liberia, if the United States Government will not give us a territory to ourselves somewhere in the United States, and I hope you will all vote this year.

STATEMENT OF SPECIFIC CASES OF OUTRAGE FROM 1866 TO 1876

[Compiled by HENRY ADAMS.]

Statements of individuals (colored)

DE SOTO PARISH

1st. My name is Bebe Oldman; lived on Joe King place in (1875); was nearly beaten to death by a white man.

2d. My name is Pete Umfort. On a plantation about three or four miles from Mansfield, I was badly beaten, in the year 1874, by a white man.

3d. My name is ———; I lived on Bell's plantation, and was cropping. I asked him for some meat for rations. He told me to plant corn. I did so; then returned and asked him again for meat; he told me to go and plant cotton; which I did, and again asked him for meat, and told him I was going to work for a man that would give me some meat to eat. Then Bells, Lans, and other white men tried to kill me; they cut me nearly to death. This occurred on his place, in the year 1874.

4th. My name is Stoney Sugers. I and my brother were badly beaten on Henry Bell's plantation, by him and other white men, in the year 1875, near Mansfield.

5th. Marches Beenman was killed about six miles from Mansfield, on the high-road, by white men (names unknown), in the year 1874.

6th. Willey, a young man, was killed about six miles from Mansfield, while going home, on the high-road, by a body of white men (unknown), in the year 1874.

7th. Gains King, killed by (whites), on Coates' place, by a white man named James Farmer, because he said that a hog that James Farmer had was his hog. This occurred in the year 1873.

8th. Bill Jones was killed by a white man because he was laughing and talking with a white lady. This occurred in Davies' place, in the year 1870.

9th. Pete, was killed by white men on ____ , in the year 1870. No cause assigned for the killing.

10th. Two colored men, names unknown, were killed on Barde David's place, by white men, in the year 1870.

11th. Charles Edward, shot by white men, on Bige David's plantation, in the year 1870.

12th. Henry, a colored man, was killed by white men on Bill Crowsby's place, at or near Mansfield, in 1867.

BOSSIER PARISH

14th. Hunter, colored, was killed by white men, at or near Red Lands, about twelve or fifteen miles from the line of Arkansas, in the year 1867.

15th. Louis Eaton, colored, was killed by white men on Eaton place, about six or seven miles from Columbus, in 1866.

16th. Selern, colored, killed by James McCalled, a white man, on Leek's plantation, in the year 1868.

17th. Cicero Simmons, badly beaten by Johnny Naterson, a white man, on Captain Abenishbou's place, in the year 1870.

18th. Bill Melton, colored, beat and severely whipped by white men at or near Cotton Valley because he quarreled with them about taking his crop. This occurred in 1869.

19th. Miss Matilda Johnson was beaten and badly whipped by white men at or near Cotton Valley, in the year 1871.

CADDO PARISH

20th. Donahoue, colored, was killed by a white man on Nick Marchu's place, in the year 1873.

21st. Miss Delia Young, beat and severely whipped by James Robinson (white) on Hayne's place, or, as called, Levee Bend, and also all her crop taken from her, in the year 1872.

22d. Margaret Bates, badly whipped by John Brown, a white man, on Levee Bend plantation, in the year 1873.

23d. Henry Hard (colored) killed by a white man, in the year 1874.

24th. Dick, a colored man, was killed by a white man, in the year 1874.

25th. Cæsar Johnson (colored) killed by Milton, a colored man, in the year 1872.

26th. Harden, a white man, killed by a white man named Oakley Rust, in 1871 or 1872.

27th. Anderson, a colored man, killed by Starks Wells, a colored man, in the year 1874.

28th. John Williams, colored, badly whipped by a white man named Mack Marchards, in the year 1873.

29th. Fred, a colored man, killed by being burnt up at the stake, on Joe Bealey's place, in the year 1872.

DE SOTO PARISH

30th. William Monroe, colored, was shot and badly wounded for voting a Republican ticket; was shot by armed white men, in the year 1874.

31st. Francis Pigion, colored, killed at or near Greenwood, by Bill Bateman, white, in the year 1865.

32d. Henry Foster, colored, killed by Halworthe, a white man, at or near Keachie, in the year 1866.

33d. Frank Weaver, colored, killed by Daniel Worker, a white man, in Caddo Parish, in the year 1873.

34th. John Beden, white, killed by Mr. Dryfufe, white, in the year 1874.

35th. Manuel Oakart, colored, killed by Bateman, white, at Greenwood, La., in the year 1865.

36th. Annie Gray, colored, killed by a white man, in 1871.

37th. Frank Tucker, colored, killed by a white man, 1866.

38th. Aaron Williams, whipped badly by Albert Grester, at or near Greenwood, in 1874.

39th. Henry Parker, colored, shot by a white man, in 1868.

40th. William Parker, colored, killed by a white man, in 1868.

41st. O. Parker, colored, killed by a white man, in 1868.

BOSSIER PARISH

42d. Aaron Nickerson, colored, killed by a white man, in 1868.

43d. Miles Nickerson, colored, killed by white men, in 1868.

44th. Henry Smith, colored, killed by white men, in 1868.

45th. Lawrence Evans, colored, killed by James Sanders and other white men, in the year 1868.

46th. Edward Starks, colored, killed by white men, in 1868.

47th. Jesse Field, colored; formerly belonged to Milton Sanders; was killed by white men, in 1868.

48th. A colored man named Williams was killed by white men, in 1868.

49th. George Morris, colored, killed by white men, in 1868.

50th. George Dillman, killed by white men, in 1868.

51st. Alex. Ariel, colored, killed and his tongue cut out by white men, in 1868.

52d. Henry Picket, killed by white men, in 1868.

53d. Ben. White, colored, killed by white men, in 1868.

54th. Murrell Grial, colored, killed by white men, in 1868.

55th. Watch Smith, colored, killed by colored men, in 1868.

56th. Julius Davis, colored, killed by white men, in 1868.

57th. Ishmon Babe, colored, hung by white men, in 1868.

58th. Robert Jackson, colored, shot at by white men, in 1868.

59th. Bob. Gilmore, killed by drunken white men, in 1868.

60th. Dick Thomas, colored, shot by white men, in 1868.

61st. Ben. Powell, colored, shot by white men, in 1868.

62d. Amos Johnson, colored, killed by a white man by the name of Smith, in the year 1868.

63d. Julius Johnson, colored, killed by white men, in 1868.

64th. James Bungtree, colored, shot by white men, in 1873.

65th. Harry Aurgan, colored, shot by white men, in 1868.

66th. James Brown, colored, shot by white men, in 1868.

67th. A colored man named Crossman was shot by white men, in 1868.

68th. Nick Johnson, colored, killed by white men, in 1869.

69th. David Jones, colored, shot at seven times by white men, in 1868.

70th. Owen Pread, colored, shot by white men, in 1868.

71st. Aaron Washington, colored, shot at by white men, in 1868.

72d. Charley Starck, colored, killed by Bob Cummings, white, in 1868.

73d. Richard Gee, colored, killed by Lige Soles and his company, all white men, in 1868.

74th. A colored man named Judge was killed on the Red River place by John Vance, Dr. Kings, John Homer, Dr. Mitchell Fields, Jack Wolgers, all living at Cash Point place, and all white men. This occurred in 1868.

75th. A colored man named Boles was killed at the same place (Cash Point) and by the same men, in 1868.

76th. A colored man named Albert was killed at the same place (Cash Point) and by the same men, in 1868.

77th. A colored man named Simon was killed on the same place and by the same band of men, in 1868.

78th. Big Charley (colored), killed by James Picket and Budd Cockes, whites, in 1868.

79th. Smith Gobley (colored), killed by Bud Blocpes on Buck Hall place, in 1868.

80th. James Smith (colored), badly shot on Wells's place, near the line of Caddo, by a white man, in 1868.

DE SOTO PARISH

81st. Oakley Carter (colored), badly whipped by W. C. Carrows (white) on Furguson's place, September 5, 1865.

82d. George Adams (colored), killed by a white man, in June or July, 1866.

83d. Samuel Hunter (colored), killed by white men, in 1868.

84th. Monday Jefferson (colored), killed by white men, in 1868.

CADDO PARISH

85th. Samuel Lawson (colored), killed by white men, in 1868.

86th. Harry Hawkins (colored), killed by white men, in 1868.

87th. Hector Hawkins (colored), killed by white men, in 1868.

88th. Joe Louis, shot by white men, in 1868.

89th. Bill Connelly (colored), killed by white men, in 1868.

90th. George Brown (colored), killed by white men, in 1868.

91st. Manuel Johnson (colored), killed by white men, in 1868.

92d. Dick Long (colored), killed by white men in 1868; accused of raising armies against the white people.

BOSSIER PARISH

93d. January Toll (colored), killed by white men on Joe Briant's place, in 1868.

94th. Gaunt Hunter (colored), shot by white men on Joe Briant's place, in 1868.

95th. Joe Squire (colored), shot by white men on Joe Briant's place, in 1868.

96th. Willey Hunter (colored), shot by white men on Joe Briant's place, in 1868. Dr. Hunter did the shooting.

97th. Reuben William (colored), shot by Dr. Hunter (white) on his, Hunter's, place, in 1868.

98th. Pink Jameson (colored), badly whipped and stripped by William Alborn and father (white men) on his, Alborn's, place, in 1868.

99th. Benton Louis (colored), badly whipped by Milton and William Alborn, brothers, both white, in 1868.

100th. Thomas Lee (colored), beaten badly by the same white men on the same place, in 1868.

101st. Miss Caroline Lewis (colored), badly whipped by Capt. William Alborn, brothers, and white men, in 1868.

102d. Miss Sarah Allen (colored), badly whipped by the captain and William Alborn, brothers (white men), on Alborn's place, in 1868.

103d. Elie Lee (colored), beaten near unto death by William Alborn and brother, on old man Alborn's place, in 1868.

104th. George Nash (colored), killed by James Acres, white, at or near Benton, on McCarley's place, in 1872.

105th. Miller Gidston, killed by Butcher Gilmore, white, in 1868.

106th. Aaron Gidston, killed by Butcher Gilmore, white, in 1868.

107th. Edward Worley, killed by Bud Chochus on Gilmore's place, in 1868.

108th. Marshal Bodly, killed by white men on Gilmore's place, in 1874.

109th. Flowers Worley, whipped by white men on Gilmore's place, in 1875.

110th. Madison and Davidson, whipped by white men on Gilmore's place, in 1874.

111th. Toney (colored), shot by old man Winn (white) on his place, in 1868.

112th. Mack Smith (colored), killed by Sam Sawer (colored) on Douglass's place, near Gilmore, in 1868.

113th. Willis Richardson (colored), badly shot by a white man at or near Shreveport about his gin screaking, in November, 1875.

114th. My name is Wash. Douglas. I was badly beaten over the head by Bloody John Gage with a six-shooter because I told him he could not come in my house, and before my face, and keep my daughter. Says he to me, "If you say any more to me about your child

I will kill you"; and if I report him, he would kill me. This occurred on Dr. M. S. Vance's place, called the Buck Horn place, about eight or nine miles from Shreveport, in June, 1875.

115th. Big Charley (colored), killed by John Aramel (white), on Be Been place, 1868.

116th. Nick Johnson (colored), killed on Be Been place by armed white men, 1868.

117th. Amos Lee (colored), killed on Be Been place by armed white men, 1868.

118th. Rev. Meen (colored), was killed by old man Dillard, on Sandy Grove's place; was run from there and killed near Shreveport, 1868.

119th. James Hickers (colored), was United States marshal; was taken out of Dr. Thomas's house at night in Benton, by armed white men, including Marion Brooks, colored, and shot dead.

120th. Vorden (colored), lived in Grela Place; was killed by white men, in 1868.

121st. Miss Nancy Carroway (colored), whipped by Captain Dority almost to death, and all of her clothes taken from her, in 1874.

122d. Bladly Evan (colored), shot at by white men; Gibson and Hamilton gave them the guns and ammunition to shoot with.

123d. Lee Jones (colored), killed by Charley Scott, colored, who got a white man to help him, in 1873; they went from Shreveport to kill him.

124th. Wash. Douglass (colored), was badly beaten over the head with a gun and wounded by the stock; this occurred on the Buckhorn place in 1868.

125th. Primus Jones (colored), was badly cut and wounded in the head by colored men on the Buckhorn place, in 1873.

126th. Robert Brooks (colored), was badly beaten by a white man, named John Gay, on Buckhorn place, 1875, in March.

127th. Cato Davis (colored), beat nearly to death by armed white men, in 1873.

128th. Cæsar Johnson (colored), killed by white men, having his heart cut out, on Cornell place, in 1873.

129th. Charley Leo (colored), beaten over the head with a six-shooter and got his skull cracked, in the town of Fillmore, by white men, in 1873.

130th. Henry Margroves (colored), burnt to death between Bellowe and Fillmore, on the high road, in 1870, by white men.

131st. Anderson Bailley (colored), badly beaten by J. White, at Fillmore, 1874.

132d. Joe Douglass (colored), beaten near to death by Dick Sanders, a white man, at Fillmore, in 1872.

133d. Joe Crugals (colored), badly beaten by Aares, a white man, in Fillmore, in 1874.

134th. Margaret Tucker (colored), badly beaten, and in a delicate state, by Briston Plates, a white man, 1871.

135th. Rose Cooper (colored), beaten by a white man on Mr. ———— Bludsan place, near Fillmore, in 1878.

136th. Frank Jeffrew (colored), killed by white men on Seward Angrel's place, 1868.

137th. Isaac Louis (colored), whipped badly by Brownlee, on Brownlee place, in 1868.

138th. Mrs. Martha Frances (colored), badly whipped by Simon Gilmore (white) on Gilmore's place, in 1874.

139th. Bill Louis (colored), badly whipped by Charley Milton (white) on Bore's place, 1872; died from the wounds.

140th. William Whiteman (colored), badly beaten by Charley Milton (white) on Bore's place, in 1873.

141st. Alex. Tramels (colored), badly beaten by white men on Brown's place, in 1868.

142d. Old man Willey (colored), badly whipped by Brown's son (white) on Brown Lee place, 1868.

143d. Bill Thomas (colored), badly beaten by Martin Marshall (white); also cut through, but not killed; done on Bore's place, 1868.

144th. George Murrell (colored), killed by white men on Sacery Groves's place, 1868.

145th. James Smith (colored), killed by Budcocks near Shreveport, in 1868.

146th. William Linchpin (colored), killed on Douglass place by white men, 1868.

147th. Bob Case (colored), killed by Joe Biley and other white men on Mrs. Dickerson's place, in 1868.

148th. Willis Dunn (colored), killed by Alex. Bard and other white men on Mrs. Dickerson's place, in 1868.

149th. Richard Neal (colored), killed by white men on J. Oneal's place, in 1868.

150th. Willis Homles (colored), killed by John Gunters, a white man, on Mrs. Dickerson's place, in 1866.

151st. Albert Ross (colored), killed by white men on East Point place, in 1868.

152d. Henry Calways (colored), killed by white men on John Orial's place, in 1868.

153d. Alex. Nelson (colored), tongue cut out, skinned and beat, and then killed by Old Dority and other white men, on John Oriely's place, in 1868.

154th. Simon Cerows (colored), killed by white men on Mrs. Dickerson's place, in 1868.

155th. William Cawles (colored), killed by white men on La Groves's place, in 1868.

156th. Thomas Lacan (colored), killed by white men on Buck Horn place, in 1868.

157th. Burrell Howe (colored), shot by a colored man on East Point place, in 1870.

158th. Dick Dowells (colored), killed by white men. He was taken from Lagroues' place to Mrs. Dickerson's place and killed, 1868.

159th. Edmond Young (colored), badly whipped by Captain Thomas on the Dickerson place, in 1869.

160th. Charley Robinson (colored), shot by Thomas Watley (white), in the year 1872.

161st. Louis Booker (colored), killed by Charley Flanagin (white) and others; also Marlio Booker, in the year 1868; also two children from off the same place.

162d. John, a colored man, killed by Oharry and others (white men) on Mr. Carrow's place, in 1868.

163d. Thimble Anderson (colored), badly whipped by James Markes (white) on J. Marks's place, in 1874.

164th. Nathan Williams (colored), badly whipped and his cotton taken away without any cause by Bill Mark, a white man, on his place, in 1874, because he voted the Radical ticket.

165th. Carter Frances (colored), badly whipped and his cotton taken away from him because he voted the Radical ticket, by Bill Marks (white), on his place, in 1874.

166th. Alex Williams (colored), shot by Joe Blaly (white) because he wanted his cotton he made in 1874, on Marks's place.

167th. Cameron Hall (colored), badly beaten by Bill Marks (white) because he wanted his cotton and corn he made on Marks's place, in 1873.

168th. A colored woman shot by Mrs. Gilmore on her Tom's place about 3 miles from Shreveport, because Mrs. Gilmore wanted to whip her and she would not take it. This occurred on the 28th of April, 1875, on Tom Gilmore's plantation.

169th. Charley Robinson (colored), shot by Bob Robinson, colored, on Bridan place, in 1873.

170th. Phil (colored), shot on James Heron's place in 1873, about his step-daughter, by a white man.

171st. Isaac Cooper, Elie Cooper, and Clarance Cooper, all colored, were badly beaten by Bill Stildon and other white men near Red Schute, about their cotton made in 1873.

172d. Maria Morris (colored), whipped by John Platt and other white men, on Hamilton place, in 1873.

DE SOTO PARISH

173d. Bob Balos (colored), killed by James Taylor Meems (white) on Meems' place, about four miles from Clinton, in 1868.

174th. Stepton Great (colored), killed by James Meems (white) on J. Meems' place, four miles from Clinton, in 1868, about killing a mule accidentally.

175th. Rose (colored), killed by James Meems and James Lafayette (white men) on Meems' place, in 1868.

176th. Henry Lane (colored), a boy, killed by Ben Hogan (white) on his place, in 1868.

177th. Simus Richardson (colored), badly beaten by a white man named Dick Ridge on Captain Cores' place and broke his arm, which is not near as well and useful as it was before; this was in February, 1875.

178th. Jane Ladreuse, badly whipped by James Meems (white) on his place, in 1871.

179th. Ligeley Houston, beaten badly by James Meems (white) on his place, in 1867.

180th. Thomas Blaine, killed by Jiles Grooves (white) four miles from Keachie, in 1866.

181st. Burth, a colored man, was killed in Caddo Parish, at Greenwood, by white men, in 1867.

182d. John Morris, killed by white men in Shreveport, La., in 1872.

183d. Smith (colored), killed by a white man in 1872.

184th. Lily George, whipped by Paterwood in Shreveport, La., a white man, in 1879.

185th. Sally Groves, whipped by Dick Wright, white, in Shreveport, in 1869.

186th. Annie, a colored woman, was whipped by old man Washington, white, one and a half miles from Shreveport, in 1870.

187th. Charley Tolsom and wife, beat and hung by whites in 1868.

188th. Pacey Harris, badly whipped by a white man in Shreveport, La., in 1868.

189th. Harris Washington, whipped by Joe White, a white man, on White's place, in 1870.

190th. Henry Thomas, killed by white men on Mrs. Alexander's place, eight miles from Mansfield, in 1869.

CADDO PARISH

191st. Phil. and Simus Cobro, were badly whipped by white men at or near Thomas Walter's place, about fifteen miles west of Shreveport, August 25, accusing them of stealing corn out of his field, in 1876.

DE SOTO PARISH

192d. Frances Louis, shot badly by a white man named William Harrison on Bill Hall's place, in the year 1870.

193d. George Barber, badly whipped by white men, at or near Grand Cane, Wiggin's place, in 1874.

194th. John Coleman, killed by a white man named James Paton, at or near Keachie, in April, 1875.

195th. George Freeman, killed by armed white men, at or near Clinton, and thrown in a creek, in 1871.

196th. Nathan Pratt, killed by armed white men, at or near Sam Edmond's place, in Caddo Parish, in 1870; reason, voting Radical ticket. Sixteen miles from Shreveport.

197th. William Smith, killed at or near Keachie, by white men, in 1874.

198th. Elias Flood, badly beaten by John Fish, white, at or near Keachie, in 1874.

199th. Thales Clarence, badly whipped by Charley Shaler, white, at or near Keachie, in 1872.

200th. Amos Smith, badly whipped by Silas Mason (white), on Mrs. Ward's place, in 1875.

201st. Antoine Williams, killed by armed white men, 1873.

202d. Houston Thomas, badly whipped by white men at or near John Holmes' place, in 1874.

203d. Brant Slone, killed by Samuel Marglaton (white), about seven miles from Mansfield, on his place, in 1868.

204th. William Jones, killed by white men, one mile from Mansfield, in 1868.

205th. Gabe White, killed by Lewis Tidwell (colored), about 1½ miles from Mansfield, and is not yet arrested—1874.

206th. Bill Wilson, killed by Owen Porter, at or near Mark ————, on Sabine River, in 1873.

207th. David Silas, killed by Joe Dickerson (white), on the river road, about two miles from Mansfield, in 1870.

208th. Henry Thomas, killed by white men on Mr. Alexander's place, in 1867.

209th. John Cotton, whipped badly by Albert Kidd (white), on his place, in 1866.

210th. Alexander Porter, beaten severely on John Sheldon's place, in 1874.

211th. Simon Hall, badly beaten by white men on J. Sheldon's place, because he was Radical, in 1874.

212th. George Barbery, beat badly by white men on John Wagoner's place, because he said he was a Radical from head to foot, in 1874.

213th. Miss Lily and Lidie Ford (colored), badly beaten, even the blood beat out of her, and two daughters badly beaten by the same white men because she would not let them sleep with her. One of them who whipped her was Bishops, on his place, about two and a half miles from Mansfield, in 1873.

214th. Frank Handy, shot by Bill Harris (white), on William Harris' place, in 1868.

215th. Climer Birdie, killed by a white man on Bob Acres' place, in 1867.

216th. Jack Davis, killed by white men on Leveny Hardee's place. Shot through the back of the house, July, 1873.

217th. Ned Casey, killed by John Moore (colored), on Remell place, in 1871.

218th. Lottie Samples, badly whipped by Wash. Samples, on his place, in 1868, '69, '70, '71, '72, and 1873.

219th. Miss Louise was badly whipped by Wash. Samples, on his place, in 1868, '69, '70, '71, '72, and 1873; also whipped my brother. We have lived with Mr. Samples for 13 or 14 years. I was whipped severely in 1872. This is my own statement.

LOUISA SAMPLES, *Colored*

220th. Sam Maybury, whipped near to death by Lord Hill and Henry Smith, white men. He afterward died from the effects of the beating. This was in Mansfield, in December, 1865. Several other white men helped to beat him.

221st. A young colored man was killed on John McMillen's place by a colored man, in 1873.

222d. Henry West, badly whipped by Butler Williams, in or near Mansfield, November 2d, 1874, and since beat him near to death.

223d. An old man (colored) was killed by Hersel ———, a white man, about cotton, while on their way to Shreveport, in the road, 1866.

224th. George, a colored man, killed on John McMillen's place by a white man, in 1873.

225th. Nancy Brooks, badly whipped by Davis, a white man, on Hammond Scott's place, in 1873.

226th. Henry Alexander, badly whipped by Justers, a white man, now at or near Shreveport, in 1871.

CADDO PARISH

227th. Hiram Coleman, whipped and beat on the head with a six-shooter by two white men, at or near Shreveport, in 1870.

228th. Old man Jack Horse and son was badly beat and shot at by white men—they were as bloody as hogs—at or near Jack Horse's place, going to the election November 7, 1870.

229th. Old man Mack Sambola, killed by a colored man.

230th. Louis Page, killed by Bill Anderson (colored), between Black's place, Holingworth, in 1873.

231st. Mary Allen (colored), whipped by Williams Henrick, on his place, in 1874.

232d. Ned Elis, badly whipped by Borne McMillan, white, on his place, in 1868.

233d. William Smith, badly beaten by David Adams, white, at or near Spring Ridge, in 1874.

234th. John Williams, badly beat by James Fullove, white, on his place, in 1873.

235th. Feary White, badly beat by Taton Fullove on his place, in 1874.

236th. John Draggs, killed by white men because he was holding colored meeting at or near Cotton Seed Point, in 1868.

237th. Pine Hill George, badly whipped by white men on Rance Cole's place, in 1868.

238th. Daniel Berry, shot badly by Bill Boatman, and died since from the effect of his wound, at or near Lick Kittles, in 1868.

239th. Reeves Lake, shot by John Lake on his place, and has since died from his wound, in the year 1867.

240th. Dick Lakes, killed by white men at or near Lickskillet, in 1867.

241st. Edmond Adams, shot by armed white men on Mr. Robinson's place, in 1867.

242d. Rufe Hunter, shot by Luke Marks, white, on Marks's place, at or near Summer Grove, in 1868.

243d. Bob Owen Hinges, killed by white men on J. W. Pickens' place, in 1867.

244th. Gustaves Guse, badly whipped by Mack Marion, white, at or near his place, at Sunny Groves, in 1873.

245th. Willis Rogers, badly whipped and throat cut and nearly killed by Capt. Wm. Cotts, on Andrew Pickens' place, at or near Sunny Grove, in 1871.

246th. Friday Ward had his arm broke by Mack Moring, white, at or near Sunny Grove, in 1872.

247th. Walton Goss, badly whipped by Dr. Harris, white, on his place; also David Goss, whipped badly by Dr. Harris on his place, in 1874.

248th. Delia Goss, badly whipped by Dr. Harris; also, he whipped my children whenever he wanted to, and I could not help myself. All was done by Dr. Harris, and on his place, in 1874.

249th. Peter McCrary was badly beaten by Cicen Steven and Davis Lee. He was staked out by his feet and hands in front of a grocery store on Widow Pickens' place, at or near Keachie, because he said they were drabs,* 1874.

250th. Jones, colored, killed by a white man, in 1872.

251st. Able Johnson, killed at or near Shreveport, by a colored man, in 1871.

252d. John Lebanon, killed by a white man, in 1874.

253d. Albert Gifford, killed by a white boy, in 1872.

254th. Members, a colored man, taken from John Johnson's brick-yard, and killed by John Johnson and other white men, in 1868.

256th. Jim Jinkins, killed about six miles from Shreveport, by Joe Bowls, David Simpson, and Sandy Jones, white men, in 1874.

257th. Old man Mead (colored), killed by Thomas Coots, in De Soto Parish, in 1868.

258th. Lamn, a colored man, wounded by Jules Pomner and Thomas Coots, white men, 1866.

---

* Men who patronized prostitutes.

259th. Frances Moses, whipped nearly to death by John Gambles (white), September, 1865.

260th. Alsee, a colored boy about 14 years of age, was beaten nearly to death on James M. Wilson's place, about or near Shreveport, Louisiana, by Neal Wilson (white), October 15 or 16, 1875.

261st. George Campbell, badly shot by W. M. Blackwell, a white man, and Markus Johnson, a colored man, accused of disturbing the peace of the city of Shreveport, in or near Shreveport, on or about the 16th day of October, in the year of our Lord 1875.

262d. Hartman Jones, killed by white men on Dr. Corres' plantation, in 1868.

CADDO PARISH

263d. Henry Clay, killed by John Harris (white), on the lake, about three or four miles from Morning Port, near Mr. Jackson's plantation, in 1873.

264th. Manuel Watley, killed by Dick Harrison and brother, on John Hamilton's plantation, 1868.

265th. Samuel Betman, killed by Dave Bithloman (white), at Albany Landing, on Caddo Lake, in 1868.

266th. George Carter, badly whipped by Bill Longley (white), on his place, in 1874.

267th. Sally Kimmon, badly beaten and her arm broken by Sam Patterson (white), in 1871.

268th. Milles Simn, badly whipped and stabbed, because she did not want to sleep with him, except he would marry her, and he would not marry her. This was done by a white man named Bill Langly, in 1872.

269th. Adam Thomas, badly whipped by Nathan Harris (white), at Parnell's store, in 1875.

270th. Pete Marlow, badly whipped by white men on Mrs. Pickens's plantation, at or near Sunny Grove, 1874.

271st. Bob Richmond, badly whipped by armed white men, at or near Harrell plantation, and his clothes taken off, 1870.

272d. Ben. Harris, killed by white men on Bill Acres' plantation, in the year 1874.

273d. Harvey Cornell, killed by white men on Samuel Edmond's plantation, in 1869.

274th. Simon (colored), killed by white men on Sam Acres' plantation, in 1870.

275th. Frances Anderson, badly whipped by white men on Bill Simpson's plantation, by Bill Simpson and others, 1870.

276th. Dick Garder, badly whipped by white men on Bill Simpson's plantation, in 1870.

277th. Handy Davis (colored), badly whipped by Joe Davis (white), on his plantation in 1873.

278th. Burritt Mitchell, killed by white men at or near Greenwood, in the year 1870.

279th. Argell Parker, killed by white men; taken from his house at night, about two miles from Mourningport, 1868.

280th. Wilson Parker, killed by white men on his father's place, at or near Mourningport, 1870.

281st. Simon Hunting, killed by white men about two miles from Mourningport, 1870.

282d. Bill Goings, killed by white men about two miles from Mourningport, in 1870.

283d. Mandid (colored), killed by white men about two miles from Mourningport; these were all killed for holding club meeting in 1870.

284th. Joe Lewis, shot by white men about two miles from Mourningport, in 1870.

285th. Albert Jackson, shot by white men, on Dick Harrison's plantation, in 1866.

286th. James Mitchell, badly whipped by Billy Harrison (white), on Dick Harrison's plantation, in 1866.

287th. Two colored men found dead at or near Carroll Jones' plantation, back of the old field grave-yard, April 23, 1875.

288th. General Green (colored), killed or beat to death by Henderson, a white man, on Little Levee Bend plantation, 1868.

289th. Louis Clarke, badly whipped by Albert Grister, on his plantation, a white man, 1873.

290th. Albert Rainey, badly whipped by Albert Grister (white), on his plantation, in 1873.

291st. Edmond (colored), killed by white men on Washington's plantation, 1869.

292d. A colored man, name unknown, killed by white men on Wimmis' plantation, about two miles and a half from Shreveport, Caddo Parish, in the year 1868.

293d. Mary Allen, colored, whipped by Henrick on old John Henrick's plantation, in 1874.

294th. John Williams, shot by white men, headed by Bill Barton, on John Jones' plantation, in 1866.

295th. George Grise, killed by a lick in the head with a rod of iron, by Eli Coleman, white, on his plantation, in 1868.

296th. Silas Porter was badly cut with a knife by Eli Coleman, white, on his plantation, in 1868.

297th. Marsh Johnson, badly beaten by Thomas Jourdan and Bill Coleman (both white), on Eli Coleman's plantation, in 1868.

298th. Dick White, shot by white men at or near Sunny Grove, in 1874, about his crop.

299th. Bob White, hung by white men at or near Sunny Grove, on Mrs. Picken's, and then thrown in the river, 1868.

300th. Richard Jones, badly whipped by Lite Marks, on his place, in 1870, simply because he was not afraid of him.

301st. Elder Marks, by Lite Marks and other white men, on Marks's plantation, in 1870.

302d. Dick Jackson, shot by armed white men near Greenwood, Caddo, in 1868.

303d. Rufus Bowles, badly whipped by Caspen Cottes, white, in 1873.

304th. Alex. Hamilton, badly whipped by Little Marks, on his plantation, in 1872.

305th. Toney Lee, badly whipped by Caspen Cottess, white, on his plantation, in 1868.

306th. John Daton was badly whipped by Sam. Madison, white, and other white men, on Madison plantation; accused of stealing a saddle, and afterward put in jail, 1874.

307th. James Henrick, killed by white men on Mrs. Morres's plantation, in 1867.

308th. Elbert, colored, killed on government land by white men, in 1870.

309th. George, colored, killed by white men at or near Converse Mills, in 1870.

310th. Elijah Johnson, colored, killed by George Johnson, white, on Micky Johnson's plantation, at or near Spring Ridge, in 1868.

311th. Cato Robinson, shot by a white, at or near Shreveport, in 1868.

312th. Neuse Reeves, shot by a white man at or near Shreveport, in 1874.

313th. Robert Johnson, killed by men, in 1868.

314th. James Watson, killed by Joe Parker, near the Four Mile Springs, for voting Radical ticket, in 1868.

315th. Asa Dorten, killed by Isaac Johnson, colored, near Claiborne Feastor's plantation, in 1870.

316th. Henry Davis, killed by Manuel, colored, on C. Foster's plantation, in 1870.

317th. Daniel Eaderoy, killed by Joe Daniels, colored, at or near Crow's plantation, 1871.

318th. Bright Mitchell, killed by white men at or near Greenwood, in 1868.

319th. Capus Holt, killed by Bill Boatman at or near Greenwood, in 1868.

320th. James Turner, badly whipped by Parson Doty and other white men on Dowty's plantation, 1871.

321st. Louis Coleman, badly whipped by William White, a white man, on White's plantation, in 1871.

322d. Coleman, colored, killed on Epps's plantation, and two other colored men, one hung, one shot, by white men, in 1867; names unknown.

323d. Manuel Gregory, hung by white men for talking to a white girl at or near Briton Bayou, six miles from Shreveport, in 1874.

324th. Mack Williams, killed by Sam Coleman on Eli Coleman's place, in 1872.

325th. Henry Bellas, killed by being beat to death by Allen Dimerice and other white men, at or near Shreveport and Bob Carres' plantation, 1870.

326th. Moses Dundo, shot on Rhodes' plantation by a colored man, in 1875.

327th. Asa Camby, killed by Jack McFalland and Wm. Lowells, in 1866.

328th. Jack Vance, killed by white men and burnt, in 1874.

329th. Frank Page, whipped badly by Jack Davidson, white, on Gasgrove plantation, in 1871.

330th. Jeff, colored, killed on Rulfort place by white men, in 1866.

331st. Anthony, colored, shot at or near Fortison Miles' by white men, 1873.

332d. Charley Williams, killed on Dr. Regan's plantation by colored men, in 1872.

333d. Abe. Young, shot by white men on Angles plantation, spouting about voting Republican ticket, in 1874.

334th. Dan Dixon, shot by a colored man on Lodon place, in 1874.

335th. Henry Stephen, shot on Jack Harris' plantation, in 1873; and Bill Young, shot by Wash. Young on Page's plantation, in 1873.

336th. Dick Jackson, whipped, tied hand and feet, and then shot near Caddo Lake, in 1870.

337th. Jack Johnson, shot by Kite Gooden, colored, near Greenwood, in 1873.

338th. Nancy, colored, killed by a colored man on Page's plantation, in 1867.

339th. Frank Dawson, whipped and shot by Willis Albert on Albert's plantation, in 1874.

340th. Marshall Cato, beaten over the head with a six-shooter by a white man, in 1874.

341st. Six colored men hung, Vance's, Good's plantation, names unknown, by white men, in 1869.

342d. Ceaser Johnson, colored, killed by Walton, colored, on Gordon plantation, in 1871.

343d. Wallace, colored, killed by Frank Black, colored, a Democrat, at Allen's brickyard, near Shreveport, 1874.

344th. Wilson, colored, killed by Jack Wiggins, colored, on Mrs. Hart's plantation, in 1872.

345th. Albert Hamilton, badly whipped by Dr. Davis on his plantation, in 1874.

346th. Hannibal Jones, badly beat by Dr. Davis, white, about his cotton accounts and crops, in the city of Shreveport, in 1873.

347th. Old man Lory, colored, killed by a white man on Frank Logan's plantation, in 1868.

348th. Louis Gray, killed by white men on the lake, in 1868.

349th. Thomas Jackson, killed by armed white men at Mourningport, in 1868.

350th. Russel Johnson, badly whipped by white men in Shreveport, in 1874.

351st. Jerry Green, colored, killed by Robert Logan, colored, on Charley Baley's plantation.

352d. Reeves Lake, badly wounded and since died, shot by Long Shaw and another white man, half a mile from Lickett, 1867.

353d. Dick Lake, killed by the same crowd at the same place, in 1867.

354th. John Bowan, killed by Jack King, colored, on Mrs. Bruin's plantation, in 1871.

355th. Walton Hill, badly whipped by Dr. Scurves, white, on his plantation, year unknown.

356th. Robert Owen, killed by armed white men two miles from Sunny Groves, for voting the Republican ticket, in 1868.

357th. Dick Albatross, colored, killed by John Lee, colored, on Gordon plantation, in the year 1872.

358th. Ander Eliza Lacy, badly whipped by white men, who went to her house in the night on Merceo's plantation, name unknown, in 1868.

359th. Calvin, colored, was run from Johnson's plantation, about six or seven miles, and then killed, in 1868.

360th. David R. Johnson, whipped by Newton Glover, white, in Homer, in 1874.

CLAIBORNE PARISH

361st. Bob Reese, badly whipped by Peter Meantio, white, in Homer, in 1874.

362d. William Madison, colored, killed by white men at or near Colquate, officers of election, in 1868.

363d. Burch Frilley, killed by white men at or near Colquate, in 1875.

364th. Miles Dickerson, badly whipped by white men on Mrs. Hill's plantation, in 1868.

365th. Scott Ranger, whipped by white men on Burch plantation, in 1868, near Homer.

366th. John Roberson, badly whipped by white men at Homer, in 1868.

367th. Sidney Rogers, wounded by white men and since died, in Homer, in 1873.

368th. M. Elmore, badly whipped by Furgerson, white, in Homer, in 1873.

369th. Sam Williams, shot by Peter Demento (white), in Homer, in 1874.

370th. John Lee, badly whipped by James Whitaker, in Homer, in 1868.

371st. Mattie Lee, badly whipped by same party, in 1874.

372d. Jeannette Litman, badly whipped by same party, 1872.

373d. Mite Parker, whipped badly by Peter Demento on his plantation, in 1868.

374th. Edmund Mitchell, badly whipped by Silas Clark, white, on his plantation, in 1869.

DE SOTO PARISH

375th. Adam Peterson, badly beaten by William Jourden on his plantation, in 1869.

376th. Moses, colored, badly whipped by white men on Charley Chase's plantation, in 1874.

NATCHITOCHES PARISH

377th. Henry Hunter, badly whipped by Charley Chase, white, on his plantation, in 1874.

378th. Singmore Louis, badly whipped by white men at or in Natchitoches Parish, names unknown, 1874.

379th. Louis Jones, killed by Charley Chase on his place, because he did not go to pounding when he told him to. This was in 1873.

SABINE PARISH

380th. Molton Pluntel, killed by a white man, name unknown, because she refused to make a fire when he told her, at or near Pleasant Hill, 1868.

381st. Brown, colored, killed by white men about two miles from Fort Jessee, in 1867.

382d. Canus Wright, killed by white men, taken out of jail and hung at Fort Jessee, in 1868.

383d. Frances, colored, beaten nearly to death by Mack Armstrong and Brooks, white men, because she refused to live with Armstrong any longer. This was on Joe Wood's plantation, in 1870.

384th. Miss Morris, colored, severely beaten by Thomas Armstrong, white, on his plantation near Rains' Mills Co., in 1868, she being enceinte at the time about five months.

385th. Tarvey Harrison, killed on Mr. D. Blackshade's plantation, a white man, in 1869, accused of voting a Republican ticket.

386th. John Jackson, killed by white men on his own place, in 1872.

387th. George Kenneday, hung by white men; he was taken from J. Vilman's plantation, and taken out on the railroad, in 1867—about doing his duty.

388th. Hannah Jackson, badly whipped by Lansing Rains, white, on his place, because she refused to let him take her child.

389th. Margeretta, colored, badly whipped by John Woods, white, on his plantation, in 1874.

390th. Elijah Molby, killed by white men named Fernis, Gear, and Brother, in 1874. They tried to take his wife away from him in the woods, in 1874.

391st. Hamp Gibbs, killed by white men because he would not live with his owners. His old master was instrumental in having him killed, Mr. Gibbs doing the deed, in 1867.

392d. George Camby, hung by white men on Jeff. Villman's plantation, in 1868, no cause.

393d. Moses Thompson, hung by white men on Jack Thompson's plantation, in 1867.

394th. Jones Jurdan, killed by Jedro Sims, white, on Jedro plantation, in 1867.

395th. Mack Armstrong, killed by Captain Finlay, white, at or near Pleasant Hill, in 1866.

396th. John Davis, killed by white men, at night, in 1870. Place unknown.

397th. Jessie Argylis, killed by a colored man at Cornells' Mills, in 1872.

398th. Sandy Martin, killed by a colored man with a rock and thrown overboard, in 1874.

399th. Andrew Mitchell, whipped by Joe Bolls, white, on his place, in 1871.

400th. Aaron Marsh, badly whipped by George Cowers, white, and brother, on his plantation, in 1874, near Spring Ridge.

401st. Elijah Swanson, badly whipped by John Caldwell, white, in his stable, in March, 1874.

DE SOTO PARISH

402d. Ross Hall, killed by B. S. Horton and his company, white men, on Ned Edmond's place, in 1865.

403d. Silas Fuller, beat with a six-shooter by John Fisher, white, on Nat More's plantation, in 1873.

404th. Peter Hunter, killed by Sam Hopgood, white, on B. Davidson's plantation, in 1869.

405th. Ben. Green, killed by Sam Hopgood and others, whites, on B. Davidson's plantation, in 1870.

406th. Asa Hogan, badly whipped by a white man, name unknown, at or near Mansfield, in 1874.

407th. Asa, colored, killed by Thomas Hopgood on B. Davidson's, at or near Grand Cane, in 1870.

CADDO PARISH

408th. Solomen Simms, killed by white men at or near Mackkidge Johnson's plantation, because he held club meetings, in 1868.

409th. Silvia Brown Lee, colored, badly whipped by Jack Ward and his men, all white, to make her tell where they would find her husband. This was in 1868.

410th. Rube Williams, colored, shot at by Doctor Blackwell, white, in Shreveport, in 1874.

411th. John McGruer, colored, killed by whites in election times. Ed. Stringer did the killing, in 1868.

412th. Bob Gray, killed by Charley Washington, white, in 1868.

413th. John Miplass, colored, killed by Daniel Adams, colored, at Shreveport, in 1870.

414th. Meams Fielas, colored, badly whipped by some party, 1870.

415th. David Robinson, colored, whipped by Dick Vincent, white, in Bossier Parish, in 1874.

416th. Thomas Reason, colored, badly whipped by Thomas Johnson, white, in Macky's brickyard, Shreveport, 1874.

417th. Albert Bates, colored, badly whipped by Thomas Anderson, white, at Shreveport, in 1875.

418th. William Gaines, colored, killed by Jim Stewart, colored, at or near Shreveport, in 1870.

419th. Newton Stevens, colored, killed by white men, on John Page's place, in 1868.

420th. Henry Dixon, colored, killed by armed white men, on John Page's plantation, in 1868.

421st. Anderson, white, killed at Bean's place, in 1868.

422d. Marshall Davis, killed at Bean's place, in 1868.

423d. Henry Allen, killed by William Harris, white, on his father's plantation, in 1873.

424th. Ralph Murrell, killed by Dan Curvis, white, an old man, Langley Plantation, about 9 miles from Mourningport, 1873.

425th. Lizzie Coleman, badly whipped by Langers Bigaman and Borington, white men, in 1875.

426th. John Semmes, badly beat, then hung by armed white men, in 1869.

427th. Davis Jackson, badly whipped, hung afterward, but not killed, by armed white men, in 1869, on public road.

428th. Ellen Jones, badly whipped by Large Thomasson, white, on his plantation, in 1869.

429th. Mary Camps, beat badly over the head by James Full-groves, jr., in 1873.

430th. George Rogers, badly whipped by Jack Hollingsworth, white, on his plantation, in 1870.

431st. Hiram Smith, whipped by William Davis, white, on Mrs. Walker's plantation, in 1875.

432d. Eliza Flood, badly beat over the head with a Derringer, by John Fisher, white, in 1874.

433d. Louisa Jones, whipped by D. A. Simpson, white, on Aleck Simpson's plantation, in the year 1867.

434th. Giles Gibbs (colored), badly whipped, and then tied to a horse and dragged about five miles through creeks, lakes, with the rope around his neck. This was done by D. D. Simpson and other white men on his place, in 1875.

435th. Adelaine Key badly whipped on his (D. A. Simpson's) plantation, and by him, in 1871.

436th. Rosamond Jones, whipped by D. A. Simpson on his plantation, in 1874.

437th. John Hopps, killed by Lards Warner (white), on Cleman's plantation, on the 10th day of September, 1873.

438th. David Rachel (colored), killed by Dick Johnson (colored), on Sam Washington's plantation, 6 miles from Shreveport, 1870.

439th. Frank Rachel (colored), killed by the same man and on the same place, in 1870.

440th. Beckitama Rachel, shot by the same man on the same place, in 1870.

441st. Leo (colored), whipped by white men at the race track, in 1870.

CLAIBORNE PARISH

442d. Jones (colored), shot about voting a Radical ticket at or near Haynesville, by white men, 1874.

443d. Green Jackson, badly whipped with a hand-saw, and will never get over it. Also several more on the same place. Done on old James Smith's place, by white men, in 1868.

444th. Ned Neally, shot and badly hurt by white men, on James Smith's place, in 1868.

445th. Richard Green, badly beat by white men, on James Smith's plantation, for voting a Republican ticket, 1866.

446th. Isom (colored), shot by James Blacksock, on James Nocks' plantation, and will not recover, in 1873.

447th. Adelaine Mackwell, badly whipped by white men, on Jack Markwell's plantation, three miles from Hayneville.

448th. Louise Tippet, killed by being beaten by white men, on Ashbury Hillie's plantation—one man did the killing—in 1868.

449th. Henry Ham, shot by Thomas Larkins (white), on Tyler's plantation, in 1873.

450th. Calvin Owens, badly whipped by Jack Daniels (white), on his plantation, trying to make her work, 1873.

451st. Wash. Casselin, badly whipped by Ned and James Vance, brothers (white), on J. Vance's place, in 1868.

452d. Nelson Moore, badly beaten by John Molton (white), on Molton's plantation, in 1873.

453d. Jack Shanbress (colored), badly whipped and shot by white men, on Bob Bower's plantation, because he was president of a Republican club, in 1868.

454th. Ben. Gardner (colored), badly beaten by white men, on Mr. Gamble's plantation, because he refused to stay on the place another year. This was in 1874.

455th. Mint Mocks, badly beaten by white men, because he refused to live on the place any longer; this was in 1872.

456th. Bob Gleeten (colored), badly whipped by white men, on Doctor Macede's plantation, in 1870.

457th. David Lane (colored), wounded by Lock Flestoon (white), on his plantation in Homer, 1873.

458th. Ben Chapman, beat nearly to death by Ned Litman, on Ned Litman's plantation, in 1874.

459th. Sam Cooper (colored), beat nearly to death by Bob Roberts (white), and also took away his son and carried him to Texas, 1870.

460th. Caroline Lee, badly whipped by Dave Penton (white), because she would not bind her children to him, on his plantation, in the year 1870.

461st. Henry James (colored), badly whipped by white men, at or near Calquarte, in 1873.

462d. John, a colored man, killed by fifteen white men, in or near Haynville; accused of asking a white lady an unfair question, 1872.

463d. Joe Norton, colored, killed by Henry Norton, colored, on old man Doton's plantation, 1870.

464th. Asa, a colored man, killed by white men at or near Lisbonville; also another colored man, name unknown, killed at the same time and place, and by the same crowd, 1870.

465th. Mingo Edmunds, whipped and run off from his home by white men, in 1868.

466th. Martin Jefferson, colored, beat, kicked, and taken from his home and has never been seen since; done by white men, in 1875.

467th. Dick Hashlin, colored, badly beaten by old man Tungles on his plantation, in 1868.

468th. Harris Payne and Emily Payne, colored, beat by white men on Aston Payne's plantation, in 1867.

469th. Pensey Long, colored, badly beat in the woods by Bill Hays and other white men, in the year 1872.

470th. Ben Jackson, colored, badly beat by Sam and Bill Hays, white, on Bill Hays's plantation, in 1872.

471st. James Hill, colored, beaten by Louis Bowen and other whites, George Price's plantation, in 1871.

472d. George Hill, colored, badly beat by white men on Westley Grater's plantation, in 1871.

473d. Jack Barrows, colored, badly beat by white men on Mrs. Norman's plantation; her son and Newte Glenner and another white man did the whipping, in 1870.

474th. Taylor Bittell, colored, badly whipped by Newte Glenner, white, on Mrs. Norman's plantation, 1870.

475th. Jerry Hamilton, colored, cut with an axe on the head by Ben Adkins and nearly killed. Adkins was a colored man; done at Homer, in 1875.

476th. Thomas Willis, colored, badly whipped and laid up three months by Joe Neally and other whites, 1874.

477th. Morris Brown, colored, badly beat by Mark and Park Shaw, white, on J. Overte's plantation, 1871.

478th. Wash McAdams, colored, badly beat by armed white men at or near Bedford Place, in 1868.

479th. John Russian, colored, badly beat by white men near Bedford Place, in 1868.

480th. James Morse, colored, killed by white men on Mr. Thomas's plantation; accused of asking a white girl a delicate question, 1869.

481st. McCready Blackman, colored, killed by white men on Dr. Skeel's plantation, 1866.

482d. Margaret Carves, colored, killed by John Love, a white man, on Dr. Carves' plantation, in 18—.

483d. John Carter, colored, badly whipped by white men on the road about two miles from Lisbon, in 1872.

484th. Wash Edmonds, colored, badly beat by white men in Homer, in 1875.

485th. Mollie Kembrow, colored, badly whipped by white men on Dr. Madruke's plantation, 1868.

486th. Eliza Smith, colored, badly whipped by Frank Hall on his plantation about not being able to work while sick, 1868.

487th. Louis, a colored man, killed by R. Brown, white, on his plantation, 1870.

488th. Steele Core, colored, killed by John Blackman, colored, on Burrell Johnson's plantation, 1870.

489th. Bedford Green, colored, badly whipped by Asa Adams and Bill Allen, whites, on Allen's plantation, 1870.

490th. Everith Alvery, badly whipped by white men on Dr. Mark's plantation, because he was president of a Republican club, 1868.

491st. Richard Meeders, colored, badly whipped by Nester, Glover, and other white men, in 1868.

492d. Blanch Anne Morgan, colored, badly whipped by old man Tungles, white, on his plantation, 1870.

493d. Lorania Parks, colored, badly whipped and beat with a six-shooter over the head by J. Tungles, white, in 1870.

494th. Wiley Morgan, colored, badly beat and his eyes knocked out by Joe Tungles, on his plantation, in 1870.

495th. Hannah Langly, colored, beat near to death by armed white men concerning cotton on Henry Clarke Porter's plantation, in 1870.

496th. Nelson Moore, colored, dragged by a horse and badly beat, from which he will not recover, simply because he would not live with John Nocks; done by white men, in 1871.

497th. Gives Bill, colored, badly whipped and kicked nearly to death by Law Ferguson, white, at Homer, in 1874.

498th. A colored man killed and thrown into the Larborn Creek, on or near George Garter's plantation, in 1874.

499th. Thomas Marks, colored, killed by white men at or near Dutch Town, in 1874.

500th. Aunt Emiline, colored, killed by Newt Glover, a white man, at or near ———, in 1868.

501st. Yerk Brown, colored, badly beat by white men on Trabor's place, in 1874.

502d. Henry Sham, colored, beat by white men on Ferguson's plantation, in 1871.

503d. Albert Brown, killed by whites on J. Garter's plantation, in 1868.

504th. Laura Henry, colored, badly whipped by white men because she refused to live on Jenkins' place, in 1870.

506th. Pleas Jash, colored, badly whipped by white men on George Garter's plantation, in 1870.

507th. Green Amos, colored, shot from back of the house by white men on George Garter's plantation, in 1873.

508th. A colored man, James, killed by George Calvin, colored, on Philip Travor's plantation, in 1873. He is now in Baton Rouge.

509th. George Hill, colored, badly beat by armed white men on Mark Garter's at or near Lisbon, in 1872.

510th. Dick Johnson, colored, badly beat and since died from the wounds; done by white men on Mrs. Cook's plantation, in 1872.

511th. Florida Johnson, colored, burned to death by white men about three and a half miles from Homer, in 1873.

512th. Henry Simmons, colored, killed while working in the field by white men five miles from Homer, in 1872.

513th. Antino Tipet, colored, killed by white men on old man Tipet's plantation, in 1868.

514th. Louis Epps, colored, badly whipped by George Garter, white, on his plantation, in 1875.

515th. Louis Epps, colored, badly whipped by George Garter, white, on his plantation, in 1875.

516th. Ned Sapps, colored, badly whipped by two of Tungles' sons about three miles from Homer on Tungles' place, in 1875.

517th. Phebe Louis, colored, shot by her husband, William Louis, colored, about one mile from Homer, in 1873.

518th. Henry Moore, colored, killed by white men and burned; accused of living with a white girl near Homer, in 1873.

519th. Luke Kenner, colored, killed by white men near Kenner's plantation; accused of harboring colored men, in 1873.

520th. Maurice, colored, killed by white men at or near Homer about his cotton, in 1867.

521st. Thomas Grisby, colored, killed by a colored man on Dr. Beatty's plantation, in 1874.

522d. Westley Gaster, colored, killed by John Grater's two sons on Godly plantation, in 1874.

523d. Louis Butler, colored, killed by colored men on Noxer plantation, in 1872.

524th. William Willis, colored, badly beaten by colored boys at or near Homer, J. Buttows, J. Carles, and others, in 1869.

525th. David, colored, killed by white men about voting on Thomas Nelson's plantation, in 1868.

526th. Berry Hill, colored, badly beaten with a six-shooter about voting, by William Allen and others, white, in 1868, Mineville.

527th. Isaac Dannel, colored, shot by Louis Brown, white, on John Harris's plantation; L. Brown trying to take his wife, in 1874.

528th. Cass Williams (colored), badly beat on Mr. Dickley's plantation, in 1874, by Jake and Keth Peckleys, whites.

529th. Randell Johnson (colored), shot by Joe Tungles (white) on George Grater's plantation, 1871.

530th. Henry Thomas (colored), killed by E. Olives (colored), on David Traler's place, 1873; was sent to penitentiary.

531st. Isaac Newton (colored), was killed by whites carrying his children from J. C. Tippett's plantation, and was put in the Middle Fork Creek, 1870.

LINCOLN PARISH

532d. Booker (colored), killed by Bolly Chambers (white), who tried to take Booker's wife from him, on Caldwell plantation, 1873.

BIENVILLE PARISH

533d. Peter Jones (colored), killed by white men on Jones's plantation, 1872.

WEBSTER PARISH

534th. Jack Crown (colored), beat to death by colored men on Crown's plantation, 1868.

535th. Eli Brigham (colored), badly beat by a white man at or near Minden, 1874.

536th. Martin Hadson (colored), shot by Cutler's sons (white) on Slanlessing's plantation, 1865.

537th. Willis Lunton (white) shot and killed Thomas Washington (colored) on T. Marzenia's plantation, 1868.

538th. Hanley Perry (colored), badly whipped by Clarence Bright (white) for wanting a settlement with him at Minden, 1865.

539th. John Wallace (colored), killed and put in a barrel, by white men, and thrown into the river eight miles from Minden, 1873.

540th. Henry Bullocks (colored), badly whipped by Willis Lucifer (white), on Thomas Marzenia's plantation, 1868.

541st. Abe McLaughin (colored), badly beat on old man Sliddell's plantation, or Killing plantation, 1868.

542d. Jane Hawkins, badly whipped by Lunchford and Runson, on Plump's plantation, both white, because she refused to live with them, 1868.

543d. Unknown colored man killed and thrown in a well by Mack and Thomas Crow (white), on Crow's plantation, ten miles from Minden, 1868.

544th. Andrew Williams (colored), whipped by Marzenia and other whites on his plantation, 1868.

545th. Dennis Cornelia (colored), badly beat by armed white men in the road three miles from Minden, 1872.

546th. Henry Wilson (colored), badly whipped by armed white men; year unknown.

547th. Jourdan Miles (colored), badly whipped by Louis Morrey and brother, white men, on McDonald's plantation, 1868.

548th. Albert Hanson (colored), whipped by Mr. Long (white), in 1868, on Cotter's plantation.

549th. Calvin, a colored man, whipped by armed white men about nine miles from Minden, 1871.

JACKSON PARISH

550th. Dick Harrow (colored), beaten by Squato Hopless in Vainville, 1871.

551st. Mason Harrison (colored), killed by white men in Trenton, 1872.

552d. Dick Hamilton (white), killed by Beales Turner (colored) on B. Shoulder's plantation, 1872.

553d. Dock Harris (colored), beaten by Sid Morcanery in Vinandrass Town, 1874.

554th. George Harris (colored), whipped by Dobe Axfort (white) in Minville, 1874.

555th. Frank Lenington, beaten by James W——— (white) in Vainville, 1872.

556th. Henry Jacobs (colored), killed by white men on Bob Yances' plantation, in 1866; also, Sam Thomas and Green Yances, killed by same white men on the same plantation, 1866.

557th. Toney Smith, burnt to death because he looked and laughed at a white girl on Lawes or Claly plantation, 1867.

558th. Harrison, colored, shot by white men on Rankins Thomas plantation, 1867.

559th. Elie Hamilton, colored, badly whipped by white men, because he voted a Republican ticket, 1868.

560th. Abram Shoulders, colored, and his three daughters badly whipped by white men, concerning his cotton and potato crop, 1868.

561st. Park Richards, colored, badly beaten, because he voted as he chose, by white men, on old man Richards' place, 1868.

562d. Aunt Polly Richards, badly whipped by John Shoulders, white, on his plantation, 1867.

563d. Peter Jones, colored, killed by Albert Pormoles, while moving from his to J. C. Jones's plantation, 1874.

564th. Cansson Tarleton, colored, beaten half to death, by Neute Smith, on plantation, 1874.

565th. Jim Whifleton, colored, beaten severely by white men; he will not recover. Done on Mr. Kide's plantation, in Trenton City, 1873.

566th. Morgan Shephard, colored, beaten by Buck Shoulders, a white man, on his father's plantation, 1874.

567th. Jessie Warrick, colored, killed by a white man named James Whorns, on Markilty plantation, in the year 1873.

568th. Mary Ann Harrow, badly whipped, and died from the wounds, on Mr. Tedd's plantation, 1866.

569th. Toney Walker, colored, killed by white men on Mr. Walker's plantation, 1873. Killed about a colored woman.

570th. Harris Romes, colored, badly whipped by white men, on Frank Price's plantation, 1872.

571st. John Coots, colored, badly beaten by white men, because he was president of a club, 1870.

572d. Wash Tarvers, colored, beat severely by white men, on Mrs. McLane's plantation, 1874.

573d. Bob Williams, colored, shot badly by Bill Casson, white, on his plantation, 1867.

574th. Jerry Kidd, colored, badly beat by white men, on Mr. Simpson's plantation, 1866.

575th. Jerry Simms, colored, badly beaten by white men, in the town of Trenton, 1872.

576th. Standford, a colored man, badly beaten by armed white men, on Mr. Jack Simms's plantation, 1874.

577th. Isaac Pearson, colored, badly whipped by armed white men, 1868.

578th. Mary Toade, colored, badly beaten by B. T. Kidd, on his plantation (white), 1867, in Claiborne Parish.

579th. John Domkins, colored, killed by white men, about five miles from Painville, 1866.

580th. Isaac Jerry, colored, killed by armed white men, on his own place, 1868.

581st. Ben, a colored man, was killed by white men, on the same place, 1868.

CLAIBORNE PARISH

582d. Barrett Telley, colored, killed by white men, on Mr. Rogers's plantation, 1874.

583d. Henry Willis, killed by white men, by being hung. He was taken from Willis's plantation, 1869.

584th. William Meeders, colored, killed by white men, because he held an office on Mrs. Smith's plantation, 1869.

585th. Beckett Wilson, colored, killed Pat McGold, colored; was sent to State penitentiary. Done 1873.

586th. Newton Hodge, colored, killed by white men; accused of having a white woman in the woods, 1873.

BIENVILLE PARISH

587th. Unknown colored man killed by white armed men, about seventeen miles from Mindon, 1873.

588th. Two colored men, names unknown, killed by armed white men, six miles from Mindon, 1872.

589th. Anderson Clark, colored, badly whipped by white men, on Mr. Lowry's plantation; accused of asking a white lady an impertinent question, 1868.

590th. Abe Jackson, colored, beat by white men on Mr. Thompson's plantation, about his crop, done 1867.

591st. A young colored man, name unknown, killed by white men and thrown into a creek called Boon Creek, near lake Bisteneau, 1868.

592d. Jasper Smith, colored, killed by white men on Vance's plantation, 1868.

593d. Henry Parker, colored, killed by a colored man named Martin Siplers, on Holler's plantation, 1867.

594th. Calvin, colored, killed by Dr. Moore, white, on Mrs. Adam's place, accused of cursing a white woman, 1871.

595th. Aunt Tapee, colored, whipped by white men on Mrs. Reed's plantation, 1871.

596th. Old man Bason, colored, killed by Mr. Lanton, white, on his plantation, 1872.

EAST BATON ROUGE PARISH

597th. Frank Hays, colored, was badly beaten and all his crops taken from him, about six or eight miles northeast of Port Hudson, on Frank Vons's plantation, and Mr. Frank Vons was captain of the crowd of armed white men who done it; all white men, 1876.

598th. Peter, colored, severely beaten by armed white men, on Mudide plantation, about four miles from Port Hudson, and all his crops taken, 1875.

599th. Jack, colored, was hung dead, by white men, on De Loche's plantation, about three miles from the town of Saint Martinville, because he sauced a white man. The white man wanted him to leave his crop and he refused, thereupon the white man got a crowd of white men and hung him, and taken his crop from his family; 1875, July.

600th. William Henry, colored, hung dead, by a large crowd of white men, about four miles east of Saint Martinville, because he refused to let them take his crop. This was done December, 1875.

601st. Five colored men, names unknown, were hung dead, by a large crowd of armed white men at or near a place called Carn Crow, about eight miles from the town of Saint Martinville. They were taken from their homes at night, in January, 1875.

EAST FELICIANA PARISH

602d. Picado Reilly, colored, badly beat by two white men, and put ropes around their necks and pretended they were going to hang them. Done on Mrs. Fletcher's plantation, about eight miles east of Bayou Sara, September, 1876.

603d. Abner Cariber, colored, badly shot by armed body of white men on Stairn Hill plantation, about five miles east of Bayou Sara, October, 1875.

604th. Louis Washington, colored, was badly beaten over the head with a six-shooter, and considerably blooded by the same body of white men, on the same place, October, 1875.

695th. Sarah Parker (colored) was badly beat and her head cut with a six-shooter by armed white men on the Share Hill plantation on or about October, 1875.

606th. I was shot at, and my life threatened, and I was run off from my crop, and it was all taken from me by a crowd of armed white men, on Mrs. Fletcher's plantation, about thirteen miles east of Bayou Sara, August, 1875.

SAMUEL CHENEY

607th. I was run off and all my crop taken from me, and my life threatened, by five armed white men on Wash Edwards's plantation, about six and a half miles east of Bayou Sara, September, 1875.

ISAAC COATES

608th. Louis Smith was run off from his crop and all taken from him by a crowd of armed white men; his life threatened; his house broke open, and he was threatened by note being posted on the roadside; done about five miles from Bayou Sara, on Alex. Lile's plantation. September, 1875.

HENRY ADAMS

U. S. Scout

BOSSIER PARISH

609th. Ishman Bob (colored), killed at Benton, by white men, 1868.

610th. Marshall Davis (colored), killed at Greely's plantation, 1868.

611th. Louis Hefft (colored), killed at M. Ball's plantation, 1868.

612th. Rev. B. Membs (colored), killed at Dillard's plantation, 1868.

613th. Henry Harris (colored), drove from home to the woods for four months, 1874.

614th. A colored woman, name unknown, killed by white men. She was cut open, and her child taken out of her, and set side of her, being cut open while she was alive. Done by Ed. Stugles and another white man, near Dixiseé plantation, 1868.

615th. Three colored men, names unknown, found dead on Woolus Sweat's plantation, belonging to Mrs. Pickett, about one mile from the house, their throats cut; they were buried by Doarity, a white man, who ran the plantation, 1868.

DE SOTO PARISH

616th. Simus Riggs (colored), whipped near to death; arm broke by Dick Riggs and son, white men; done 1874.

617th. John Clinton (colored), runned off from Robert Scott's plantation, and his life threatened, 1875.

618th. Robert Parks (colored), beaten near to death over the head with a six-shooter, by Irvin Premins, a white man, in a grocery called McCracken, at or near Kingston, 1875.

619th. Silas Moore (colored), badly beat by Bill Samples (white), on his plantation, because he refused to vote the Democratic ticket, November, 1874.

620th. Simon Blandley (colored), beaten by white men, at or near Mansfield, because he voted the Republican ticket, November, 1874.

621st. Peter Hunter, killed by armed white men, on Bige Davidson's plantation, about fourteen miles from Keachie, southeast, and his crop taken away from his family, 1869.

622d. Asa Steward, colored, killed by armed white men in the night on the same place and by the same men; his crop also taken; done in 1869, and burned his corn.

623d. Andrew Johnson, colored: I was badly beaten and my arm broken by James Payton, a white man, at or near Keachie, in August, 1874, and my wife was run off his plantation and our things taken from us, also our child's things.

CADDO PARISH

624th. Samuel Smith, badly whipped and bloodied by Captain Scott, white, because he went to church without his consent; then made him run away and leave his crop; done July 4, 1875.

625th. Henry, colored, shot badly by Marion McMillen, white, on McMillen's plantation, and he has not been seen since. All of his crops was taken from him. Done July 5, 1878.

626th. Patsy McCready, colored, badly whipped by John Ellis, white, on his place; accused of pulling a watermelon. Done June, 1875.

627th. Jesse, colored, killed by Sam Coleman, white, and all his crops taken from his family. Done in June, 1875.

628th. Asa Giggs, colored, killed by white men on John Harris's place, over the lake, about eight miles from Mourningport, 1868.

629th. Wilson Parker, killed on John Harris's plantation by white men.

630th. Simmon Hunter, colored, killed by white men in the woods, 1868.

631st. John Jackson, colored, killed by Dr. Harris on John Harris's plantation; had his head shot off and cut open, 1868.

632d. Joe Fields, colored, shot by the same crowd of white men, on John Harris's plantation, 1868.

633d. John Waingus, colored, killed by the same crowd of white men on the same place, 1868.

634th. Parker, killed by the same crowd of white men and a hole dug and two colored men drove into it, 1868.

635th. Henry Johnson, colored, killed in 1873.

636th. Albert Mason, colored, killed in 1873.

637th. Lane McLane, colored, killed in 1872.

638th. John Angland, colored, killed in 1871.

639th. Reilly Fortbearry, colored, killed in 1871.

640th. John Philips, colored, shot in 1875.

641st. Isaac Bruce, colored, shot in 1871.

642d. Thomas Anderson, colored, shot in 1874.

643d. Archey Onealus, colored, shot in 1875.

644th. Corneus Potter, colored, wounded in 1875.

645th. Anthony Tramnel, colored, killed in 1875.

646th. Merrick Tramnel, colored, killed in 1875.

647th. Allen Coleman, colored, killed in 1875.

648th. Robert King, colored, killed in 1875.

649th. Nathan Virgin, colored, killed in 1875.

650th. Cannon Ermin, colored, killed in 1874.

651st. Nallie Rhodes, colored, killed in 1874.

652d. Sarah Frindle, colored, killed in 1874.

653d. Rev. Phil. Frenley, colored, killed in 1874.

Names of 24 unknown, colored, killed in 1874.

One hung, unknown, colored, killed in 1874.

MARION COUNTY

654th. Wash Porter, colored, killed in 1874.

655th. Miss M. Bateman, colored, killed in 1875.

656th. Henry Ragland, colored, killed in 1875, July.

657th. Jerry Peter, colored, killed in 1875, May.

658th. Two men, names unknown, colored, found dead in 1875, April.

659th. One woman, unknown, colored, found dead in 1875.

660th. George Hill, colored, killed in 1874, October, and a large number, whose names are unknown to us, killed in 1871, 1872, and 1873.

GROSBECK COUNTY

661st. Robert Sellers, colored, was killed on the night of July 15, 1875; some ten or fifteen white men came to his house and took him and shot him to pieces. He was living on McDaniel plantation.

662d. Nace Burgess, colored, was put in jail and taken out by a mob of white men in the same year.

663d. Sumner Abion, colored, was hung by white men. Old man Allen Strand was killed by the same crowd, and Bob King was shot by the same crowd—shot in pieces. All done at Springfield, Texas.

664th. Ten or more colored men were shot and cut to pieces. T. M. Hood was captain of them, and some of that same crowd told me they were going to kill every colored man for six miles around; and I know that ten colored men had to slip out to save their lives; and in Limestone, particular, the colored have to live in the swamp and woods to save their lives.

PARISH OF ORLEANS—ALGIERS

665th. James Murphy, colored, killed by a colored man at or near the ferry-boat, on or about January, 1875.

666th. An unknown colored man, by a white man, about three-quarters of a mile from the ferry-boat, in December, 1875.

667th. Eight colored men in New Orleans, La., were run off from West Feliciana, where they were given only six days to leave there. January, 1876.

668th. James Washington, colored, killed at or near Shreveport, Caddo Parish, in 1866.

669th. David Montgomery, colored, killed at or near Shreveport, by Joe Parker, white, 1870.

670th. Tim Taylor, killed by a white man in Caddo, in 1868.

671st. Miss Mandy Jackson, colored, whipped by two white men named Williams, 1874.

672d. Morris Simson, colored, whipped by a white man named Candy, 1874.

673d. Mango Reeves, shot by a white man in Caddo, in the year 1874.

674th. Julia Davis, colored, killed by Smith, the boss manager on the plantation, 1874.

675th. Dick Turban, colored, killed by a black man in Bossier Parish, in 1873.

676th. Ralph Morris, colored, killed by Dean Carey, white, at or near Carey Lowe, 1873.

677th. Henry Clay, colored, killed by Bill Harris, a white man, on his own plantation, 1873.

678th. Manuel Johnson, colored, killed by white men on John Hamilton's plantation, 1868.

679th. Cæsar Turner, colored, beaten near to death by J. Stephens, white, on Joe Thomas's plantation, 1875.

680th. Martin Singwell, colored, whipped by Calvin Crown, white, at or near Winghart, 1871.

681st. Henry Nichols, badly beaten by James Nolt, white, in the year 1871.

682d. Miss Salena Jetts, colored, whipped by Bill Alburt, white, on Youngblood plantation in 1874.

683d. James Metimus, colored, beaten by Billy Willfort, a white man, on Dr. Spempe's place, because he did not get out to work as soon as he wanted him to, 1868.

AFFIDAVITS OF COLORED MEN

No. 1.

De Soto Parish,

State of Louisiana:

My name is Edmond Jones. I have a place in this parish, but was run off from it for about thirteen months. So I then left the parish with my family. Mr. Joe McMolloine told my son that if I did not move back on my place that he and other white men would run anybody else off of that place that goes on it by my order, and put any one on it they please and ask me no odds, simply because I had agreed to rent it to a friend of mine, as I seen I could not live on it myself.

his
EDMOND + JONES
mark

Witness:

 Henry Adams

No. 2.

De Soto Parish,

State of Louisiana:

My name is Anthony Witch. I live in De Soto Parish. I had to pay this year, 1874, twelve dollars tax, and I only had one horse and one cow and calf. Do not own any land, nor never owned any land, and a large number of us have been made to pay that much on three horses and cows; and if we do not pay the money right away they take our stock, and then make us pay a great deal more as taxes. We have all been prosecuted about taxes again this year, but we don't know what the amount will be, as we have only a few horses & cows.

his
ANTHONY ✕ WITCH
mark

No. 3.

CADDO PARISH,

   State of Louisiana:

My name is Mary Johnson, and I live in this parish by a white man named James Hill, at Flour Grove Plantation. I was accused of a crime I never dreamed of nor done. This was in 1872.

her
MARY ✕ JOHNSON
mark

Susanah Williams was badly beaten and whipped by a white man named Bill Allen, on his place, in the year 1868.

MARY JOHNSON

No. 4.

SHREVEPORT, CADDO PARISH,

   State of Louisiana:

I, Cæsar Robinson, make the following statement: I am a colored man. I settled a place on overflood land about three and a half miles west of Shreveport, at or near the lake; and I have about nine or ten acres improved and four houses built on it; and I have lived on the place for the past five years; and in the year 1875, in December, I went to Natchitoches to the United States land office, and I paid them fifteen dollars, and got my title to the land. The land agent told me to carry my papers to W. D. Willey and tell him to have them recorded for me in the court-house at Shreveport, and I did so, and Mr. Willey charged me nine dollars to have them recorded, yet he did not have my land recorded, nor did he give me my money back, neither my papers, nor can I get them from him. At the land office at Natchitoches they told me there was thirty acres of land in that tract. In January, 1876, Mr. Jewell told me to leave that place, also Mr. Willey. Mr. Jewell told me he would send me to State prison if I did not leave that place and leave everything there that I had made and built on that place. Nor would he let me move anything.

I am about eighty years of age; have a wife and one child. I had a good garden, but they have turned the stock in on it and destroyed it. I also had a very nice lot of fruit trees, such as apples, plums, peaches, &c., and he would not let me move any of them. This is the truth, so help me God.

his
CÆSAR X ROBINSON
mark

No. 5.

CITY OF EAST BATON ROUGE,
    State of Louisiana:

  At or near the city of East Baton Rouge, I seen on board of the Col. A. P. Kouns a colored man and his wife and one child, I think about six or seven years of age, who had taken passage from New Orleans to West Baton Rouge. But the captain on the A. P. Kouns carried them about twenty or twenty-five miles above Baton Rouge landing, for we passed Baton Rouge about 2 o'clock p. m., and they were put off about half past 4 o'clock p. m., on the same day. The captain did not land at Baton Rouge, but put them off on a coal barge about the distance as stated above, and left them to get back the best way they could. It was rainy and very cold, and rained nearly all night on the poor people who were then on the coal barge on the Mississippi River, a long ways above the town. This was about the 15th of March, 1876. The colored man begged the captain to land and put them off, as he had paid his fare for himself and family. But the captain would not land, but carried them up the river and placed them on the barge.

H. ADAMS

No. 6.

PARISH OF NATCHITOCHES,

State of Louisiana:

My name is Henry Albit. I went on board the steamer Col. A. P. Kouns, at Coushatta, and took passage in Red River Parish, and took passage to Grand Ecore, in Natchitoches Parish. But the captain would not land at the wharf for me to get off. I then asked the captain to put me off at Grand Ecore wharf, and he told me he would do so (that was when I took passage and was paying my fare), but when he landed his boat for me to get off it was at Alexandria, and he then told me if I did not get off or pay more fare he would go for me, and he would not be long about it either. So I was put off there, and had to pay my fare back to Grand Ecore on another boat. This February 8th, 1876.

REV. HENRY ALBIT

No. 7.

CADDO PARISH,

State of Louisiana:

We, George Underwood and Bellun Harris and Isaiah Fuller, make this statement: We live in the parish of Caddo, and worked, or contracted to work and make a crop on shares, on Mr. McCrowning's place, for one third we make or made, and McCrowning to furnish provisions or rations. But, in July, when we were working along in the field, Mr. Mack Morring and Mr. Mack Borrington came to us and said, "Well, boys, you all got to get away from here, for we have been going as far as we can, and you all must sign agreements, or you all must take what follows." They then went and got their sticks and guns and told us we must sign the papers, and we told them we would not sign it, because we did not want to give up our crops for nothing. They told us we had better sign, or we would not get anything. They said they only wanted justice; so we told them we would get judges to judge the crops, and to say what it is worth. But they told us no judges should come to see the crops, and we did not want to sign the paper. But they beat me (Isaiah), and then we got afraid and we signed the paper. We had about thirty acres in cotton, and it was the best cotton crop in that part of the parish, and we had about twenty-nine acres in corn. The corn was ripe and the fodder was ready to pull, and our cotton laid by. They then run us from the place, and told us not to come back any more. We owed Mr. Mack Morring one hundred and eighty dollars altogether. They then told us if they ever heard from us again they would fix us. During the time we was working and living on the place they did not half feed us, and we had to pay for half of our rations, or whatever we eat. We worked just as hard as if we were slaves, and in return was treated like dogs.

his

GEORGE + UNDERWOOD

mark.

his

BELLUN + HARRISS

mark

his

ISAIAH + FULLER

mark

No. 8.

Parish of De Soto,

   State of Louisiana:

My name is Albert Thomas; I work on Joe Williams's plantation, about two miles southeast of Keachie. On December 26, 1875, I was badly beaten by George Crow, a white man, on the above-named place.

ALBERT THOMAS

No. 9.

DE SOTO PARISH,

State of Louisiana:

My name is Hiram Smith; I lived on Joe Williams's place, about two miles southeast of Keachie. I asked Mr. Williams to pay me what he owed me on my cotton; also seventy-five dollars he had taken away from me, what another man had paid me. He jumped on me and beat me so badly I fear I cannot live. He made me crawl on my knees and call them my God, my master, the God of all power. They then drew revolvers on me; all because I had asked for a settlement. This was done on the 16th of March, 1876.

HIRAM SMITH

No. 10.

DE SOTO PARISH,

State of Louisiana:

My name is Primus Albert; I lived on Joe Williams's place. On the 5th of February, 1876, Mr. Joe Williams gave me a terrible beating with a buggy trace, striking me one hundred and two licks. I did nothing to merit it unless it was I worked for him too much like a slave.

PRIMUS ALBERT

No. 11.

BOSSIER PARISH,

State of Louisiana:

My name is Simon Dickson; I worked for Miss Lizzie Dickson, on her place, about sixteen or seventeen miles from Shreveport, north, on the bank of Old River, in the year 1873. I was due her the sum of twenty dollars. I made six bales of cotton and each bale weighed about six hundred pounds. I was to give her one hundred pounds to the acre, but she took all I made that year for the amount I owed her, twenty dollars. In 1874 I made eight and a half bales of cotton, weighing on an average about five hundred and twenty-five pounds to the bale. I was to give her one-half of what I made. But she again took all, and would not let me have any. I then owed her about forty dollars. She said I owed her about one hundred and fifteen dollars, so she taken all of my crop every year, for what she claimed I owed her, yet she would never tell me what anything cost. In 1875 I asked her to tell me what such and such things cost, but she refused to tell me. I asked her for the account sales of my cotton, but she would never give them to me, nor to any of us on her place, though she has about two hundred and fifty hands working on her place, and out of them all there are but three she will give anything like justice. She even takes our cotton seed. She furnishes us a mule to plant with. This place is near Benton, La., and belongs to Miss Lizzie Dickson.

his

SIMON + DICKSON

mark

THE WHITE LEAGUE
IN LOUISIANA

The following description of the White League organization in Louisiana, its object, and design of its leaders, as submitted by witness, was ordered to be printed as part of the evidence:

The existence of an organization in Louisiana known as the "White League" is a fact so well known that nobody can feign ignorance of it or question it, except, perhaps, Louisiana correspondents of the Northern press, who are accustomed to represent it as a mere myth, a malicious Republican falsehood, intended to furnish the President a plausible pretext for sending troops to Louisiana to control elections, &c. We shall not stop here to controvert these groundless but often repeated assertions, which constitute only a part of a stupendous effort of the white leaguers and their friends at home and abroad to conceal from the world the nature and designs of this organization; but will proceed at once to make a brief exhibit of the organization as shown by the sworn testimony of White League witnesses before the Congressional committee, together with utterances of the Democratic press throughout the State.

WHAT THE PRESS SAYS.

The following extracts from the White League papers of Louisiana will serve to elucidate more fully the real design of the originators of the league, and their modes of accomplishing that design.

[From the Shreveport Times.]*

The Radical or negro party has not yet, so far as we know, nominated a parish ticket. The movements of that party are usually

---

* The first two paragraphs quoted are from the *Shreveport Times* of September 13, 1874, while the third paragraph is from November 15, 1874.

conducted in the manner of those of a thief, stealthily, and while honest people are asleep; therefore their nominations may be agreed upon, though not yet known to the honest portion of the community. We think not, however. We are of the opinion that the plan of the carpet-baggers, scalawags, and negroes has been to wait until the white man's ticket was in the field, and then to move. It has been surmised from expressions which have fallen from some of the chiefs who have leaky mouths, that the negro party would nominate on their ticket white men of average character and seek by that means to break our ranks and divide our strength.

If such is the design it certainly will fail, for we cannot conceive that any man who has any honesty or pride or decency or self-respect would, in this crisis, accept a nomination from the negro party against the white people's ticket. Should any white man outside of the carpet-baggers and well known scalawags have the temerity to accept such a nomination he would be banished from decent society and universally condemned by the community. No white man could at this juncture accept such a nomination without perpetrating a crime against his fellow man. Should the radicals or negroes tender their nomination to white men in any measure identified with or possessing the respect of this community, it will be not for the purpose of putting good men in office but with the view of dividing our strength and perpetuating the reign of ignorance and rascality.

We have no appeal to make to our fellow-citizens of New Orleans. We know that the men of the 14th of September* will do their whole duty as freemen and Louisianians zealous of their liberties. But throughout the country parishes there should be concert of action, and that action should be prompt and emphatic. In every parish where the officers elected by the people may be counted out by the returning board, the people should use hemp or ball on the defeated candidates counted in. To localize the proposition—if

---

* See Chronology, 1874.

Geo. L. Smith is counted in over Wm. M. Levy, or if Twitchell is counted in over Elam, let Smith and Twitchell be killed; if Johnson and Tyler, in De Soto, are counted in over Scales and Schuler, or if Keating, Levisee, and Johnson, in Caddo, are counted in over Vaughan, Horan and Land, then let Johnson, Tyler, Keating, Levisee, and Johnson be killed; and so let every officer from Congressman down to constable in every district and parish of the State be served, whom the people have defeated and whom the returning board may count in.

[From the Shreveport Times of May 20.]

We are going to redeem this State from the rule of villainy and ignorance, or we will force the Federal Government to establish a military government.

[From the issue of July 29, 1874.]

There has been some redhanded work done in this parish that was necessary, but it was evidently done by cool, determined, and just men, who knew just how far to go, and we doubt not if the same kind of work is necessary it will be done again.

We again say that we fully, cordially approve what the white men of Grant and Rapides did at Colfax.

The white man who does not is a creature so base that he shames the worst class of his species. We say again we are going to carry the election in this State next fall.

Then let the negroes of Louisiana beware. Whenever the Anglo-Saxon and African have met in arms the result has not been a battle but a butchery, as it has been in Bossier in 1868 and at Colfax in 1873.

[From the issue of August 5, 1874.]

It has been charged that the white man's party expects to achieve success by intimidation. This is strictly true. We intend to succeed by intimidation, and we place little confidence in our numerical strength as shown in the figures above given from the ninth census.

Perhaps the fusion legislature was one of the ablest and most conservative bodies assembled in Louisiana in many years, and yet its vacillation lost the cause; its timidity betrayed the trust the people reposed in it. There were some bold and resolute men in that body and they sought to rally their fellow-members to action, but in vain.

There were too many men in it afraid of trouble, afraid of a little blood-letting, afraid of making things worse.

The people of Louisiana are fast making up their minds that this state of things shall exist no longer.

Either the next government will be composed of the tax-payers of the State, or else a strong military government brought about by their action.

There are two other classes who do not seem to comprehend these things—a small class of white men who refuse to register and aid their people in carrying the election and avoiding this crisis, and the negroes who are again rallying to the support of the thieves they have put in power, and are thus invoking upon their heads a terrible and bloody retribution.

[From the Natchitoches Vindicator of July 18, 1874.]

The white men intend to carry the State election this fall. This intention is deliberate and unalterable from the fact that their very existence depends upon it; and that you (the colored race) may enjoy the blessings which will naturally follow such an event, blessings made doubly sweet when you know that you are partly instrumental in bringing them about, we desire your co-operation and we simply ask you, Will you assist us in redeeming your State from the degradation and ruin she now is in, or will you follow still the advice of those who have placed her thus? Take time to answer it, and let your mind, should you decide affirmatively, be at rest for your future welfare and happiness. We propose to do for you more than any party has yet done for you. On the other hand, should you imagine that the teaching of your former rulers is correct, and you elect to attempt—for it will only be an attempt—to continue their rule, then you must take the consequences, for we tell you now, and let it be distinctly remembered, that you have fair warning that we intend to carry the State of Louisiana in November next, or she will be a military Territory.

[From the Mansfield Reporter of July 4, 1874.]

"There is nothing to be gained by pleadings or concessions, but everything is within our reach, if we will move forward and grasp it. Let our action be such that everybody will know what we want, and let them see that we are in earnest and we are determined to carry out the programme regardless of consequences."

The following from the same paper, of July, affords some idea of what this "programme" was:

"The lines must be drawn at once before our opponents are thoroughly organized, for by this means we will prevent many milk and cider fellows from falling into the enemy's rank.

"While the white man's party guarantees the negro all his present rights, they do not intend that carpet-baggers and renegades shall be permitted to organize and prepare the negroes for the coming campaign. Without the assistance of these villains the negroes are totally incapable of effectually organizing themselves, and unless they are previously excited and drilled, one-half of them will not come to the polls, and a large per cent. of the remainder will vote the white man's ticket."

[From the Minden Democrat.]

The remedy for all the evils that afflict our State and every Southern State under negro and carpet-bag rule is very simple. The incendiaries who flood our country at the approach of every election must be looked after. The proceedings of midnight gatherings in dark and gloomy places must be known.

Incendiary teachings of the carpet-baggers and scalawags, to inflame the minds of the negroes, must not be tolerated again.

[From the Sugar Bowl.]

Yes. Let us kneel on the grave of the "lost cause" and swear to Heaven to defend our rights.

[From the Caucasian.]

The question presents itself here that we have heard on the lips of every one for some time—what are we to do? To that question there can be but one answer, and that answer is comprised in a single word, fight. When, where, and how must be determined by future developments. For the present we can do nothing but make sure we are well prepared to go anywhere on short notice, and that we are ready to obey any call.

[From the Franklin Enterprise of August 6, 1874.]

We ask for no assistance; we protest against any intervention. We own this soil of Louisiana by virtue of our endeavor, as a heritage from our ancestors, and it is ours and ours alone. Science, literature, history, art, civilization, and law belong to us, and not to the negroes. They have no record but barbarism, and idolatry; nothing since the war, but that of error, incapacity, beastliness, voudouism and crime. Their right to vote is but the result of the war; their exercise of it a monstrous imposition, and a vindictive punishment upon us for that ill-advised rebellion.

Therefore are we banding together in a White League army, drawn up only on the defensive, exasperated by continued wrong, it is true, but acting under Christian and high principled leaders, and determined to defeat these negroes in their infamous design of depriving us of all we hold sacred and precious in the soil of our nativity or adoption, or perish in the attempt.

[From the Shreveport Comet.]

While we are willing, and aways have been, to give to the negro everything he needs and should have to make him happy, free, and contented, we are not and never will be in favor of his ruling the State of Louisiana any longer; and we swear by the Eternal Spirit that rules the universe, we will battle against it to the day of our death, if it costs us a prison or a gallows!

Let each white man make it his special duty to watch pot-house scalawagers, as they have spotted skins, and damned black hearts. Of course these scoundrels have misrepresented everything they took occasion to describe in their infamous letters and dispatches.

Somebody ought to make these black-hearted villains angels at once, for from the present temper of the State the quicker such monumental liars take unto themselves wings and fly away, the better.

Let the negro be made to know his place; treat him as he should be treated; but never, no never, will we submit more to his laws, as we were born free and will die free in spite of all the powers this side of hell.

[From the Baton Rouge Advocate.]

We have struck the key-note of redemption, and let us not close the glorious work until East Baton Rouge and the whole State has slipped from the grasp of thieving scoundrels, who are morally, intellectually, and totally unfit to be our allies. We hope the great work commenced by the White League throughout this parish will be continued from this time on until there is not a single corrupt or ignorant scamp left in office. The Rads need not congratulate themselves upon the probability of the White League dissolving if they are defeated this year. Such will not be the case. Their work has just commenced and defeat will only redouble their energies to overcome the Radical horde in the future. The White Leaguers are not regular politicians to retreat when they are defeated. They are not that class of men. Should they be repulsed this time, they will be up and at the enemy again with redoubled vim and energy that will strike terror to the hearts of those who think they have an easy foe to overcome.

The White League is a fixture in the political history of this State, and many a carpet-bagger will wish he had never been born, ere the Leaguers let them alone. The time has come when Louisianians have determined to get rid of the rule of this class of vampires. We hope there is nothing in this bit of information that will cause them to rub their hands with glee or to feel that they are bully boys, with or without a glass eye. Such they may rest assured is the policy of this people, and let them defeat the object if they can.

EXTENT OF THE LEAGUE

[From the Minden Democrat of August 29, 1874.]

The New Orleans Bulletin says that "in the White League of Louisiana are now organized and armed fourteen thousand men, one-half of whom are inured to battle and privation." The Bulletin has certainly made a mistake in its figures. Why, there are ten thousand in North Louisiana alone who are ready and willing to march at the first clarion note of the bugle that calls them in the defense of their rights; and the deep sense of the wrongs they have been compelled to submit to in the bayonet government will make them no ordinary force in the event a conflict is precipitated upon us.

OSTRACISM

[From the Franklin Enterprise.]

"At Alto on the 11th of July the following was adopted: 'That we regard it the sacred and political duty of every member of this club to discountenance and socially proscribe all white men who unite themselves with the Radical party, and to supplant every political opponent in all his vocations by the employment and support of those who ally themselves with the white man's party; and we pledge ourselves to exert our energies and use our means to the consummating of this end.'

"There should be kept and carefully preserved for future reference a *black list* or book of remembrance in every parish, wherein should be inscribed the names of those white men who *in this emergency* prove recreant to the duties and instincts of race and cast their lot with the African. The infamous record should be as conspicuous for all time to come as the pictures of notorious criminals in the rogues' galleries of large cities. These men must not be forgotten. Let their names be written in the black list with a pen of adamant, that they and all who descend from their loins to the fourth generation may be pariahs, forever cast out from all association with the Caucasian race. Let all who adhere to the negro party in this political contest be reckoned as negroes and treated as such. Let the black list for St. Mary be opened. Let the names of those who pant for immortal infamy be enrolled. Whose names shall head the list? We know two, father and son, who have equal claims to the distinction."

The above passage is reproduced in the New Orleans Picayune of August 1, 1874, with tacit commendation.

[From the Natchitoches Vindicator.]

We advise our native white fellow-citizens of Louisiana who have arrayed themselves against their white brothers to retrace their steps while there is still time left to do so. When a war of races is imminent—and we tell them it is imminent—they should be found but on one side, battling with the Caucasian race; words of sympathy will not do. The people will be satisfied with nothing short of acts, plain and unmistakable. They have yet time to redeem themselves. They know full well that the white men of this State are no mere beginners in the arts of peace or war, and that in going through such an ordeal all those who are not with us must certainly be against us, and none such will be allowed to remain in our midst, to take us in flank or rear at the opportune moment. When the conflict will have commenced it will be too late then. The contest will be quick, sharp, and decisive. Let them take warning in due time, for the die is surely cast.

Words cannot express our abhorrence of the man or men who would thus aid our foes. Every man who votes a split ticket, who gives his support to an independent candidate, is not only an enemy to our citizens, but a traitorous foe to his own race and to civilization.

Let us never cease to make war upon them, both in their official and private capacities; discountenance any person who meets them as gentlemen on the street. Shut your doors and your hearts to them; let them be outcasts to every feeling of mercy you have, so that living they may only encumber the earth, and dying descend to hell covered with the curses of every virtuous man in Louisiana.

[From the Baton Rouge Advocate.]

The White League Club of Sandy Creek puts it thus:

"*Resolved*, That we consider it beneath our moral and social dignity to associate with any white man who refuses to enroll his name among those who have openly declared themselves to be white men with principles favoring a white man's government."

The Baton Rouge White League No. 1, on the 5th of September, 1874, delivers itself as follows:

"*Resolved*, That all the members of this organization compose a committee, with the secretary as its chairman, and that it be the duty of every member of said committee to report to the chairman the names of all white men who, through indifference to the future welfare of the white race of Louisiana, have failed to register; and that a list of those names be kept for publication after the election, together with all white men who voted the Radical ticket."

[From the Shreveport Times.]

If any white man accepts a Radical negro nomination, place upon him the ban of public scorn and contempt; and if any man seeks to divide our strength by attempting the independent dodge, treat him as a public enemy.

THREATS TO DISCHARGE NEGRO LABORERS FROM EMPLOYMENT

The New Orleans Bulletin of 2d July, 1874, says this:

"We intend to tell the merchants, lawyers, doctors, and all others of our people who employ black men as porters, that they are supporting the best and most intelligent of the Republican party; and because they are the best and most intelligent, therefore the most dangerous."

The Catholic Messenger, in its abounding love and good-will to all men everywhere, having also an eye on politics, makes the following deliverance:

"That (the blacks) are and have been carrying on a relentless war upon the whites is unfortunately too true. It is not, indeed, a war of arms, for in that they would not have the shadow of a chance, and they know it well, but it is a legislative war—a war of ruin and extermination through the army of sheriffs and their deputies.

"And how has the white race met this war? We must answer, weakly, very weakly. They have shown no courage, no spirit of sacrifice, no public spirit whatever, in meeting the emergency. On the contrary, they have met this open, insolent defiance of these unscrupulous partisans with the most accommodating submissiveness. So far from breaking off relations with them as a public enemy, which they are in every true sense of the word, every planter, every employer has run a race with his compeers as to which of them could employ the greatest number of negroes. They are kept fully occupied everywhere. By this means they are furnished with the ability to carry on that very war which they wage so relentlessly against their employers. The white man supplies them with food, clothing, and money. They grow fat and insolent. They go to the polls and defiantly vote to ruin the very man who weakly and stupidly warms into life and strength the reptile which he knows is stinging him. There is but one way to manage the negro. He is, as a class, amenable to neither reason or gratitude. He must be starved into the common perception of decency."

INTIMIDATION AND VIOLENCE—THE LAW AND THE DUTY OF SELF-PROTECTION

Under the above caption, the Shreveport Times of October 17 says:

"Without delay every man in Shreveport, whatever his business may be, should give every negro voter in his employ to understand that if he votes the Radical ticket he will be instantly discharged. The planters should pursue a like policy. They should warn the negroes on their plantation that if they vote the Radical ticket, they must leave their plantations."

ACTION OF THE MERCHANTS

Under the above head, the Shreveport Times instant has the following editorial remarks, approving the proscription of Republicans now going on in Northern Louisiana:

"We call attention to the two cards signed by the merchants of Shreveport, published in this morning's Times. The merchants have acted promptly, and it is to be hoped the example they have so nobly and fearlessly given will be everywhere followed. Let the negroes be made to fully and clearly understand that their insolence and misrule has gone as far as it can go, and that they must either co-operate with us to re-establish good government and the prosperity of the State, or depend upon their Radical friends for employment and support. We would suggest, now that our merchants and business men are in earnest in this important matter, that they immediately correspond with their friends in Saint Louis and Cincinnati, and make arrangements to have a brigade of draymen and porters sent here when needed. Draymen and porters in Saint Louis and Cincinnati are working for one-third less than the negro draymen and porters are getting in Shreveport, and will be glad to come if they are assured of regular work. The planters of Summer Grove and the merchants of Shreveport have spoken. Let us hear the next voice."

*   *   *   *   *   *   *

The cards referred to are found in the same paper, signed by about sixty names of persons and firms calling themselves merchants of Shreveport. The first reads:

"SHREVEPORT, *October 14th*, 1874.

"We, the undersigned, merchants of the city of Shreveport, in obedience to a request of the Shreveport Campaign Club, agree to use every endeavor to get our employés to vote the people's ticket at the ensuing election, and in the event of their refusing to do so, or in case they vote the Radical ticket, to refuse to employ them at the expiration of their present contracts."

The above is signed by sixty-nine merchants and commercial firms. The second card says:

"SHREVEPORT, *October* 14, 1874.

"We the undersigned, merchants of the city of Shreveport, alive to the great importance of securing good and honest government to the State, do agree and pledge ourselves not to advance any supplies or money to any planter the coming year who will give employment or rent lands to laborers who vote the Radical ticket in the coming election.

"We are constrained to this course from a principle of self-defense. Knowing that the negroes are being banded together for the purpose of foisting upon the country incompetent and dishonest men for office, and if they persist in their determination to support a ticket which plunders the white people of their subsistence, they must look to others than the white people for the means of subsistence."

Above is signed by sixty merchants and commercial firms.

NOTE.—It appears that steps were taken to arrest some of the signers of the above cards under the enforcement act, pending which the following editorial comments appear in the Shreveport Times:

*   *   *   *   *   *   *

"The position assumed by our merchants and property-holders has had its effect upon the negro dupes of the thieves who lead the Radical party. It has opened their eyes, and many of them have determined to vote with their best friends, the white people. The object of this movement of the Kelloggists* and Federal authorities is simply to counteract the influence of this movement upon the negroes; it is to intimidate the gentlemen who entered into the agreement, and force them to withdraw from it; to make them slink out of a *brave and proper action* by threatening them with the terrors of arrest and confinement in stockades and of Federal courts as they exist in Louisiana. If this is accomplished and our people back down, the negroes will become insulting, arrogant, and intolerable. Led by their chiefs, they will literally ride rough-shod over the community; and this section of the State will be carried by them in the election. This is what this proceeding means—nothing more nor less.

---

* See footnote on page 65.

"If these men, fellow-citizens, make this issue, force them to develop the dastardly outrage in its full proportions, that the whole country may see it in all its hideousness.

"Our word for it, no one will remain in General Merrill's* stockade or guard-house many hours after the news of the outrage is telegraphed North and East.

"Citizens, stand firm! Dispatches have already been sent over the United States in relation to the threatened outrage upon your rights and liberty, and the eyes of the American people are upon you. Your action in this matter now will excite the sympathy or derision of the country, according as it is courageous and manly, or weak and contemptible.

"You are not alone; the whole community supports you. Lists are now circulating throughout the city, pledging the signers to the same line of action you agreed upon. One hundred additional names have been signed and every man in Shreveport will share your responsibilities. The planters of Summer Grove, Spring Ridge, Greenwood, and Mooringsport neighborhoods have unanimously signed similar pledges. Even the ladies of our city are signing cards that will make them as guilty as you are."

*   *   *   *   *   *   *

The following is the heading of the list referred to above: "We, the undersigned, agree to use every endeavor to get our employés to vote the people's ticket at the ensuing election. And in the event of their refusal so to do, or *in case they vote the Radical ticket, to refuse to employ them at the expiration of their present contracts.*

*   *   *   *   *   *   *

"The signers of the obligation will, every one of them, stand squarely up to what they have done. Indeed, so far from scaring

---

* See footnote on page 65.

anybody into backing down, the citizens are now more absolutely than ever determined to stand firm, and yesterday 180 additional names were signed to the pledge, representing nearly every business house in this city. The same obligation has been signed by the planters in the different neighborhoods throughout the parish, while a large number of ladies signed an obligation to hire no servants whose husbands affiliated with the Radical party. Thus, if General Merrill and Commissioner Levisee carry out their programme, they will have by tonight under arrest about three-fourths of the white population of the parish.

"The temper of the people is splendid, and their resolution is to test this question, and learn whether they are free men or the minions of a brutal military despotism.

"The people of this city are much excited over the outrage which General Merrill and the United States Commissioner Levisee have threatened to perpetrate upon them this morning, and unless caution is observed by the deputy marshal in executing the warrants of these worthies some desperate act may be perpetrated. We doubt if any deputy marshal's life will be safe if he attempts alone to arrest citizens here upon these scandalous processes. We admonish any civil officer, therefore, in perpetrating the outrages, to be accompanied by Federal troops."

[From the Baton Rouge Advocate.]

"We understand that the leading merchants are seriously considering the propriety of entering into a solemn compact to supply no man next year who either votes against the interests of the property-holders in the coming election, or gives employment to those who do. We would suggest also that they adopt a method to do away with both the renting and share system. Both of these systems are ruinous to both planter and merchant. By concert of action the merchants and planters can and will put down the disastrous rule of political thieves in this parish and State, and we know they do not lack the courage and the will to do it. They hold their fate in their own hands; therefore let them wield their influence for the future good of all.

"That we, the white people, do solemnly promise and bind ourselves not to employ or aid in any manner any person, whether white or black, who votes against our interest, as well as their own, at the coming election in November."

A similar resolution was passed by the meeting of the people's party of ward No. 1, parish of East Baton Rouge.

[From the Shreveport Times of October 17.]

"Whereas there has been a preconcerted plan carried into effect by the Radical party, since the enfranchisement of the colored race, to unite them in leagues, bound by the most solemn oaths, to support none but Radicals for office, which has brought our country to the verge of destruction:

"Be it resolved by the white people's party of ward No. 2 (parish of Caddo), that we pledge ourselves and our sacred honor, that we will, under no circumstances whatever, employ as laborers, rent to, or in any other manner give employment to, any man, white or black, who votes the Radical ticket at the coming election.

"We hereby pledge ourselves to discountenance any one who refuses to sign or who fails to comply with this agreement, by refusing to associate with him in any manner whatever."

[From the Shreveport Times of September 19.]

"With the Federal Army and Navy at his command, the President may reseat Mr. Kellogg; he may replace in some of the parishes the local officials, but if he would keep them there, he must keep troops in every parish in the State, and it will require an army of 20,000 men to hold in place the rotten and contemptible usurpation. Nor will this quiet the State. The people of Louisiana cannot fight the Federal Government, but they will not bear tamely or patiently the outrage, and it will be as much as a man's life is worth to accept office from Kellogg. We doubt if Kellogg himself will live twenty days after his reinstallation, even surrounded by an army. Lawlessness will break out everywhere; the worst elements of society, under no fear of public opinion or law, will follow their evil instincts. Carpet-baggers and scalawags and negroes too *we fear* will be killed."

The following editorial comment on the Coushatta massacre* is from the Shreveport Times of September 3: "If the civil commotion of the last few days in Red River Parish had no counterpart in other parishes of the State, it might be surmised that lawless men there had outraged the law and outraged humanity, but the simple fact that similar occurrences are transpiring in other and distant sections of the State, and that the white people in every section of it sympathize in these occurrences, is evidence that a general and powerful cause has provoked them.

"And now looking at the killing of the creatures that were caught in Red River Parish, engaged there in organizing a war of the blacks against the whites, from this stand-point, we believe that justice has been done.

"It may have been, in the language of some of our friends, bad policy to kill the men who were engaged in organizing ruin and death in Red River Parish, but we differ with them.

"The ringleaders of the war in Red River are dead. As for our part, while we do not exult over their death, we have no tears with which to bedew their graves, and no censure to bestow upon the men whose homes, whose lives, whose wives and children were threatened.

"The eagles have struck down the foe and swept away. Now let the buzzards of radicalism squat upon the carcasses, and scream

---

* Members of the White League murdered three black and six white Republicans near Coushatta on August 29 and 30.

and chatter and flutter; their noise strikes terror to not a single heart in Louisiana."

The foregoing extracts are only samples of the torrent of a like nature that poured forth daily from the White League press all over the State. The careful reader, however, of all the foregoing testimony, will readily see that the White League in Louisiana was a military organization extending through the whole State; that its formation in the several parishes was nearly contemporaneous, thereby indicating a general unity of purpose all over the State; that the organization of the league was effected generally throughout the State, about the month of June and the 1st of July, 1874. That this organization was probably not less than twenty-five thousand strong, of well armed men in the State. That these men, having more or less of military experience, were regularly formed into companies and regiments, and were armed, officered and drilled, ready for military action; and that they could all be massed if the exigency required it.

The intelligent reader will also perceive that this organization was formed for a political purpose. That the direct object of the formation of the League was to wrest the government of the State from the hands of the Republican party, and to place it in the control of the White League party. That to accomplish this, they adopted the dangerous policy of uniting the white population *as a race*, against the colored population *as a race*, thus making a strictly race issue of the matter. And to reach the desired end (of possessing the government) it was necessary to pursue two lines of action at once, viz: "To drive incompetent and corrupt men from office," that is "to get rid of the Kellogg officials" and "to carry the election."

How the election was to be carried, the reader can have no trouble in determining from the foregoing extracts; intimidation, violence, threats, and proscription in its most aggravated forms were freely used.

CHRONOLOGY

1843   Born March 16 in Georgia. (In 1872 Adams recorded his birthplace as Jasper County, his parents as Milly and Samuel Carter, and listed ten siblings. He later wrote in 1878 that he had "formerly belonged to a man named Houston in Newton county, Georgia, and was then called Henry Houston.")

1850   Brought with his parents to DeSoto Parish in northwest Louisiana, probably by slaveholding plantation owner Caleb Adams.

1858   Caleb Adams dies. Henry becomes the property of Nancy Emily Adams, Caleb's youngest daughter, and is hired out to a planter named Ferguson, possibly her brother-in-law Aaron Ferguson. Works in northwest Louisiana and northeast Texas. During his enslavement he will marry a woman named Malinda and have four children with her, Lucy, Rena, Josephine, and Henry. They are separated by slaveholder Columbus Henson, who will take Malinda and the children to eastern Texas before emancipation.

1860   Census records Louisiana population of 708,000, including more than 357,000 white persons, almost 19,000 free people of color, and more than 331,000 enslaved Black persons. Election of Abraham Lincoln begins movement for secession in the South.

1861   Louisiana convention votes to secede from the Union and join the Confederacy. Civil War begins.

1862   Union forces capture New Orleans and Baton Rouge, although most of the state will remain under Confederate control until the end of the war.

1863   Emancipation Proclamation frees "all persons held as slaves" in Confederate-held territory. Lincoln administration begins establishing Unionist government in Louisiana.

1864   Michael Hahn elected governor of Louisiana. Unionist voters approve new Louisiana state constitution abolishing slavery.

1865   Henry Adams and the other enslaved people working on the Ferguson plantation in DeSoto Parish are told on June 16 that they are free. Adams refuses to sign a labor contract and leaves the plantation in September. After being robbed by armed white men while traveling to Shreveport he begins working as a peddler.
        Hahn resigns and is succeeded by Lieutenant Governor James Madison Wells. Congress refuses to admit senators and representatives from the former Confederate states. Ratification of the Thirteenth Amendment is declared complete.

1866   Adams enlists in the army for three years in September. Serves at Shreveport with the 80th U.S. Colored Infantry, a Civil War volunteer regiment, before joining the 39th Infantry, a newly formed Black regiment in the regular army, at Greenville outside of New Orleans.
        White mob attacks supporters of a new state constitution in New Orleans on July 30, killing thirty-four Black and three white persons.

1867   Promoted to quartermaster-sergeant in March. Posted to Fort Jackson downriver from New Orleans. Learns to read and write.
        Reconstruction Act places Louisiana and nine other southern states under military rule and requires them to adopt new constitutions providing for Black male suffrage in order to regain representation in Congress.

1868   Biracial convention in Louisiana adopts new state constitution enfranchising Black men and declaring that all persons "shall enjoy equal rights and privileges" on public transportation.

Voters approve new constitution in April and elect Republican Henry C. Warmoth, a carpetbagger from Illinois, as governor. Louisiana is readmitted to Congress in June. Ratification of the Fourteenth Amendment is declared complete in July. White terrorists murder hundreds of people, most of them Black, in Louisiana during the summer and fall in an effort to suppress the Republican vote in the November election. Democratic nominee Horatio Seymour wins the presidential contest in the state as Ulysses S. Grant receives 30,000 fewer votes than Warmoth.

1869   Adams joins the new 25th Infantry in April and serves with the regiment until his discharge from the army in September. Returns to Shreveport, the seat of Caddo Parish, where he buys property in town with his cousin.

1870   Works as woodcutter. Joins other Black army veterans in organizing a secret committee to "investigate the condition of our race" in the southern states. Examines contracts and agreements signed by Black laborers and tenant farmers and advises them on their rights. Votes for the first time after urging fellow members of the committee to cast their ballots for the Republican ticket.

Ratification of the Fifteenth Amendment is declared complete in March. Republicans win races for state auditor and treasurer in election marked by less violence than the 1868 contest. Census records Louisiana population of 727,000, almost evenly divided between "white" and "colored," and Caddo Parish population of 22,000 that is 73 percent "colored."

1871   Adams visits Texas as an investigator for the committee.

1872   Becomes manager of Shreveport wood yard owned by white farmer W. C. Hambleton. Attempts to vote for the Republican ticket in the November election but is barred from the polls by a white mob.

Voting in Louisiana results in conflicting returns in national, state, and parish elections. Republican William P. Kellogg, a carpet bagger, and Fusion candidate John McEnery, a conservative who is supported by Democrats and Liberal Republicans opposed to Grant, both claim victory in the gubernatorial contest. Congress refuses to count the state's electoral votes in the presidential election.

1873   Adams begins managing one of Hambleton's plantations near Shreveport. Serves on Caddo Parish grand jury.

Kellogg and McEnery establish rival state governments in January. Grant recognizes Kellogg government, which takes control of New Orleans. White posse attacks local militia guarding the Grant Parish courthouse in Colfax on April 13, massacring at least eighty Black men. Grant sends troop reinforcements to Louisiana and issues proclamation in May ordering pro-McEnery forces to disperse.

1874   Adams is fired by Hambleton for being a Republican and resumes working as laborer. The committee organizes a Colonization Council to promote Black migration out of the South, and in September the Council sends a petition to President Grant signed by a thousand people asking to be removed to either the federal territories or Liberia. Adams serves as an election supervisor in Caddo Parish.

Paramilitary White League is formed to overthrow the Kellogg government. White Leaguers murder three Black and six white Republicans near Coushatta in Red River Parish, August 29–30, and on September 14 White League militia in New Orleans defeats the Metropolitan Police and seizes control of the city in fighting that kills thirty-five people. Grant orders troop reinforcements sent to New Orleans and Kellogg is restored as governor. Election in November leaves control of the state house of representatives unresolved.

1875   Adams serves as an undercover scout for the U.S. Army in Louisiana in the spring and summer. Submits statement to the military describing the violence against Black people he has witnessed since 1866. (It is printed in 1877 along with other documents sent to Congress by the War Department.) Visits

Arkansas and Texas to gain support for the Colonization Council. Attends convention of Black ministers in New Orleans in December.

Democrats attempt to gain control of Louisiana legislature on January 4 by forcibly installing five members in the house of representatives. At Kellogg's request, federal troops eject the five Democrats from the statehouse; the action is widely denounced in Congress and in the northern press as an illegitimate military intervention in civil affairs. Committee of the U.S. House of Representatives arranges "adjustment" under which the Democrats gain control of the Louisiana house in return for a promise (not kept) to accept the legitimacy of the Kellogg administration. In the fall White Line militia in Mississippi uses violence to intimidate Republican voters and win control of the state legislature.

1876   Adams visits Texas for the Colonization Council. Attends Republican state convention in New Orleans and helps organize Republican clubs in northern Louisiana. Serves as deputy U.S. marshal in Bienville Parish on election day, November 7.

Presidential contest between Republican Rutherford B. Hayes and Democrat Samuel J. Tilden results in disputed electoral count caused by conflicting election returns in South Carolina, Florida, and Louisiana, and disqualification controversy over an Oregon elector. In Louisiana both parties claim victory in the state elections.

1877   Adams visits Arkansas and Texas for the Colonization Council. Begins corresponding with the American Colonization Society in Washington about migration to Liberia. Public meeting held in Shreveport on September 15 adopts petition to President Hayes asking for federal support for colonization.

Electoral commission created by Congress awards all of the disputed electors to Hayes, giving him an electoral majority of one. President Hayes orders federal troops withdrawn from the statehouses in South Carolina and Louisiana. Stephen Packard, Kellogg's Republican successor, leaves office and Democrat

Francis T. Nicholls becomes governor of Louisiana on April 25, completing the "redemption" of the southern states from Republican rule.

1878   Adams continues to speak at public meetings promoting colonization. Places notice in the *Southwestern Christian Advocate* on June 20 seeking information about the wife and children he was separated from during enslavement; writes "I married again and have children." Writes to U.S. Attorney General Charles Devens shortly after the November election about the violence, intimidation, and fraud used by the Democrats to suppress the Black vote. Travels to New Orleans in December to testify before a federal grand jury investigating the election.

1879   Remains in New Orleans, fearing that he will be murdered if he returns to Caddo Parish. Signs petition to President Hayes requesting federal employment along with fifty-three other witnesses in the election investigation. Works in the U.S. custom house and on the levees. Attends convention of Black clergy, teachers, and other leaders held in New Orleans in April to discuss emigration. Appointed to committee established to aid migrants to Kansas. Travels through the Louisiana parishes and western Mississippi observing the "exodus."

1880   Testifies in Washington before the Senate select committee investigating the "Negro Exodus," March 12–13. Returns to New Orleans, where he works in the custom house, in the mint, and on the levees.

1882   Collects signatures for a petition urging government support for establishing direct mail steamer service between the United States and Liberia.

1884   Adams writes to the America Colonization Society on August 27, predicting that the election of a Democratic president will renew interest in emigration from the South to Liberia. There is no known written record of the remainder of his life.

The text in this book is set in 10¼ point Fairfield, an old-style book typeface created for the Mergenthaler Linotype Company in 1939 by the Czech-born American type designer Rudolph Ruzicka, who later wrote, " 'Type is made to be read' implies a reader [who] expects nothing but to be left in optical ease while he pursues his reading." The font family was revived and expanded for digital use by Alex Kaczun in 1992. The chapter titles, running heads, and other display elements are set in Benton Sans, designed by Tobias Frere-Jones in 1995 and further developed by Cyrus Highsmith in 2003. They were inspired by the industrial typefaces created by Morris Fuller Benton in the early decades of the twentieth century.

The paper is an acid-free stock that exceeds the requirements for permanence of the American National Standards Institute. The binding material is Allure, a polycotton blended cloth with an aqueous acrylic coating. Composition by Westchester Publishing Services. Printing and binding by Versa Press, Inc., East Peoria, Illinois.

2 04